ACTORS AND AUDIENCES

Actors and Audiences explores the exchanges between those on and off the stage that fill the atmosphere with energy and vitality. Caroline Heim utilises the concept of "electric air" to describe this phenomenon and discuss the charge of emotional electricity that heightens the audience's senses in the theatre.

In order to understand this electric air, Heim draws from in-depth interviews with 79 professional audience members and 22 international stage and screen actors in the United Kingdom, United States, France and Germany. Tapping into the growing interest in empirical studies of the audience, this book documents experiences from three productions, *The Encounter, Heisenberg* and *Hunger. Peer Gynt,* to describe the nature of these conversations. The interviews disclose essential elements: transference, identification, projection, double consciousness, presence, stage fright and the suspension of disbelief. Ultimately Heim reveals that the heart of theatre is the relationship between those on- and offstage, the way in which emotions and words create psychological conversations that pass through the fourth wall into an "in-between space" and the resulting electric air.

A fascinating introduction to a unique subject, this book provides a close examination of actor and audience perspectives which is essential reading for students and academics of Theatre, Performance and Audience Studies.

Caroline Heim is a senior lecturer in Theatre at Queensland University of Technology, Australia.

ACTORS AND AUDIENCES

Conversations in the Electric Air

Caroline Heim

Routledge
Taylor & Francis Group

LONDON AND NEW YORK

First published 2020
by Routledge
2 Park Square, Milton Park, Abingdon, Oxon OX14 4RN

and by Routledge
52 Vanderbilt Avenue, New York, NY 10017

Routledge is an imprint of the Taylor & Francis Group, an informa business

British Library Cataloguing-in-Publication Data
A catalogue record for this book is available from the British Library

Library of Congress Cataloging-in-Publication Data
Names: Heim, Caroline, author.
Title: Actors and audiences: conversations in the electric air / Caroline Heim.
Description: Abingdon, Oxon; New York, NY: Taylor & Francis, 2020. |
Includes bibliographical references and index.
Identifiers: LCCN 2019053706 (print) | LCCN 2019053707 (ebook) |
ISBN 9781138210066 (hardback) | ISBN 9781138210073 (paperback) |
ISBN 9781315456096 (ebook)
Subjects: LCSH: Theater audiences–Psychology. | Actors–Psychology. |
Theater audiences–Interviews. | Actors–Interviews. | Theater.
Classification: LCC PN2193.A8 H44 2020 (print) |
LCC PN2193.A8 (ebook) | DDC 306.4/84–dc23
LC record available at https://lccn.loc.gov/2019053706
LC ebook record available at https://lccn.loc.gov/2019053707

ISBN: 978-1-138-21006-6 (hbk)
ISBN: 978-1-138-21007-3 (pbk)
ISBN: 978-1-315-45609-6 (ebk)

Typeset in Bembo
by Newgen Publishing UK

Dominus illuminatio mea

CONTENTS

ACKNOWLEDGEMENTS

A book on actors and audience members is not complete without the voices of these two troupes of performers, and I am deeply grateful for the generosity of the actors and audience members I had the privilege of interviewing from many parts of the globe. I am particularly indebted to those actors and audience members that permitted me to share their thoughts on some very sensitive topics.

The interviews would not have been possible to secure without the assistance of some very helpful and connected theatre professionals: Tony Sheldon in New York, Janet Fullerlove in London, Doreen Röder in Stuttgart, Carl de Poncins in Paris and Natali Seelig in Berlin. A special thank you goes to my dear friend and fellow actor Kimberly Hollingsworth not only for introducing me to some of New York's finest actors, but also for her constant support, interest in and keen insights into actor–audience relationships in the short- and long-distance conversations we had while I was writing this book.

The theatre companies that staged the productions in my case studies were all gracious with their time and assistance. Thanks to the Manhattan Theatre Club for continuing to support my work and particularly to the very gifted David Shookhoff who introduced me to one of the most unique audience enrichment experiences I have ever attended. I, like your devoted audience-fans, take my hat off to you. Thanks to the Deutsches Theater for their help and for welcoming difficult conversations. I am very grateful to Claus Caesar and Ulrich Beck for opening up the doors of the Deutsches Theater to me and for going out of their way during a very busy season to secure interviews with their actors and audience members. The Schauspiel Stuttgart, Théâtre à Paris and Complicité were also accommodating.

Queensland University of Technology (QUT) and my colleagues at QUT have been very supportive of this project. Many thanks to Mark Radvan for his encouragement and his generosity in giving me time to write, and to Dianne Eden who always believed in the electric air. My gratitude also goes to Emma Felton, Bree

Hadley and Kathryn Kelly who always had an encouraging word, and a cup of tea or chocolates waiting to sustain me. Thanks to Ben Piggott at Routledge for our continuing work together and to Jonathon Pitches for his excellent feedback on Chapter 1.

Like theatre, the heart of life is relationships. I am very privileged to have wonderful relationships in my personal life with some very special people that I would like to acknowledge. My dear friend Joy Lawn for her constant encouragement and belief in my work, particularly in those last furious weeks of writing. Mark Grenning for his spamming of emails on audiences and Robin McKenzie for always asking the right questions when I was stressed. My wonderful parents who, even at the age of 90, were always there flying the flag and understanding. My son Benjamin for his beautiful electric air cover image, his transcriptions and his arguments with his brother about *The Encounter*. My son Reuben for his insights into *The Encounter*.

The relationship that sustained me the most during writing – both in its electric air moments and in its comfortable times – was my relationship with my husband Christian. My heartfelt thanks for the long hours spent editing my chapters, sharing powerful insights, attending productions, translating German, protecting my writing time, contributing to my ideas during long walks along the beach, taking over all the cooking and cleaning, and generally being a wonderful, encouraging support. My best memories of writing were a sweet combination of Chopin Nocturnes from Christian's piano playing and the scent of gardenias wafting in from our garden. Every writer needs time, space, belief and love to muse. On a more personal level, I am deeply grateful to him for giving me all four in abundance.

INTRODUCTION

There are two sides to every conversation. In any exchange of ideas there are different points of view. Conversations are not only reciprocal, they are relational. Theatre is relational and replicates life not only in that it is what Maxwell Anderson called a "hieroglyph" of the relationships in the society we live in, it is relational onstage, in the auditorium and across the footlights.[1] In the theatre, myriad verbal conversations are held among the artistic team, the actors and the audience members in preparation for a production. The most vital conversations of the theatrical event arguably occur between actors and audience members during the performance. If, as Jerzy Grotowski describes, the essence of theatre is: "what takes place between spectator and actor,"[2] then actor–audience conversations – psychological, emotional and, even sometimes, physical and verbal – are the *raison d'être* of the theatrical event. They bridge the aesthetic distance and Edward Bullough's psychical distance between stage and auditorium, creating what Bullough calls "the utmost decrease of Distance without its disappearance."[3] This book imbricates the aesthetic and psychological as a way of describing a phenomenon of the theatre that actors and audience feel in moments of epiphany during a performance: a heightened state of excitement or thrill.[4]

Theatre and Performance Studies scholars, myself included, have neglected these aforementioned conversations, or given a view from backstage or off-stage rather than listening to the actor–audience conversation. This book will go some way to addressing this gap. Concentrating on the under-researched actor–audience relationship, this book not only considers the intrinsic worth of each side of the actor–audience conversation, but also explores the relational aspects of those conversations, arguing that it is the relational co-creation between actors and audiences that charges the air in the theatre, creating those thrill moments in the theatrical experience that audience and actors alike often describe as "electric."[5]

Nicolas Bourriaud's *Relational Aesthetics* explores the importance of relationships and the value of relational art as an antidote to the continued fragmentation of society. Although Bourriaud's understanding of relational art concentrates on the relationship between audience members and the audience's "rendez-vous" moments in visual art, the relational imperatives and their value can be related, even more convincingly, to attending a performance. It has only been over the past ten years that audience research has ventured beyond demographic questions to explore audience meaning-making. The next step is to ask, who are we making meaning "with" and what does the experience of that meaning-making or co-creation feel like? To answer these questions, it is essential to include the actor's and performer's perspectives. As theatre is relational, it is crucial that theatre research, and specifically audience research and performance research, includes a discussion of the relational by interviewing all participants in the co-creative conversation to capture more of what it means to experience the theatrical event, from onstage and in the auditorium. For actors who have spent much of their professional life on stage, the relational in theatre works as an antidote to the fragmentation of society. As one actor interviewed for this book divulged, "that's the beauty of theatre, it teaches me how to be a better human."[6] This is achieved for actors, by embodying flawed characters and sharing their stories of triumph and failure with other flawed human beings, or who actor Edward Hibbert calls "a dysfunctional family,"[7] across the footlights.

Theatre has become one of the few sanctuaries that offer opportunities for live, emotion conversations. One male audience member interviewed for this book explained, "[at the theatre] I am able to experience emotional responses that I actually don't have in real life."[8] Actors too are often drawn to the theatre for this very purpose or, as Stella Adler argued, "because their soul is not filled up by life."[9] This book attempts to describe the emotional and psychological conversations about the human condition that occur between actors and audience members across the footlights to which the audience member was referring. At times, these conversations make the liveness of the theatre experience so vital that it is felt viscerally and can indeed fill the "soul" where life does not.

Why conversations?

Conversation is defined in current usage as an "interchange of thoughts and words."[10] An interchange or an "exchange" or "interaction" is well suited to describe the reciprocity that occurs between actor and audience. Significantly, conversations are words *and* thoughts. The psychological and emotional conversations observed in this book are, in one sense, thought conversations.

In theatre studies, there is a significant body of research that considers affect. A large percentage of this research takes a neuroscientific approach. For example, there has been some interesting interrogation of the workings of mirror neurons in actor–audience thought-life and meaning-making by recent audience theorists. Cognitive neuroscience has much to offer in explaining the workings of the mind in meaning-making but it is, as yet, underdeveloped and as Erin Hurley argues in

Theatre & Feeling, cognitive neuroscience is "not the last word on theatre and feeling [...] the *nature* of the brain is decidedly influenced by the *nurture* of its environment."[11] It is the environment of theatre, or the atmosphere of theatre, created by the psychological and emotion conversations that this book also aims to describe. Although various emotional and psychological audience responses are recorded, whether these experiences are affective, cognitive, psychological or embodied is not the primary concern of this book which seeks to describe the thought conversations between actors and audience members as phenomenological experiences.

For the purposes of this book, conversation is predominantly the thought discourse between actors and audience at the theatrical event that is psychological and emotional. In some chapters, these conversations are described in aesthetic terms. Elsewhere I have described the more audible and physical conversations between actors and audiences, the paralingual, gestural and verbal expressions that also form part of the audience conversation.[12] This research goes beyond the utterances and physical dialogues to explore the feeling and psychological states of actors and audience members. Interestingly, in the sixteenth century, the term "conversation" was understood to mean "sexual intercourse."[13] A thought conversation can be a very intimate experience in theatre, as explored in several chapters. As in intimacy, the close exchange, or even in what some actors describe as "feeding" the audience, thought conversations work to decrease the psychological distance between stage and audience.

No one understands the stage–audience theatrical interchange as a conversation better than actors. As German actor Elias Arens insists, "the audience asks for a dialogue. They always do."[14] Actors also understand the relational aspects of the interchange. British actor Ian Bartholomew explains, "It's such a febrile relationship: a group of actors and an audience. [...] Sometimes the conversation is 'oh great let's get on with it.' At other times it is 'Like you care. I'm not talking to you again.'"[15] Frequently, in the actor interviews undertaken for this book, actors spoke what they perceived as the audience's inner dialogue such as in this example. Actors' thought conversations with audiences are multifarious and work on a complexity of levels as explored in the discussions of double consciousness. The conversations described in this book are metaphorical, but as we shall see, conversations as thought dialogue or emotional transference are also very real to actors and audiences and create a certain felt tension in the air.

Why electric air?

During audience interviews for my last monograph, *Audience as Performer*, I was intrigued by how many of the 106 audience members interviewed relished the opportunity of discussing the live atmosphere of a theatrical event. Their demeanour would actually change as they commented, "Ah the energy, the energy! [...] The theatres of New York just have a different electricity [...] It's live, that's the operative word,"[16] with a nostalgic sparkle in their eyes. It was, however, the few actors that I interviewed that predominantly referred to the atmosphere in terms of electricity.

Actor Paul Schoeffler exuded: "You can feel it. It's like electricity: an electric, tactile thing that you can feel. It's a participatory thing, a dialogue with the audience."[17] Having had the privilege of performing[18] on both sides of the footlights, I have experienced the sensation of this electricity and was eager to explore it more rigorously. While there are some theatre texts discussing liveness, there is a dearth of literature on the actual atmosphere. While this book predominantly explores the figurative atmosphere, at times I will touch upon the physical atmosphere such as the temperature in the auditorium or stage effects that create a physical atmosphere.

The writings of German philosopher, author of *The Aesthetics of Atmospheres*, Gernot Böhme serve as a point of departure. As more fully explored in Chapter 1, Böhme describes atmospheres as a space-filling phenomenon that emotionally radiates in between objects and subjects. Atmosphere fills this in-between space with "a certain tone of feeling."[19] For Böhme, atmospheres are "something spatial and at the same time something emotional."[20] This book explores the atmosphere that fills the in-between space between actors and audience members that is both spatial and emotional. They are descriptions of Böhme's "common reality of the perceiver and the perceived."[21]

Audience reception is informed by age, gender, socio-economic background and other aspects described in this book. The actors' performance is framed by casting, skill, experience and other aspects also described. This book concentrates on audience engagement during the performance itself with aspects that "heighten" the experience of theatre for actors and audiences alike to the degree that they become what I posit as electric air experiences.

There are, however, times in the theatre when the electric air is noticeably absent. There is no buzz, thrill, excitement, or charged atmosphere. *New York Times* theatre critic Alexis Soloski argues that this "theatrical deadness" is endemic in productions that have a "slickness, a complacency; they might be pre-recorded for all the notice they take of [the audience] watching."[22] These descriptors reflect Peter Brook's concept of the deadly theatre. A theatre that works to a formula that is so ingrained and predictable that even though the now obligatory standing ovation is given at the end of the production, the audience member and the actor "secretly find [the play] excruciatingly boring."[23] Often the criticism of these productions unfairly falls on the actors rather than the unseen creatives. What Soloski's and Brook's perspectives pre-suppose is that audience and actors expect some sort of heightened live, rather than dead experience in the theatre.

There are some times, however, when actors, as New York performer Lynn Cohen explained, "don't show up."[24] This too creates the deadly theatre experience. The audience are also sometimes at fault. As the interviewed actors emphasised, at times the audience are culpable of creating a deadly theatre experience; they too "don't show up." They have full stomachs, they go to sleep, they are preoccupied with their phones, the weather affects them, they are in a bad mood, they have dinner-party conversations during the performance. Or they are sometimes Richard Schechner's integral audience of theatre industry professionals or hardened critics that have been known to cross their arms, sending a challenge to the stage to "try and move me or get me interested." They "don't show up" emotionally. As theatre is relational and reciprocal, these moments deaden the atmosphere. There are two sides to every theatre conversation and when one is not participating there is less potential for electric air experiences. These moments are also explored in the forthcoming chapters.

What is an audience member?

In their discussion of audience emotions, Doris Kolesch and Hubert Knoblauch have argued that

> The common tendency to think of an audience as a single entity cannot do justice to the heterogeneity assembled in an audience or to the variety of audience emotions. Audience emotions are the collective experience of a momentary corporeal synchronization and of a sensuous transmission.[25]

The psychological conversations explored in this book are individual experiences. The transference or identification with a character from either actors or audience members is clearly an individual response and is notated as such. For the purposes of this research, however, and to allow a space to even discuss audience and actor behaviour, I will at times homogenise the audience. It would almost be an impossibility for me to talk about the audience without doing so. I see the audience as heterogeneous not homogenous and as individuals as well as a collective, but I will often refer to them as a collective. They are individual audience members that join together to form a collective called "audience." As argued elsewhere, they become a collective due to the effect of emotional contagion and collective effervescence

Kolesch and Knoblauch also argue that the use of highly metaphorical language such as "electricity" has engendered a suspicion of a discussion of audience emotions in theatre studies.[26] This current research, consistent with phenomenological methodology, will make use of such "loaded" terms as they are frequently used by the interviewed audience members and actors alike.

Conversations in the theatre are more of Bakhtinian dialogic rather than a dialectic. They are not only informed by multiple histories of multiple individual personalities, they are relational and heterogeneous. They engage in a reciprocal process that proffers myriad articulations and re-articulations of a fictitious world being experienced by actors and audience members.

Writings about actors and audiences

The relationship between the artwork or performance work and the audience has been discussed since Aristotle's *Poetics*. This aesthetic relationship has been explored most prolifically and contains the central precept of most contemporary audience research: the audience's meaning-making. The relationship with the performance work is also the central focus for most contemporary discourse on co-creation: how the audience co-create the performance work. As argued above, the "how" of audience co-creation is now being considered, but not the "with whom." Erika Fischer-Lichte comes closest, perhaps, to describing the actor–audience conversation in her descriptions of the auto-poetic feedback loop, arguing that theatre requires the bodily co-presence of actors and audience members.[27] In his seminal book *The Emancipated Spectator*, Jacques Rancière explores similar ideas to Bourriaud in his ideas of emancipation in art. Rancière argues that theatre is communitarian, a site for community, primarily because of the "living bodies onstage address[ing] bodies in the same place."[28] Rancière includes the actors in his discourse of co-creation and proposes that the narratives co-created in the theatre have the potential to "change something of the world we live in."[29] Lindsay Cummings[30] has begun to approach questions of empathy as dialogue and Maria Turri[31] has considered some of the psychological conversations occurring in the theatre. Yet all of these texts still distance themselves somewhat from engagement with the actor's meaning-making strategies and, more crucially, from their conversations with and relationship with the audience.

Similarly, there are many books on the actor's relationship with the artwork or performance piece and/or the character they are portraying. Many of these tend to be primarily skills based. A proliferation of actor training manuals commenced in the nineteenth century most notably with Johann Goethe's *Rules for Actors*. Some of the most significant contributions in the field of realistic acting exploring actor's perspectives were from Denis Diderot's highly contested *Paradoxe sur le comédien* and the writings of Konstantin Stanislavski. Many of these argue for or against certain acting techniques and contain discourses on the embodiment of character. It is only in what have now been considered more non-traditional approaches to performing that the actor–audience conversations surface. A closer consideration of the actor–audience relationship can be found in the writings of Jerzy Grotowski, Michael Chekhov, Peter Brook, Augusto Boal and, of course, Bertolt Brecht. Some more contemporary acting texts have touched on the emotion conversations between actors and audiences. Elly Konijn's *Acting Emotions* takes a more cognitive approach in the field of emotion psychology which includes, at times, the conversations with audiences and the role they play.

There is no extant discourse on the phenomenon of the electric air in theatre studies. There has been much discussion in Theatre and Performance Studies on what I argue is a component of the electric air – the subject of liveness in the theatre – but little on atmosphere. These related but dissimilar terms will be explored in Chapter 1. The liveness debate, introduced by Philip Auslander and Peggy Phelan and contested for many years in Performance Studies scholarship, is refreshingly re-conceptualised in *Experiencing Liveness in Contemporary Performance*. This anthology moves away from a discussion of liveness *per se* towards the performers and audience's experience of the live. Some conversations between actors and audiences are explored, yet the perspectives tend to be more audience-centric or actor-centric rather than relational. There is also an emergent group of scholars beginning to consider feelings as atmospheres in the theatre: Martin

Welton,[32] George Home-Cook,[33] and Joseph Roach.[34] Given the seeming hostility towards anything to do with psychological approaches or emotions in Theatre and Performance Studies, these directions, and the discussions undertaken by Kolesch and Knoblauch, and Turri cited above, are overdue.[35]

Once a performance commences, the most crucial relationship that actors and audiences have in the theatre is with each other. It is in that liminal space across the footlights that they co-create, in relationship. That relationship is temporal and ephemeral and yet, as I have argued elsewhere,[36] it is what actors are most preoccupied with and, as I posit in this book, what audiences go to the theatre for: conversations in the electric air.

The interviews

In initial preparations for this book, I planned to conduct general interviews with actors and audience members that were independent of any particular production. To this end, 14 one-hour interviews were undertaken with actors from New York, London, Paris, Berlin and Stuttgart, aged from 29 to 85. The majority of these actors were what I call veterans of the stage and screen: award-winning actors who have performed regularly on Broadway, West End, or capital city French or German stages for many years. Some of them also have significant film credits, and all have worked across both genres. Professional actors with vast and significant performance credits were selected as I needed to interview actors that had experienced myriad stage–audience conversations. Their biographies are included in the Appendix. In addition, 12 one-hour interviews were undertaken with audience members from New York, London, Paris and Stuttgart. The majority of the audience members were regular theatregoers that attended the theatre between 3 and 52 times a year with the average attending once every fortnight. It was imperative that I interviewed what I call "professional" audience members, "ordinary"[37] audience members that attend many productions. If I were to interview an audience member that was going to the theatre for the first time, they would only be able to draw on their experience of one set of actor–audience conversations or relationships. Audience members who go to the theatre often have experienced multiple stage–audience relationships with many casts of actors, so their individual views become more representative. Many of the audience members I interviewed drew on hundreds of conversations and relationships. Further, during the interviews I was quite astounded by not only how regularly they attend the theatre, but also how often they reflect on their role as an audience member. These interviews with professional actors and professional audience members formed the basis of Chapters 2 and 3.

While these interviews were fruitful in constructing the general perspectives of the relationships between actors and audience members and their prevailing motivations for experiencing theatre, I soon realised that I needed to observe and discuss the conversations at a particular performance to capture both sides of a specific conversation. The discourse embedded within plays was a fertile field to begin with and provided the necessary scaffolding for a discussion of the actor–audience conversations across the footlights. As actor Arens argued, in a play "there is a specific subject, and what I am trying to do is discuss that specific subject with the audience at that moment onstage."[38] To capture that specific subject discussion, case studies of three productions and subsequent interviews with actors and audiences attending those productions were undertaken. Details on these productions are outlined below. A total of 79 phenomenological audience interviews[39] were conducted across the three productions. I also interviewed either the full cast or half of the cast members of each production.[40] In total, for this book, 22 in-depth interviews were undertaken with actors, and 91[41] with audience members.

The conversations in the electric air are a subjective experience, so, consistent with that, the comments included in this book are subjective. Furthermore, since the purpose of this book is to investigate the nature of an acknowledged phenomenon, I aimed to investigate and record what audience members and actors said about the conversations between stage and audience and the presence or absence of the theatre atmosphere that I call the electric air. I was not searching for specific responses.

My research journey was, however, challenging. Drawing from my own lived experiences as an actor and as an audience member, I had already written my first chapter theorising on, and describing, some of the elements that I considered made up the electric air. Further, in undertaking my first few interviews, I realised that my background, assumptions and beliefs heavily influenced the intersubjective dynamics of the interview.[42] This consideration resulted in a complete re-evaluation of not only my questions but also my position as a researcher.[43] To minimise biases, I ameliorated several aspects of the interview methodology for subsequent interviews. Rather than commencing with an expert-led description of my book, I reduced my initial introduction to a few sentences: "My book talks about the 'magic' of theatre between actors and audiences. In this interview I am interested in hearing about your experiences of theatre." For the case study interviews, this was followed by "I'm going to start with some general questions, then move on to some specifics of this production."

I used no leading questions and avoided any words that were part of my own philosophy of the electric air such as "atmosphere," "electricity," "suspension of disbelief," "conversation" and so on. I did not reveal the title of the book until the conclusion of the interview. The questions were invitations to describe a lived experience such as "Could you describe for me the first moment when you perform in front of an audience – maybe the first preview after rehearsals – what does it feel like for you?" Or, for the case studies: "Can you recall a special moment you had in this performance and why it was special?" When words were not found to describe experiences, I left them hanging in the air and did not complete sentences or offer suggested descriptors. It was essential for me to endeavour to put aside any preconceived ideas, hidden agendas and predetermined theories in order to allow the actor and audiences' lived experiences room to flow, unimpeded by a desire on their behalf to provide answers that they thought I was wanting. This was of importance in the actor interviews. Second-guessing what the interviewer desires and giving the interviewer what they think they want to hear can be habitual for actors.[44]

The process of interviewing revealed some limitations of the process of interviewing. Some of the actors and audience members had preconceived notions of what an interview should be and, at times, failed to elaborate on their experiences. Furthermore, although experiential descriptions were an easy task for actors who were used to accessing their imaginative world and emotional reservoirs, it became a little more problematic with the initial round of audience interviews. Some audience members arrived with a list of productions they had seen and were keen to talk about these details rather than their experiences. During the later interviews it was confirmed that I did achieve some success as the impartial, undirected researcher when comments were made such as "is this something of what you want?" or "please let me know if what I am saying is not helpful." Because of the phenomenological method of enquiry, much of the content in the book is informed by the interviews, particularly the actor interviews. Through this journey, the list of undercurrents of the electric air in Chapter 1 was revised and extended.

In her investigation into audience research, Kirsty Sedgman argues that not only should the audience voice be included in discussions of theatrical events, but "Arts and culture scholars should value the knowledge and engagements of the publics they study."[45] Some audience research has begun to include the audience voice, valuing and privileging the audience comments as part of a larger "expert" discourse.[46] There are many more inroads that need to be made in this area. Sedgman goes on to emphasise that "[i]t is so important for audience researchers to analyse discourse in context."[47] The context of the theatrical event and the consequent context of the relational aspects of theatre are often overlooked in theatre research. The expert voice of the theatre scholar has traditionally prevailed over the voice of the audience member *and* the actors.

Actors have a vast repository of untapped insights and illuminating understandings of what occurs in the conversations between actors and audiences. They are acutely aware of how relational theatre is. That theatre theorists have not yet accessed this treasure store of information, and favour, instead the voice of the playwright or the director, is a conundrum. Further, as Gay McAuley notes, "actors gain a great deal of intuitive knowledge about audience response through their years of performance practice, but, as is so often the case in the theatre, this has rarely been written down or systematically collated."[48] This book is an initial attempt to begin to address this lacuna in theatre research.

The performances

Mainstream, commercial theatre productions continue to be under-researched in Theatre and Performance Studies. Consequently, actors and audiences co-creating at these productions are rarely interviewed. This book considers three productions that took place in commercial theatres in a Western dramatic indoor theatre tradition. They include a realistic drama, an intermedial one-person production and a post-dramatic work.

The first production was Manhattan Theatre Club's 2016 innovative Broadway staging of Simon Stephens's *Heisenberg*. For this production, the Friedman Theatre was entirely re-configured and rather than a proscenium arch experience, almost half of the audience sat on erected raked seating on one side of the stage facing the other audience members. This created more of a theatre-in-the-round intimate experience usually unobtainable in Broadway theatres. Manhattan Theatre Club also have an innovative audience engagement programme in which they offer audience members experiential workshops and play-theme-related classes and events that extend the conversation before and after the theatrical event. Actors often attend and participate in the workshops. Both of these aspects, the close proximity of actors and audience during the play, and the extended conversations before and after the production worked to make *Heisenberg* a unique and relational experience for the actors and audience members alike.

The second production was Complicité's *The Encounter*. Actor/co-deviser Simon McBurney's rich descriptions of his "virtual" conversations with audience members while onstage were so extraordinary that the questions I devised for the audience were informed by his responses. The production toured worldwide and audience interviews were conducted at three of the productions: New York in 2016, Adelaide in 2017 and London in 2018. Because of the nature of the play, *The Encounter* interviews were short "vox pops" carried out directly after the production on the New York theatre sidewalk, in the Adelaide Dunstan Playhouse foyer and the London Barbican foyer. *The Encounter* was an intermedial production. Audience members wore headphones for the entire performance. The headphones worked to create an intimate sensory experience and a very different conversation between actor and audience member.

A 2018 staging of Peter Handke's *Offending the Audience* at the Deutsches Theater in Berlin was the original choice for my final production. It was an outstanding production that historicised and contained a commentary on the original 1966 production. After interviewing three audience members, two actors and the dramaturg Bernd Isele, I discovered, however, that due to the audience familiarity with the play and its objectives, it was no longer relevant to my discourse on actor–audience conversations. I encountered another production that had just premiered at the Deutsches Theater that was commencing its repertory season: Sebastian Hartmann's *Hunger. Peer Gynt*. Although the production was not deliberately constructed to offend the audience, one-third of the audience members walked out of both of the performances I attended. My intended *Offending the Audience* case study was quickly replaced by *Hunger. Peer Gynt* which could, perhaps, have been aptly named "Offending the Actors." The audience walk-out, the atmosphere created onstage and the non-narrative approach to the production which ran anywhere between three and four hours made it a prime study for this book.

For the case study interviews, the same questions were asked of the actors and the audience members. For example, the actors were asked, "who are you onstage, the actor, the character or both? Why?" The audience were asked "who did you see onstage, the actors, the characters or both? Why?" There were some questions that were a little more specific than those asked in the autonomous interviews as necessarily informed by the productions. For example, during the *Hunger. Peer Gynt* case study audience members that left at interval were asked "why did you walk out?" and the actors were asked "what did you feel when audience members began to walk out?"

In addition to actor and audience interviews, participant observation played an important role in understanding the context of the productions and the ecologies of the theatre spaces. I saw multiple performances of each production taking on the role of observer-participant.[49] Observing the behaviour of other audience members and the interactions between actors and audience members was crucial in understanding the conversations specific to each production. This observation was particularly important during the *Hunger. Peer Gynt* walk-outs and equally so during *The Encounter* where I took my headphones off several times for long periods to listen to and record the sounds and comments made by audience members. My proximity to the stage also played an important role in this. In *Heisenberg*, for example, I sat on the staged seating for one performance and then in the auditorium for another. Participant observation also became important in experiencing the atmosphere of the productions as it rolled off the stage spatially in *Hunger. Peer Gynt*, or was co-created emotionally in the psychological conversations during *Heisenberg*. *Heisenberg*, *The Encounter* and *Hunger. Peer Gynt* each had experimental elements in them. The experimental elements and the very differing natures of each of the productions led to a diversity of actor–audience conversations.

Book structure

The book is divided into two parts. Part I "Electric Air" describes the theories and contributors to the electric air. Part II "Conversations" discusses the different conversations held across the footlights in the three case studies. As atmosphere and distance emerge as important concepts when considering psychological and emotional conversations in the theatre, frequent references are made throughout Parts I and II to the writings of Gernot Böhme, Hermann Schmitz, Edward Bullough and Jean-Paul Sartre. These theorists, unlike many of their contemporaries,[50] all consider the emotional, psychological and the relational in their discourses on atmosphere and distance. Further, it is important to note that as this book considers physical bodies in spaces – the actors on stage, the audience in the house – the physical and the emotional qualities of atmospheres are considered. Similarly physical distance and psychological distance in theatre are also examined.

Why are some moments in the theatre "just electric"?[51] What is about the audience that actors say "makes [them] spark" onstage?[52] In the process of considering these questions, Chapter 1, "The electric air of theatre," provides the theoretical lens for the book. It describes the unique climate of live theatre and the "electricity" that is transferred and reciprocated between actors and audience members through their conversations. Since the electric air is an intangible phenomenon, the chapter includes what I posit as descriptors and undercurrents of the electric air. Referring to the research of Gernot Böhme, Michael Chekhov and Jane Goodall, I describe the electric air in terms of atmosphere, liveness and electricity. Some theatrical, psychological and sociological undercurrents of the electric air are explored: suspension of disbelief, the encounter, ephemerality, narrative, transference, projection, identification, empathy, presence, celebrity magnetism and community. These descriptors and undercurrents establish the paradigm through which the actor–audience conversations are analysed in the rest of the book where some descriptions of the undercurrents are expanded.

Drawing from the in-depth interviews with actors in the first iteration of interviews, Chapter 2, "The view from the stage," considers the questions: Who is the actor while onstage and what is the actor's perspective of the audience? The actor's view from the stage is both visual (the audience they see) and relational (the audience they feel). The subjects under discussion are very much informed by the content of the interviews. The above-cited question "who are you onstage" prompted a large discussion of double consciousness that was not previously considered. A further question "how do you feel onstage" elicited, among other feeling states, considerations of actor insecurity. This not only resulted in a discussion on stage fright, it affected the structure of the chapter which follows the actor's journey from their security backstage to their insecurity onstage. Actor insecurity was inextricably linked to their relationship with an audience. The actor's presence, defined in terms of Böhme's radiation of ekstases, and the actor's encounter with the audience, emerged as important undercurrents that work to create the electric air experience for actors. Actor comments about their craft and their emotional and psychological conversations with audiences are disseminated throughout the chapter. Chapters 2 and 3 include a discussion of the electric air experiences and the times when there is no electric air. They also both conclude with an evaluation of the curtain call.

Chapter 3, "The view from the audience," considers the audience members' perspective of the actors. I commence with a discussion of what role the audience plays and then consider the audience member's view of the actors from the "house": who they see and how they experience the actors. Many audience members experience the theatre world as a hyperreality. Proximity to the stage emerged as an important aspect in the audience interviews. Edward Bullough's and Edward Hall's theories of distance are explored to describe the psychological and spatial conversations between audience members and actors. Similar to the previous chapter, the encounter with the actors and double consciousness became important audience views from the house. In the interviews, audience members were often preoccupied with actor presence. Audience perceptions of the actor's presence as drawing power, charisma, a space-filling phenomenon and as being "comfortable" onstage are discussed at length. Audience member comments about their relationships with the char/actors are discussed throughout the chapter.

During each of the case study interviews, certain undercurrents of the electric air were discussed and naturally shaped each chapter. Chapter 4, "*Heisenberg*'s psychological conversations," draws from the rich descriptions proffered in the cast and audience interviews to explore the psychological discourses across the footlights that created electric air experiences for actor and audience members alike. The intimacy of the play's staging, narrative and disclosures generated a palpable tension in the air between actors and audiences. Moments of transference, identification, projection and empathy that were experienced by audience members during the production are explored in detail. Because of what he called a "collective resonance" in the theatre during each performance, the actor, Denis Arndt, was intuitively aware of the psychological actor–audience conversations occurring, particularly identification and empathy. The suspension of disbelief, double consciousness and the "gaps" in the narrative of this production worked to create a propitious climate for the psychological conversations to occur. As the production included a celebrity, Mary-Louise Parker, the audience and actor perspectives of celebrity are also explored. The chapter concludes with a discussion of Manhattan Theatre Club's *Heisenberg* workshops and how they worked to extend the play's conversations before and after the production. As the psychological concepts explored in this chapter are quite thorny and complex, a psychiatrist was consulted several times to ensure that a clear explication of the terms was achieved.

While Chapter 4 focuses more on psychological undercurrents, Chapter 5 "Encounters with *The Encounter*," considers the theatrical undercurrents. In this one-person production, and given the titular nature of the performance, the encounter motif was central to the conversation. The actor–audience encounters with each other are described by Simon McBurney and the interviewed audience members. Encounters also occur between actor and narrative and audience and narrative. Owing to the intimacy created through the use of technology and the felt experience of the actor "inside the head," the relationship between actor and audience member changed significantly on both sides of the footlights. Actor and audience double consciousness and the understanding of presence are also recontextualised working on many different levels and creating a different experience of the electric air. The most noticeable difference in the actor–audience conversations in *The Encounter* is that they occur in a virtual atmosphere in what is posited by audience members as a "theatre of the mind." The chapter concludes with a discussion of the experience of the theatre of the mind for one audience member that was visually impaired. Interestingly, it is in this production that the conversations between actor and audience are most attuned.

The final chapter, "*Hunger. Peer Gynt*: a thirst for conversations," returns to evaluate the questions of what makes up the electric air experiences in the theatre, and under what circumstances is it absent. The chapter commences with an interrogation of the German word *Stimmung*. *Stimmung* in common parlance is essentially a conflation of atmosphere and mood. Its etymological origins as a musical term are used in this chapter. Conversations are re-imagined as the actors' and audience members' labour of "tuning." The chapter explores how the actors and audience tune to, or are out of tune with the space, the artwork and each other. *Hunger. Peer Gynt* can almost be perceived as an experiment exploring Böhme's conception of spatial and emotional atmospheres. The audience walk-out and how it affects or its lack of effect on the actor–audience relationship emerges as one of the most controversial yet important conversations of the production. The Deutsches Theater actors' often profound insights shed new light on their onstage, artwork and audience relationships. The audience comments highlight the importance of direct relationship with the actors in this production where many felt the actor–audience relationship was compromised. The chapter concludes with a discussion of the actor's attempts to reach across the border between stage and audience in one of *Hunger. Peer Gynt*'s subsequent performances.

The conclusion clarifies how this research brings together all the aspects that contribute to the conversation across the footlights. Drawing from the findings in the actor and audience interviews, I discuss the undercurrents and conversations that were of most relevance to the actors and audience members. The chapter concludes with a discussion of the importance of the relational: in the theatre, in actor and audience research, and as an antidote to the disconnect often experienced in these early decades of the twenty-first century. The essence of theatre is relationship.

Notes

1 The term "footlights" is used throughout the book. It refers to the border between the stage and the audience referencing the actual footlight lamps of the seventeenth, eighteenth and nineteenth centuries that were lined along the edge of the stage to illuminate the actors' faces.
2 Jerzy Grotowski and Eugenio Barba, *Towards a Poor Theatre* (New York: Routledge, 2002), 32.
3 Edward Bullough, "'Psychical Distance' as a Factor in Art and an Aesthetic Principle," *British Journal of Psychology* 5, no. 2 (1912): 99.
4 Jill Dolan describes these epiphanies as "utopian performatives." See *Utopia in Performance: Finding Hope at the Theatre* (Ann Arbor: Michigan UP, 2005), 5.
5 See Chapters 2 and 3 for actor and audience comments that describe the "electric" or "electricity."
6 Keith Randolph Smith, personal interview, 7 November 2018.
7 Edward Hibbert, personal interview, 21 September 2016.
8 Michael Reichgott, personal interview, 31 October 2016.
9 "Stella Adler: Awake and Dream! from 'American Masters'," Stella Adler School of Acting, accessed 16 August 2019, www.youtube.com/watch?v=4Yo4BLH87YY.
10 *Oxford English Dictionary*, accessed 20 July 2018, www-oed-com.ezp01.library.qut.edu.au/.
11 Erin Hurley, *Theatre & Feeling* (Basingstoke: Palgrave Macmillan, 2010), 38, 39.
12 Caroline Heim, *Audience as Performer: The Changing Role of Theatre Audiences in the Twenty-First Century* (London: Routledge, 2016).
13 *Oxford English Dictionary*.
14 Elias Arens, personal interview, 24 October 2018.
15 Ian Bartholomew, personal interview, 11 July 2017.
16 Mary Purdy, personal interview, 2 February 2014.

17 Paul Schoeffler, personal interview, 28 April 2013.

18 This refers to the argument of *Audience as Performer*, 2016.

19 Gernot Böhme, *The Aesthetics of Atmospheres*, ed. Jean-Paul Thibaud (London and New York: Routledge, 2017), 12.

20 Ibid., 5.

21 Ibid., 20.

22 Matthew Reason and Anja Mølle Lindelof, eds., *Experiencing Liveness in Contemporary Performance Interdisciplinary Perspectives* (New York: Routledge, 2016), 12.

23 Peter Brook, *The Empty Space* (New York: Simon and Schuster, 1997), 10.

24 Lynn Cohen, personal interview, 9 November 2018.

25 Doris Kolesch and Hubert Knoblauch, "Audience Emotions," in *Affective Societies: Key Concepts*, ed. Jan Slaby and Christian von Scheve (London: Routledge, 2019), 258.

26 Ibid., 260.

27 Erika Fischer-Lichte, *The Transformative Power of Performance: A New Aesthetics* (London: Routledge, 2008).

28 Ibid., 16.

29 Ibid., 23.

30 Lindsay B. Cummings, *Empathy as Dialogue in Theatre and Performance* (London: Palgrave Macmillan, 2016).

31 Maria Grazia Turri, *Acting, Spectating, and the Unconscious: A Psychoanalytic Perspective on Unconscious Processes of Identification in the Theatre* (London: Routledge, 2017).

32 Martin Welton, *Feeling Theatre* (Basingstoke: Palgrave Macmillan, 2011).

33 George Home-Cook, *Theatre and Aural Attention: Stretching Ourselves* (Basingstoke: Palgrave Macmillan, 2015).

34 Joseph R. Roach, *The Players Passion: Studies in the Science of Acting* (Anne Arbor: Michigan UP, 1993). This is more of a historical account rather than related specifically to atmospheres.

35 While there is a large body of work on the contested field of affect in theatre and performance studies, much of it is drawn from cognitive neuroscience rather than actor–audience lived experiences and it is outside the scope of this book to discuss.

36 Heim, *Audience as Performer*.

37 Helen Freshwater, *Theatre & Audience* (Basingstoke: Palgrave Macmillan, 2009).

38 Elias Arens, personal interview, 24 October 2018.

39 A phenomenological method of inquiry was adopted for this research for several reasons. Firstly, since, in essence, I am researching a phenomenon in the theatre – the electric air – phenomenological research was the logical starting point. Secondly, it was important that the questions probed beyond standard closed audience questions. The questions needed to elicit a discussion of experiences and feeling states. Thirdly, phenomenological interviews and interpretation is, perhaps, one of the most appropriate methods of inquiry for setting aside hidden agendas of the researcher and allowing more equality in the researcher/interviewee dynamic. It is important to note that biases will never be controlled fully.

  Having conducted semi-structured interviews for previous research with actors and audience members, I was very aware that actors in particular relish the opportunity of giving thick descriptions of their experiences through story, anecdote and revelations of feeling states. Phenomenological approaches seek the actors' and audiences' subjective feelings, perceptions and understandings of their theatrical experiences.

40 One production only had 2 actors, another only 1 and the third 10 actors.

41 Commensurable with the actor interviews, only 24 of these were in-depth interviews. The remaining were short interviews or vox pops.

42 My initial theorising not only biased my questions, but also changed the interviews from a 'context of discovery' to a 'context of justification.' Thomas A. Schwandt, "Constructivist, Interpretivist Approaches to Human Inquiry," in *Handbook of Qualitative Research*, ed. Norman K. Denzin and Yvonna S. Lincoln (London: Sage, 1994), 41–43.

43 In phenomenological research it is essential that the researcher "brackets" or suspends their theories and even their own experiences in order to enter into the world of the experiencer. It is also imperative that the respondent is valued as the expert, not the researcher. See Amedeo Giorgi, "The Theory, Practice, and Evaluation of the Phenomenological Method as a Qualitative Research Procedure," *Journal of Phenomenological Psychology* 28 (1997): 240; and Jason Cope, "Researching Entrepreneurship through Phenomenological Inquiry: Philosophical and Methodological Issues," *International Small Business Journal* 23 (2005): 179.

44 Patrick Tucker, *Secrets of Screen Acting* (New York: Routledge, 2003), 16.

45 Kirsty Sedgman, "Audience Experience in an Anti-expert Age: A Survey of Theatre Audience Research," *Theatre Research International* 42, no. 3 (2017): 307.

46 For some particular examples see Kirsty Sedgman, *Locating the Audience: How People Found Value in National Theatre Wales* (Bristol: Intellect, 2016); Reason and Lindelof, *Experiencing Liveness*; and Chris Megson and Janelle Reinelt, "Performance, Experience, Transformation: What Do Spectators Value in Theatre?," *Journal of Contemporary Drama in English* 4, no. 1 (2016): 227–242. See also the work of Ben Walmsley, Matthew Reason, Jennifer Radbourne, Hilary Glow and Katya Johanson.

47 Sedgman, "Audience experience," 307.

48 Gay McAuley, *Space in Performance: Making Meaning in the Theatre* (Ann Arbor: Michigan UP, 2000), 238.

49 Raymond Gold, "Roles in Sociological Field Observations," *Social Forces* 36, no. 3 (1958): 220.

50 Daphna ben Chaim argues Bullough and Sartre's distinction in this area in *Distance in the Theatre: The Aesthetics of Audience Response* (London: UMI Research Press, 1981).

51 June Weeks, personal interview, 27 July 2014.

52 Janet Fullerlove, personal interview, 20 July 2014.

PART I
Electric air

1

THE ELECTRIC AIR OF THEATRE

As an audience member, I have often sat in the theatre auditorium enthralled by the charge of electricity in the air that seems so combustible that a spark could ignite it. As an actor, I have often stood on the stage intoxicated by the heady atmosphere that rolls across the footlights and sharpens my senses and quickens my heartbeat. The electricity in the air changes the emotional temperature in the theatre. Every audience member or actor I have spoken with has experienced it in some way. It is addictive, exhilarating and gratifying. This is what I call the electric air. It is not confined to the performance alone. The electric air can be perceived from the moment an audience member enters the auditorium, the moment when the actors hear the familiar buzz of the audience from behind the curtain. The question "what is the electric air?" does not lend itself to a fixed answer. It is sensed, experienced and perceived. Is the electric air physical? Is it psychological? Does it move from the subjective to the objective in our bodies like excitement shows itself in increased heart rate? Audience members and actors describe the electric air in terms of feeling states: "It makes you tingle," "It gives you a rush."[1] Like many of the enchantments of the theatre, it defies quantification. In this chapter I am not providing an explanation; I am describing the experience of the electric air and suggesting some elements that contribute to it.

In order to situate the electric air as part of the contemporary discourse in theatre studies, I begin with a description of closely related phenomena: atmosphere, liveness and electricity. In many ways the electric air is the atmosphere encountered in the theatre that is created by the live co-presence of two groups of people, facing each other, playing specific roles: that of actors and audience. There is a certain energy and vitality that is produced by the encounter of these two groups that I describe in terms of electricity: magnetic attraction. When we hold two magnets opposite each other a magnetic field that is powerful, tense and visceral is intensified. The electric air in between the actors and the audience has this magnetic quality: two poles strongly attracted.

The aesthetic properties of atmosphere have been discussed since the early eighteenth century and the experience of atmosphere in the theatre for actors and audience members grew to prominence in the early twentieth century. Debates about liveness in the theatre have raged since the early twentieth century. Discussion of electricity in the theatre was prevalent in the eighteenth and nineteenth centuries. Since then, study of it as a theatre phenomenon has dropped into relative obscurity. Atmosphere, liveness and electricity are what I call descriptors of the electric air. There may well be other descriptors and I acknowledge that there is certain slippage between description and allusion in these terms. The electric air as an entity or a felt experience is, however, constituted by so much more than atmosphere, liveness and electricity. They are, perhaps, descriptors that are easily conceived. In order to understand the electric air more fully, in the second half of this chapter I proffer a number of different elements that can be seen to be undercurrents of the electric air in the theatre.

Descriptors of the electric air

Atmosphere

When we walk into a room we immediately sense or feel its atmosphere, that "something in the air." It could be a welcoming atmosphere, a hostile atmosphere, a tranquil atmosphere, an oppressive atmosphere. We can immediately gauge the kind of atmosphere not because we are trying to comprehend it, but because we are feeling it. The few theatre scholars that describe theatrical atmosphere in some form[2] predominantly draw from the writings of the German philosopher Gernot Böhme. Böhme notes that we tend to describe atmospheres in terms of their character.[3] We can talk about the atmosphere's character in meteorological or emotive terms or a conflation of both. Often meteorological terms are used to describe emotive atmospheres. The atmosphere in a space can be warm, cold, sultry, icy, sunny, dark or electric. If we are in a gloomy mood, the cheerful atmosphere of a room can change our mood in a kind of emotional contagion as we "attune" to the atmosphere. In the Heideggerian sense, when we are immersed in an atmosphere it can attune us "through and through."[4]

Atmospheres are ethereal, yet people have no hesitation in describing them. A coffee shop can have a cosy atmosphere; a humid summer's day can have a stifling atmosphere; parks can have a pleasant atmosphere; political rallies can have a stirring atmosphere. Phenomenologist Mikel Dufrenne argues that atmospheres have a "certain quality which words cannot translate but which communicates itself in arousing a feeling."[5] Atmospheres are felt, but they also manifest in a material form. They are, perhaps, the convergence of the physical air in a particular place and a mood or feeling. Atmospheres described by people are not, therefore, purely metaphoric or abstract, they also have physical qualities. They occupy spaces and they can be felt.

Atmospheres are considered to have three principle properties:[6] they pour out spatially, they work in in-between spaces and they are felt bodily. If, as Böhme suggests, "[a]tmospheres pour out into, and thus, shape spaces,"[7] then the theatre atmosphere is shaped by several entities, including people. While Erika Fischer-Lichte concentrates on how smells, lighting and sounds emanating from the stage or the auditorium create atmosphere in the theatre, she also suggests that the bodily co-presence of actors and audience members helps create atmosphere:[8] the live presence of two groups of people, face to face across the footlights. Theatre lighting and sound designers are experts in creating atmosphere. Stuart Grant argues, however, that atmosphere requires "bodies to experience it [and] bring it forth."[9] Atmospheres are experienced spatially and bodily.

For Böhme, atmospheres float "in-between" things and their perceiving subjects.[10] In the theatre, the gulf between audience members and actors is an in-between space. It can be highly charged and magnetic. Böhme describes atmospheres as "spheres of presence" with "ekstases" – Böhme's re-articulation of Walter Benjamin's auras – radiating out from them.[11] When the actors and audience meet across the footlights, I suggest that the energies or ekstases radiating out of the two groups create that tension, spark, thrill and buzz of theatrical atmosphere. The magnetic attraction or repulsion in the collision of these ekstases enlivens the atmosphere in the in-between space between the actors and the audience. Konstantin Stanislavski argued that one essential element of the "dramatic state" experienced in the theatre "is produced by the atmosphere surrounding an actor on the stage and by the atmosphere in the auditorium."[12] It is the collision of these two atmospheres that creates the sensory tingle of liveness felt in the theatre that is akin to what I call the electric air.

It is important to note that, as Patrice Pavis cautions, audience members' reading and understanding of atmospheres in the theatre can tend to take a "universalist" approach. "Rather," he argues, atmospheres "encourage us to start out from an understanding of our multiform identities so we can then have a better appreciation of how these cultural, ethnic, sexual and economic identities influence the way we decipher atmospheres."[13] Or, I would argue, create atmospheres. The audience member's mood and equilibrium at the time of viewing the production can not only affect their perception, and thus their reception of the theatrical event, it can also help to shape the atmosphere. Unfortunately, in his definitions of atmosphere, Pavis fails to include the actors and their labour in creating atmosphere in the theatre.

Actor and director Michael Chekhov, nephew of the Russian playwright Anton Chekhov, urged actors to be influenced by the atmosphere that surrounds them, contending that atmosphere can support and inspire creativity in the actor if they open themselves to it.[14] Atmospheres became a working technique to evoke emotional responses in his actors. Chekhov's use of atmospheres as a space-filling phenomenon pervaded the actor exercises he devised.[15] He taught his actors that "[a]tmosphere exerts an extremely strong influence upon your acting [...] The atmosphere urges you to act in harmony with it."[16] He also argued that atmosphere creates a nexus with the audience across the footlights:

> The actors who possess or who have newly acquired a love and understanding for atmosphere in a performance know only too well what a strong bond it creates between them and the spectator. [The spectator is] enveloped by it too.[17]

This bond is similar to magnetism. It is felt but not seen. When the actors and audience members are attuned to one atmosphere, a fertile climate for creativity is produced.

For audience members, the atmosphere felt in a theatre – whether it comes from the stage design, from the actors, from the emotional states of those sitting in the auditorium or even from, as Martin Welton argues,[18] the physical temperature in the room – envelops them and often induces physical sensations. We can experience prickly chills all over our body, a warm glow or shortness of breath. For actors, the atmosphere can be perceived from the minute they hear the audience filling the house and is felt acutely on their first stage entrance as the pervasive atmosphere in the auditorium spills onto the stage and into their being. Actors can receive a cool or warm reception; they can sense an atmosphere of hostility or even indifference. The atmosphere of the house is invariably discussed backstage as actors prepare each other for the kind of reception they will receive.[19] As they are entering into another room when they first enter the stage, and although actors sometimes use techniques to try and overcome this, the atmosphere felt in the auditorium can change their mood. Chekhov argued that a strong atmosphere overwhelms a weaker atmosphere.[20] The atmosphere on stage can also overwhelm the atmosphere in the audience. During the course of the performance, the actors and the audience eventually attune to or acknowledge the atmosphere co-created by each other. Even if the atmosphere is divisive, it is still a shared space. In this, atmosphere is relational. As Friedlind Riedel argues, "Atmosphere is invoked as that which mediates between two terms, integrates both, or precedes their distinction."[21] Atmosphere mediates between actors and audience members.

Atmosphere exists in nature and in bodied spaces such as theatres. Atmosphere is sensed and felt. As Welton states, in the theatre, emotions, feelings, mood and atmosphere are used almost interchangeably.[22] I would add "electricity" to this list. Atmosphere fills the air and all the cracks, crevices and in-between spaces of a place with emotions that are felt bodily by the people inhabiting those spaces. The magnetic attraction between actors and audience in the in-between space across the footlights can at times charge the atmosphere with an electric force: the electric air.

Liveness

The live, physical presence of actors and audience creates a certain thrill in the theatre. If I am sitting in the audience, I am aware that I could get out of my seat and touch the actors on stage. If I am onstage, close proximity to audience members means that I am acutely aware of their presence. As Matthew Reason and Anja Mølle Lindelof argue, "The live experience is a real embrace."[23] Liveness heightens excitement. It is the titillating experience of the *now*, generated by the co-presence of two groups of people encountering each other. Having worked both on the stage and on a film set, I am acutely aware of the difference that this live encounter makes to an actor. A live audience responds to, performs for and gives energy to actors. There is, of course, an "audience" present on a film set: the directors and film crew who occasionally offer some reaction. They do not, however, play the role of audience and their energies are focused elsewhere. Film actors and film audiences live separate, unconnected lives. There is no thrill of liveness for a film actor or a film audience. Liveness also opens the opportunity for co-creation to occur. Audience members *live* the experience with the actors, co-creating the narrative.

Since the early twentieth century, liveness has been defined in terms of its seeming antithesis: the recording of performances. Two of the primary theorists of liveness in theatre and performance studies, Philip Auslander and Peggy Phelan, have opposing perspectives. Auslander argues that theatre and recorded performances – television, film – are both live. Phelan argues that only the non-reproductive elements of theatre – co-presence and ephemerality – make it live. Film and television both lack this. In their definition of liveness, Paul Allain and Jen Harvie note that "performance's liveness gives it its distinctive energy, interest and social significance. It is in live performance that people – performers and audiences – encounter and potentially interact with one another."[24] There is a live, dynamic, magnetic pull across the footlights. It is this energy cultivated by the encounters and interactions with actors and audience members that works to make the atmosphere electric. Fischer-Lichte is adamant that energy in the theatre is not a phantasm but is physically perceptible.[25] Recent study in *Experiencing Liveness in Contemporary Performance* attempts to move the debates surrounding liveness "[a]way from liveness and towards experiencing live."[26] In this text, Howard Barker argues that "[o]verwhelming lacking is research on the meaning and value of 'liveness' to actual audiences."[27] This book makes some attempts to address this deficiency by including the audience and actors in the discussions of liveness.

I extend the meaning of liveness to include what has been obfuscated by the live/recorded discourses on liveness: a discussion of liveness that is related to or sparks a sense of electricity. A predominance of definitions of the word "live" refer to either electricity or the potential energy stored in an element. In the theatre this liveness is the buzz, the charge, the current or the spark in the air that is live. These words are often used by actors and audience members when describing the theatre atmosphere.

Electricity and liveness have always been associated with the theatre. Actors and audience members alike have even attempted to capture their physical properties. Patricia Fara relates a story of an electricity experiment in the eighteenth century where a member of the British Royal Society was acting in a performance of Henry IV and ran out of the theatre with a curtain rod during a thunderstorm in an attempt to capture the electricity from the lightning into a bottle.[28] Fascination with electric atmospheres continues today. In this second decade of the twenty-first century, various audience members have used plastic bags to capture the electric atmosphere at rock concerts and subsequently sold the bags of air online for sums as large as US$60 000.[29] In this age dominated by virtual encounters, the live encounter is becoming a valuable commodity.

This last example illustrates the connections between liveness and what is called an "electric experience" at a live event. Liveness is the very presence of bodies onstage and in the audience that creates a spark or thrill of electricity in the air. The television viewers at home, not present in the atmosphere of the event, do not experience the electricity in the air. They need to be what Barker calls "alive" in a "whole-body way"[30] to experience it. Liveness is therefore embedded in the co-presence of bodies onstage, the potential stored up in expectations, the possibility of the unpredictable, the excitation aroused in the actors and the audience. It is this potential that creates the electricity in the air.

Electricity

Audience members use the term "electricity" and its associated descriptive elements metaphorically to characterise aspects of theatre events.[31] Actors are sometimes said to embody a certain electricity. This is part of their personal magnetism and charisma and what attracts us to them: their performances are considered electric. Magnetism is part of this discussion of electricity but it is used more to describe the magnetic pull between audience members and actors.[32] Theatre has a rich history of allusions to the electricity embodied by actors. Much of it is anecdotal or inscribed by critics, actors and audience members in reviews, journals, letters, autobiographies or playgoer's memoirs. Although electricity in its figurative sense is "a state or feeling of great excitement, a thrill, a spark,"[33] there was a time in history, as alluded to in the above Henry IV story, that literal electricity was thought to be an actual force in the theatre.

We have historical evidence, at least, that electricity in the theatre was seen as physical. In *Stage Presence*, Jane Goodall gives a comprehensive historical overview of how electricity, the energy resulting from charged particles, was first equated with an actor's presence and only consequently became a metaphor for good acting. In the eighteenth and nineteenth centuries, performances displaying scientific experiments with electricity were staged to awe the public. Goodall explores how the public fascination with the power of electricity soon became an analogy for the stored up energy in actors and their potential of transmitting that energy or electricity to an audience.[34] Only 17 years after the discovery of electricity, the eighteenth-century actor David Garrick made one of the first allusions to this stored up electricity when he described how the "[e]lectrical fire, shoots through the Veins, Marrow, Bones and all of every spectator."[35] The discovery of electricity meant that this term could become figuratively mandated for use in the theatre. Electricity was seen as a life force that was a necessary part of star actors' onstage personal magnetism. Garrick's performances were considered "electrifying,"[36] William Hazlitt frequently described Charles Kean's "electric effect," and the "electric shocks"[37] he gave to audiences. Edwin Booth had "[e]lectric fire that [...] seemed to zigzag like forked lightening from the eyes."[38] Matilda Woods was considered "a complete battery of electric sparks herself."[39] Electricity came to figuratively denote talent, particularly in the early nineteenth century.

From historical accounts, it is clear that the actor's electricity was emotionally contagious. As critic Clement Scott noted, "When Mrs John Woods appears the whole theatre seems to be charged with electricity."[40] Very little research, however, has considered the electricity generated by audiences or the thrill and spark of electricity in the air in-between actors and audience that enlivens the atmosphere. In historical and contemporary actor's memoirs, letters and autobiographies, there are frequent references arguing that the "audience gives the inspiration and the electricity"[41] to the actors. From all accounts it is clear that the generation of electricity, in the figurative sense, was reliant on the performances[42] of actors *and* audience members who transmitted a certain energy, vitality and life force to each other through their conversations across the footlights. The term "electricity" is able to embody, in its figurative sense, the qualities of physical electricity.

I have used atmosphere, liveness and electricity as starting point descriptors of the electric air. The relationships among atmosphere, liveness and electricity in the theatre have a fascinating history. The liveness of actors and audiences – in Allain and Harvie's sense of co-presence – creates live electrical currents in the in-betweenness, infusing the atmosphere to create the electric air. This is why some theatre scholars and historians feel that theatres have "a semi-sacred atmosphere […] a sort of electric current that charge[s] the audience."[43]

Undercurrents of the electric air

The electric air has undercurrents. Eleven undercurrents of the electric air provide the basis for the discussions in the rest of the book: suspension of disbelief, the encounter, ephemerality, narrative, transference, projection, identification, empathy, presence, celebrity magnetism and community. There may well be other elements that could also be seen as undercurrents. I have chosen these elements as they are all, on some level, relational and conversational. Each of these undercurrents initiates or forms part of the conversation across the footlights. Collectively, they can be seen to contribute to the electric air. In order to give the undercurrents an orientation, they have been placed under three rubrics. Theatrical undercurrents include the suspension of disbelief, the encounter, ephemerality and narrative. The psychological undercurrents explored are transference, projection, identification and empathy. The sociological undercurrents include presence, celebrity magnetism and community.

Theatrical undercurrents

Suspension of disbelief

There is one rarely discussed phenomenon that occurs when the lights go down and the play begins and helps create the enchantment of the electric air: the suspension of disbelief. The suspension of disbelief essentially describes the act of a person willingly entering into and believing in an imaginary world. The term was coined by Samuel Taylor Coleridge in 1817 in relation to the reading of poetry,[44] but it has since been appropriated for the reception of many art forms. Coleridge, also a playwright and avid theatregoer, extended his discourse on the suspension of disbelief in the theatre after a viewing of Shakespeare's *The Tempest* describing how audience members "*chuse* to be deceived" by Shakespeare's drama. The phrase has also been used interchangeably with "dramatic illusion."[45] Coleridge himself uses the phrase to describe the reception to literature, poetry and plays interchangeably.[46] Interestingly, Coleridge was also one of the first poets to use the word atmosphere to describe a psychological climate.[47] In the theatre, suspending disbelief means laying aside our knowledge that the characters we see onstage are portrayed by actors and that the action occurring in front of us is not real but a piece of fiction. It also involves opening our minds to be emotionally moved by a narrative. Coleridge's "willing" is often excluded from the phrase, yet this is an essential part of the process. We consensually agree to step into the fictitious world and belief is suspended in the ether. As psychotherapist and theatre practitioner Roger Grainger argues, suspension of disbelief is a game we agree to play.[48] We open ourselves to believe in an imaginary world.

There are numerous humorous incidents throughout theatre history, particularly in the nineteenth century, when audience members believed the imaginary was the real world, mistaking fiction for reality. They would, for example, jump onstage to give money to a dying widow, challenge a character to a fight or plead with a character to stop his criminal behaviour.[49] What was going on in the minds of these audience members? They suspended disbelief to the point that they believed the narratives were actually happening. We may laugh, but these are actions that every audience member unconsciously or consciously plays out in their imagination as they watch a piece of theatre. Not jumping up on stage but believing in the character and their actions by investing the situations observed onstage with what Grainger calls "imaginative truth."[50] As audience members we know the story is a fabrication, yet the imaginative truth can move real emotions. Much of the existing research on the suspension of disbelief concentrates on literary and film studies. In his book *Suspending Disbelief*, Grainger argues that that there is a certain mutuality or sharing of imaginative truths that occurs in the theatre between actors and audience[51] that does not occur in the cinema.

Audience members have a unique relationship with actors in the theatre as they enter into the imaginary together. The audience's willingness to suspend disbelief draws them closer to the actors who too have suspended disbelief in order to recreate the fictitious world. Actors are experts in suspending disbelief, second, perhaps, only to children who intuitively suspend disbelief every time they play. As argued by Stanislavski, the imaginative work of the actor demands an extra layer of "believing" that is not required of the audience; s/he must not only believe in the fiction of the play, but "most of all [s]he must believe in what [s]he is doing."[52] One of Stanislavski's primary tenets that revolutionised acting in the late nineteenth and early twentieth centuries was his appeal to actors to believe in the imaginary circumstances of the play in order to inhabit their characters. As he argues:

> Everything that happens on the stage must be convincing to the actor himself, to his associates and to the spectators. It must inspire belief in the possibility, in real life, of emotions analogous to those being experienced on the stage by the actor. Each and every moment must be saturated with a belief in the truthfulness of the emotion felt, and in the action carried out, by the actor.[53]

Stanislavski argued that this belief is interrelated to the audience's imaginative truth.

Stanislavski's "belief" is not dissimilar to the suspension of disbelief. When an actor has suspended disbelief convincingly, the audience member "is drawn into the very thick of the life that [s]he sees on the stage" through [her/]his own belief.[54] The mutual suspension of disbelief across the footlights provides a fertile environment for conversations to occur. The consensual sharing of imaginative truths creates a bond between the actors and the audience members. The actors' and audience's belief in the fictitious world saturates the electric air with infinite possibilities.

The encounter

From the moment actors backstage put on their costumes and make-up and the audience members at home dress to go to the theatre, they are preparing to encounter each other. Much of the energy they contribute at the theatre has been stored up in those delightful states called excitement and anticipation that tease and provoke us in preparation for the theatrical encounter. As audience members, our "horizon of expectations,"[55] all the ideas, beliefs, preconceptions, past experiences that we have had, frames and informs our reception to and reading of the performance we are about to see on stage. Anticipation of what is to come builds the excitement and thrill. Anticipation surrounds audience members in an almost visible aura as they enter the theatre. Backstage, actors also share this anticipation as they prepare for that first step onto the stage to encounter the audience.

Applying one of Paul Watzlawick's communication axioms to the theatre encounter, Fischer-Lichte argues that when actors and audience members meet each other face to face, they "cannot *not* react to each other" (italics in original).[56] Their gaze, their gestures, their emotions, their words, even their silence necessarily affect each other. In the theatre there are two troupes of performers: actors and audience.[57] The physical co-presence of these two troupes facing each other is an essential part of the liveness of theatre and contributes to the electric air. At the beginning of each performance, the energies that each troupe bring in with them – filled with excitement and anticipation – enliven the air. Actors have a considerable amount of stored up energy which Joseph Chaikin argues can create an "electric field."[58] When the energies of the two troupes meet in the encounter, a highly charged interactive conversation commences in the magnetic in-between space across the footlights.

Audience members contribute just as much to the conversation as do the actors. When a scene or a character affects them, audiences cannot *not* react. Their verbal, paralingual and physical gestures and utterances affect the actors who, in turn, cannot *not* react. This interactive conversation and the co-creation of the narrative that ensues is detailed in Chapters 2 and 3.

The encounter, as Fischer-Lichte argues, is interactive and is also confrontational.[59] Jerzy Grotowski also refers to the encounter as confrontation and as struggle.[60] Actors confront insecurities in themselves as they embody characters and sometimes have confrontations with other actors or directors in rehearsals or backstage which get played out onstage in character. The biggest confrontation that actors face is with the audience. They would not exist as actors without this encounter. Although all of an actor's training and rehearsals prepare them for this meeting across the footlights, the actor's encounter with an audience can be so confrontational that many suffer stage fright.

For the audience, the most immediate confrontation is the fictitious world created on stage. Arguments with partners, children or friends are predominantly forgotten as they are engrossed in the encounter with actors. Their lives are suspended as they enter into the play's imaginative world which often powerfully overwhelms cares of the outside world. Grotowski, who believed that the core of theatre is the encounter, discussed the actors' and audience members' confrontation with themselves at length.[61] He also argued that actors have encounters with the audience, with the characters they are playing, with other creatives and with the play text. In the dynamic magnetic pull of the encounter, a powerful bond is formed between the actors and the audience members as they interact and confront each other across the footlights. Encounters create a *frisson* of energy that is an undercurrent of the electric air.

Ephemerality

Performances exist in a temporal time frame and then disappear.[62] No two performances are ever the same. The actors' and the audience's performances differ from performance to performance because, as Antonin Artaud argued, "the theatre is the only place in the world where a gesture, once made, can never be the same way twice."[63] This gives the experience of theatre that sense of newness and occasion every time. Performances live in the moment. An idiom that is part of Stanislavski's legacy but was coined by members of the Group Theatre in the early twentieth century is "moment-by-moment" acting. Actors are encouraged to live in the moment that the play is occurring: the fictitious and the real-time moment. Audience members experience and respond to the play in each ephemeral moment.

The ephemerality raises the stakes of the experience. "Raising the stakes," originally a poker term, has been appropriated as an acting term.[64] It is idiomatic for increasing risk. Performing in front of an audience can be risky for actors, but it is precisely this that makes acting enticing and exhilarating. It is like walking on a tightrope. One of the most thrilling aspects of live performance is that something can go wrong. As Matthew Reason argues, it is not that the "interest and tension" of the audience are actually dependant on something going wrong, "but the awareness of that possibility."[65] For the actor, the stakes are very high because they are vulnerable. They are using the sum total of their skills. Do they have what it takes? Are they good enough? Can they convince us enough so that we suspend disbelief? This vulnerability can create moments of sheer terror for actors as they risk breaking out of their character, forgetting their lines or are overwhelmed by stage fright. One actor losing concentration and forgetting the sequence of their lines or actions can lead to other actors losing their way. Actors are vulnerable together. Some actors recover quickly when things go wrong, while others freeze. This ephemeral unpredictability of things going wrong in theatre heightens its enjoyment.

Unpredictability also provides the conditions in the theatre for something to go more than right: those moments when actors or audience members have what Jill Dolan calls "utopian performatives" and Marvin Carlson "epiphanies"[66] that dazzle the senses, liberate the emotions or sharpen the intellect. Both scholars argue that these moments which lift us out of the quotidian occur precisely because of the ephemerality of theatre. These are moments that are often described as "magical" by audience members. Actors describe them as moments when they were "flying." They are captured moments that can never be repeated and are all the more magical precisely because they are transient and unpredictable. The stored-up potential of the unpredictable electrifies the air.

An important part of the ephemerality of performance is the potential for the audience to spontaneously interact with the actors, verbally or physically, outside of the expected boundaries of conditioned response. The audience may speak back to the stage, stop the show with their applause, snort so loudly while they are laughing that the audience starts laughing at the audience. What I call audience performance – any verbal, gestural or paralingual behaviours of the audience, invited or otherwise – was so prevalent up until the end of the nineteenth century, that it was not regarded as anything extraordinary. Since the 1850s, any audience performance outside of moderate laughing, controlled crying and applause at the end of the performance is relatively rare.[67] The potential that some unpredictable audience performance can happen is, however, present at every performance. The temptation hangs in the air.

All of these aspects of ephemerality – theatre's transience, its newness and unpredictability – give theatre that edge. Since each performance is a one-off event, it is a unique shared experience that creates a nexus between actors and audience members: those "I was there when that happened" moments treasured by actors and audience members alike charging the air with an intense electricity.

Narrative

I have often listened to a friend relate the story of a play we had just seen to someone who had not been present. I am invariably surprised by the narration and recall one or two occasions when the description was so foreign to my experience of the event that I questioned my co-attender's lucidity. They created a different narrative in their minds from my narrative. For the purposes of this book, narrative is defined as "an account of a series of events, facts, etc., given in order and with the establishing of connections between them; a narration, a story, an account."[68] Wolfgang Iser argues that literary texts have "gaps" in them which "each individual reader will fill in" from his or her own experiences "mak[ing] [her]his own decisions as to how the gap is to be filled."[69] Although Iser is referring to books, the same process applies to the theatre. Jacques Rancière argues that the audience member "composes her[his] own poem with the elements of the poem before her[him]."[70] Plays have gaps in them that audience members fill in, drawing from their own life experiences. Because each person's experiences, beliefs and emotional make-up and imagination is different, each narrative is different.

The playwright's written narrative goes through several iterations and transformations before being perceived in an audience member's mind. The playwright's narrative is transformed by the director and[71] the actors, and is again transformed by each audience member. Actors, the conveyers of the playwright's narrative, fill in the gaps of the narrative in their telling of the story but in a different way than audience members. Each audience member and each actor fill in the gaps differently, yet they are all part of the same narrative. It is this conjoining that makes narrative an undercurrent of the electric air. Actors draw from their own experiences and their imaginations to create characters. Iser argues that the virtual dimension of any piece of literary work is "the coming together of text and imagination" and goes so far as to argue that if there were no gaps in texts, we would not be able to use our imagination.[72] If we imagine a production of *Hamlet* where a different actor played Hamlet in the send act, the two characterisations of Hamlet would differ. While this is explained as "just different interpretations," in interpreting, each actor is filling in the gaps in Shakespeare's text, drawing from her/his life experiences, her/his own personality and her/his imagination[73] to create the narrative of that character for their particular performance.

Another narrative in the theatre is created in the in-between space between audience and actors. Audience and actors co-create this narrative. This narrative is co-created through emotion-, body- and word-conversations across the footlights which are described in the case studies in Part II of this book. Jean-Paul Sartre acknowledged the collaborative role of audiences when he stated that "[t]he audience writes the play quite as much as the author does."[74] I would include the actors in this collaboration. A narrative that is co-created by actors and audience is significantly different than the written play. It also differs from performance to performance and, as I have argued, from person to person. Co-creation of the theatrical narrative is relational and it is unconsciously collaborative. Similar to the mutuality experienced in the suspension of disbelief, narrative co-creation creates a nexus between audience and actors that contributes to the electric air as stories are interwoven in the space between the stage and the audience.

As part of the theatrical experience, actors and audience members willingly suspend disbelief to enter into the imaginative world of the story that is being performed. The narratives that are played out on stage and in the imaginations of the audience hover in the electric air. Actors describe their immersion in the flow of the narrative as "riding a wave" that is created by the intersubjective co-creation of actors and audience during the encounter. The co-created story exists for only those few short hours in a particular space, at a particular time in the encounter of two troupes of performers across the footlights. As Phelan argues, the theatrical performance defines itself through its disappearance.[75] It is ephemeral, and all the more enchanting because of its disappearance.

Psychological undercurrents

Transference

Have you ever felt an instant dislike for someone because they reminded you of someone you knew? You cannot place who it is, but you just feel it. Your controlling sister, perhaps, or your cantankerous grandfather or that child that bullied you at school. This is transference. As Sigmund Freud described, you "replace some earlier person for the person"[76] in front of you. You transfer aspects of a past relationship to a present relationship. As a consequence of this, what Freud calls "substitution," there is a reawakening of the emotions associated with these experiences in the imagination and "a whole series of psychological experiences are revived, not as belonging to the past, but as applying to the person […] at the present moment."[77]

Although Freud described the process of transference primarily in a psychoanalytical context, he was quick to argue that transference is a "universal phenomenon of the human mind […] and in fact dominates the whole of each person's relations to his human environment."[78] I posit that just as transference is one of the central tenets of therapeutic relationships in psychotherapy, in the theatre transference is one of the fundamental cornerstones of the actor–audience relationship. As the theatre involves relationship between actor and audience member, and character and audience member, transference would be, according to Freud, inherent in theatrical relationships. If, as Eric Nuetzel argues, "[t]ransference [occurs] everywhere that human beings interact in emotionally meaningful ways,"[79] then the theatre is a fertile environment for the transference phenomena to occur. There are, however, few discourses on transference in the theatre.

Maria Turri is one of the few theatre and psychology scholars who is equipped to and has, therefore, attempted to undertake a psychoanalytic reading of the actor–spectator relationship. She suggests that "spectatorship may imply, at an unconscious level, a form of self-analysis."[80] An interesting proposition that certainly played out in the many interviews undertaken for this research. Turri further explains how the process of self-analysis can occur in the theatre when discussing other psychological processes such as identification: "Through her interpretation, the actor gives meaning to the spectator's repressed emotions, bringing them into his consciousness."[81] Transference is relational. The actor as the vehicle of relationship is vital in the psychological processes occurring for the audience member. Stanislavski, adapting Leo Tolstoy's idea that "art communicates felt experience, rather than knowledge, 'infecting' its audience with the artists' emotion," argues that "the actor 'infects' the audience when a performance stirs an audience's affective memories."[82] Transference and all the other undercurrents are relational and are part of a conversation between actor and audience member. Each individual audience member's transference experiences are unique.

In transference in the theatre, the audience member is confronted with a character on stage, aspects of the past relationship are imprinted onto the character–audience relationship. A strong nexus is formed. There is a revival of a whole series of psychological experiences related to those relationships that can fill the air with emotions, colours and sensory responses that contribute to the electricity experienced across the footlights.

At times it may be a situation or an incident that occurs in the play which sparks the transference. Powerful emotions prompted by the transference are suspended in the air between audience members and actors. This can create a visceral tension in the encounter between the actors and the audience members which heightens the experience and raises the stakes of the performance. The audience member is significantly invested in the experience as the play's narrative is interwoven with the audience member's personal narrative.

Actors sometimes use what is called in the actor's lexicon "substitution" for characters onstage. Interestingly, this is Freud's word for transference. In this process, actors may substitute their own daughter for the fictitious daughter their character is in relationship with in the play. Uta Hagen argues that many actors use substitution unconsciously also.[83] The actor playing Blanche in *A Streetcar Named Desire* can unconsciously transfer aspects of a past relationship from her real life onto her relationship with the character of Stanley in the play. Powerful emotions are evoked which heighten the tension in the air between the two characters as the narrative is played out. This, in turn, is felt by the audience.

Transference is relational. In the theatre actors form bonds with each other and their characters, and audience members form bonds with the actors and the characters onstage. Myriad unconscious conversations permeate the atmosphere. Transference is, perhaps, the most important and potent of all these conversations because it forms interpersonal bonds that, as seen in the *Heisenberg* case study, repel or attract, resulting in a highly charged electric air.

Projection

Projection comes from the Latin for "throwing out of oneself." It is seeing aspects of oneself in the outside world. In the theatre, audience members mentally throw (project) aspects of themselves – their longings, fears, joys, sorrows and hopes – out onto the characters onstage. In psychotherapy, projection is customarily understood as a defence mechanism: "The defensive attribution of unwanted thoughts, wishes, feelings and related mental contents to some other person."[84] I hate myself being selfish, so I get annoyed when I see this fault in someone else rather than acknowledging it in myself. Freud entertained a more expansive view of projection and considered its sensory and creative qualities:

> [Projection is] a primitive mechanism, to which [...] our sense perceptions are subject, and which therefore plays a very large part in determining the form taken by our external world.[85]

In the theatre audience members individually project a kaleidoscope of perceptions and emotions onto the fictional world in front of them, building up that world until it becomes a vast sphere of images, desires and sensory perceptions which are relevant to them personally. Projection becomes an intoxicating experience in the theatre: live bodies in the audience projecting emotions onto live bodies onstage. Unresolved individual conflicts, private dreams, repressed emotions thicken the air between audience and actor. Projection is one mechanism through which audience members experience the play. Projection contributes to the electric air as audience members have similar yet quintessentially unique experiences.

As Patrick Tucker argues, projection is most apparent when a celebrity takes the centre attention of the audience:

> If any celebrity, with recent notorious behaviour were to appear in a movie [or a play], audiences around the world would project onto her their [personal, intolerable] feelings about her exploits so lovingly detailed in all the newspaper and magazine articles such things attract, and she correspondingly would be required to act less.[86]

The past experiences, in many ways, acts for her/him. This often results in uncrafted acting by some celebrities when they "return to the stage." The audience's affective memories act for them.

Projection closes the gap between audience and actors. In a process that is not dissimilar to scapegoating, audience members throw their emotions and unresolved conflicts onto the characters onstage. Projection is relational and contributes to the thrill experienced in the electric air of liveness in the encounter between actors and audience members.

Identification

Although Freud introduced the term identification in psychoanalysis in 1897, it was not until 1914 that it came into parlance in the psychoanalytic sphere. Identification is essentially the "that's me!" experience. I can identify with that character onstage because I am like them. I can identify with that situation as I have experienced it before. It is the process of seeing your identity in something else: taking something from outside and making it part of yourself. Freud proffered his own theory of theatre spectatorship arguing that identification with the characters was pleasurable for audience members knowing "firstly, it is someone other than himself who is acting and suffering on the stage, and, secondly, that after all it is only a game, which can threaten no damage to his personal security."[87] His latter assumption is not always the case, as explored in the first case study.

Jean Laplanche and Jean-Bertrand Pontalis argue that projection and identification have often been used interchangeably, but that this is erroneous as projection and identification are separate mechanisms.[88] Projection is throwing out. Identification is seeing yourself and taking in. Identification for the audience member has been written about extensively in theatre and performance studies. Several theorists – Bertolt Brecht included – consider Aristotle to be the first to describe identification, but call it "catharsis."[89] Pavis argues that Friedrich Nietzsche gives a vivid description of identification in *Birth of Tragedy*.[90] Several memoirs, journals and some theatre books of the eighteenth and nineteenth centuries also describe the process of identification in the theatre without naming it as such. In his epochal 1912 essay on psychical distance, Edward Bullough gives a vivid description of identification in the theatre. Although he named it "concordance," he described how an audience member, that "has cause to be jealous of his wife" in his natural life, may experience concordance while watching a performance of *Othello*. His description illustrates our contemporary understanding of identification. As Bullough argues, the audience member "will the more perfectly appreciate the situation, conduct and character of Othello, the more exactly the feelings and experiences of Othello coincide with his own."[91] Sartre also describes identification in these terms: "In the theatre, we remain outside and the hero meets his fate before our eyes. But the impact on us and our feelings is all the stronger in that the hero is also ourselves, even if outside us."[92] Interestingly, similar to Bullough, Sartre's argument contains a discourse on distance.

Brecht wrote and taught on the pitfalls of identification for the spectator arguing that it leads to a more passive and uncritical role for the audience member.[93] His discourses on the hazards of identification for the spectator heralded the beginning of a large range of pejorative and some complimentary discourses on audience/actor identification. From Jill Dolan's[94] and Elin Diamond's[95] Feminist perspectives to Henri Schoenmaker's projected desires[96] and David Krasner's conflation of identification and empathy. Turri's psychoanalytical perspectives have given further insights into the specific mechanisms involved.

In actor training, identification has been used interchangeably with the term "involvement." As Elly Konijn argues, involvement entails the actor seeking similar emotions to that of the character they are playing "based on the presumption that the meaning of the situation for the character has some congruence with the situational meaning from the actor's point of view."[97] Identification becomes a tool for actors to build a character. Method actors particularly search for aspects in the character they are portraying that they can identify with. They then draw from these aspects in their emotional make-up to create a character to, perhaps, make the character seem more "real" for the audience. The actor playing Blanche from *A Streetcar Named Desire* has, perhaps, a flighty or a fragile emotional make-up which she will then draw from in her interpretation of the character Blanche. This kind of acting based on identification, if taken to an extreme, sometimes becomes introspective and can deaden the atmosphere and distance an audience.[98] Actors can be so preoccupied with their own life story and their own emotions as actors in a play that their characterisations become self-absorbed and they shut out the audience. Similarly, Patrice Pavis and Kent Cartwright argue that an audience's identification can lead to introspection which in turn creates a gulf across the footlights.[99] As an antidote to this introspection, Brecht not only advocated against spectator identification, he also disapproved of the actor's emotional identification with their characters. He taught his actors to be "demonstrators" and gave them techniques to become "witnesses" of the events they were portraying onstage to ensure they are detached from emotionally identifying with the character to safeguard against identification. Ultimately, at the end of his life, he saw that this did not work in practice, and revised some of his original positions.

Empathy

Empathy is a relatively new term in English only appearing in parlance in the early twentieth century, translated by Edward Titchener from the German *Einfühlung* in 1909. It is predominantly understood, through its various aesthetic and psychological meanings, as the process of one person "feeling into" the emotional states of another. Long before Titchener's translation and dating back to the Ancient Greeks, empathy's antecedent "sympathy" was used to describe feeling with another's thoughts and feelings.[100]

Contemporary performance theory has concentrated on the affective impact of empathy and has looked to scientific qualification, specifically the workings of mirror neurons in the brain, to describe how we can imitate and/or are affected by a character's emotions onstage when we attend the theatre.[101] While this understanding of empathy as a reflexive response goes some way to describing what happens, it does not elucidate the intricacies or the mechanisms of the more personal aspects of empathy where we are drawing from our own experiences, personality and imagination to feel into the emotions of another.[102] We do this all the time as audience members watching a play.

The opportunity to feel into the emotions of a character onstage is one of the primary reasons many audience members go to the theatre. Empathy is an experience shared with the actors. As Theodor Lipps, one of the first philosophers to describe empathy in the theatre, argues, "Empathy means, not a sensation in one's body, but feeling something, namely oneself, into the esthetic object." Empathy is relational. Lipps goes on to describe it as an "echo" across the footlights.[103] These are the moments in the theatre where we can feel powerfully into the emotion states of a character onstage and it often manifests in physical states. It can make our heart pump that little bit faster, make us hold our breath or move us to tears. Recent theatre research has also begun to explore how empathy is dialogic.[104]

Everything an actor does ideally facilitates understanding, movement of emotions and an experience for the audience. In this way, the actors are being empathic towards the audience. They do not actually empathise with an audience, but they facilitate empathy. For example, it is generosity on the part of the actor that allows the audience to cry. As Hagen argues,

> The misuse of the emotional instrument is flagrant on today's stage. Many [actors] make it a primary goal to prove to themselves and to the audience that they have feelings, that they can produce tears. [...] They leave the stage, so to speak [to] make the water flow. The audience [...] usually remains unmoved.[105]

Often, if the actor cries, the audience tears are stolen. It is almost as if an actor needs to give the audience permission and space to cry. The actor chokes up, they find it difficult to deliver their lines, they just hold it together, they do not cry, the audience cries for them. This is one of the most moving experiences in the theatre and illustrates the powerful workings of empathy. At these times the chasm between actor and audience member is bridged in an empathic encounter.

A very basic and brief summary of these processes is the following. Transference is *transferring* from the past. Projection is *throwing* yourself. Identification is *seeing* yourself. Empathy is *feeling* into. All these processes are interrelated and are often experienced concurrently in all of us in every human interaction. Thunder and lightning are a useful analogy. We use two different descriptors for the audible and visual but no name for the actual phenomenon. Similarly, psychology has used different names – transference, projection, identification and empathy – for each aspect of the one phenomenon.

More than any of the other undercurrents cited in this chapter, the psychological undercurrents help create Bullough's "utmost decrease of Distance without its disappearance."[106] They draw the audience and actors into the fictional world together. The psychological undercurrents underpin the idea that each audience member is an individual within a collective. Each audience member brings in with them their unique life experiences which lead them to personally transfer, personally project, personally identify with and personally empathise with the actors and their portrayal of characters onstage. The cumulative result in the theatre is that all of these "moving" psychological experiences contribute to a collective experience of that charge in the air that we call electric. There are times when you could almost cut the tension across the footlights with a knife. Psychological experiences are those "I was on the edge of my seat" moments where, in the process of transference, your brother is staring at you from the stage, you are living vicariously through a character having projected yourself up there or you are feeling into a character through empathy. This is why Stanislavski argued that we do not go to the theatre for visual effects but "impressions made on the emotions, which leave a lifelong mark on the spectator and transform actors into real, living beings."[107]

Sociological undercurrents

Presence

When we say a person has "presence" what do we mean? Someone enters a room and all eyes are drawn to them. Their presence absorbs our attention. We may stop conversations or activities, lose concentration and even feel a thrill expire through our body as their presence affects us. They have a strong "energy" that emanates from them. Their demeanour "suggest[s] inner strength, force of personality"[108] which we perceive as negative or positive. In the theatre actors are set apart from the audience. They are, for a short while, different human beings. They are mini celebrities at least. They may have "presence" conferred on them by this status. Some actors are seen to have a strong presence, what Joseph Roach calls "it"[109] and Stanislavski calls "charm."[110] Dolan argues that actors that have a "virtuosity and charisma [...] offer intense moments of electrifying presence."[111] "It," charm, virtuosity, charisma, inner strength, force of personality – however described – presence is a highly explosive and contested term in theatre studies. For this reason alone it is very relevant to my discussion of electric air. Jane Goodall talks extensively of the drawing power of those with presence. Actors that have "it" seem to possess an extra glow of Benjamin's aura or Böhme's ekstases that flow out of them modifying the spheres of atmospheres surrounding them. Their ekstases touch us across the footlights and make us spark.

As established above it is the co-presence of actors and audience members in the encounter that makes theatre live. Can audiences, however, like certain actors, exude a strength or force of personality? If you were to ask an actor this question, you would receive a resounding yes. Actors know the difference between a Friday and a Tuesday audience. What makes a Saturday audience different from a Thursday audience? Could it be this term presence? As discussed above, actors also feel a cold or warm reception from the audience. When an actor backstage comments, "Hello, is anybody out there?" or "They are really with us tonight,"[112] they are talking about the presence of the audience, not the amount of people in the auditorium. Being "with" the actors can be seen as synonymous with being present for the actors. It is crucial to actors that the audience have a strong presence. If an audience "are really dead" or are "really quiet today," then their weak presence or what Herbert Blau refers to as their absence[113] affects the actors' performance. Conversely, if an actor comments that the audience "are so in the moment" or "they're listening closely," they are fully present, and this assists the actors' performance. There is an exchange of energy. It is also vital that the audience are receptive. If "It's a hard audience" or the actors comment that "The audience hate us, they think we're awful," then actors often feel they have to double their efforts to change the temperature in the theatre. As can be seen from these comments, the actors view the audience as a collective presence. Audience presence is not, perhaps, the kind of presence that has drawing power, but a strong, charismatic or even a hostile presence can certainly emit an electricity into the atmosphere that affects the actors' performances. Actors' and audiences' experience of each other's presence across the footlights creates a reciprocal energy which is part of the electric air.

Celebrity magnetism

There are numerous and constantly evolving contemporary definitions of a celebrity. Etymologically, celebrity comes from the Latin *celebrum* which carries associations with being "famous" and "thronged." As Chris Rojek argues, celebrity is essentially relational.[114] The celebrity is constructed by the public and perpetuates celebrity status through being "thronged" by a large group of admirers or dissenters. It is because of its relational aspects that it contains a certain magnetism in the theatre. The celebrity magnetism is what happens between a celebrity and their audience. Celebrities have that certain "wow" factor. Their reputation and identity, whether fabricated or real, are larger than life. In one sense, they are walking narratives that subsume all the ideals, aspirations and fantasies – negative or positive – that are projected onto them by their followers. When seen in the flesh, rather than on a celluloid screen, their presence and the ekstases seemingly radiating out of them creates an excitement among their audience that is magnetic and contagious. Celebrity is a broad category.[115] One of the most revered of all celebrities is the star actor or the "Hollywood star."[116]

Whenever Hollywood star actors make their Broadway or West End stage debut or "return to the stage," their stage presence is scrutinised. Critics will argue that Gwyneth Paltrow has a "striking physical presence," that Orlando Bloom "lacks stage presence"[117] or that Michael Emerson has a "magnetic presence."[118] Numerous websites have lists detailing whether the star actors have that enigmatic but vital stage presence that seems to give actors more credibility. Whether they possess a stage presence or not, their magnetic celebrity presence has drawing power. Not only box office drawing power but also celebrity drawing power: ekstases that emanates from the star, filling the air with electricity that can so overwhelm a production onstage that the star becomes the play. Narrative, production, characters seemingly fade as the celebrity presence subsumes all. As Michael Quinn observes, "The personal, individual qualities of the [star] actor always resist, to some degree, the transformation of the actor into the stage figure required for the communication of a particular fiction."[119] Hamlet is Benedict Cumberbatch. Therese Raquin is Keira Knightley. Although the critics may disparage the stage presence of the actor, the celebrity presence remains intact. Regardless of whether the star can act, the celebrity presence, as Stanislavski argues, "transforms even his[her] deficiencies into assets."[120] What is this magnetism that can so transfix an audience that it obfuscates all other elements of the drama?

Star actor productions attract many first-time theatre audience attendees: celebrity fans. Celebrity fans have a pre-formed fictive relationship with the star through, among other elements, larger than life cinematic close-ups.[121] Once the star is actually *present*, their presence eliminates all else. The electricity that is generated onstage and in the audience through the celebrity magnetism is extraordinary, contagious and visceral. The effects on an audience are visible. Traditional theatre etiquette is often unobserved by the celebrity fans and applause, screaming and verbal or paralingual utterances are frequently performed during the acts, charging the atmosphere with a fervour that is infectious even for regular theatregoers. Interestingly, while anticipation and excitement are heightened, belief in the character or the fictitious world of the play is not always suspended. The star actor remains the star actor.

Celebrity presence provides a fertile environment for transference and projection. Su Holmes argues that in contemporary society the fan–celebrity relationship gives an illusion of intimacy. Celebrities become like close friends "standing-in" for real friends.[122] This is a form of transference. Transferences naturally strengthen through frequent contact. When a fan has been following a star actor on screen, the close proximity to the live body of that star on stage is potent, evoking a powerful transference. Something inside the audience fan is fulfilled simply by seeing the actor live on stage. Seeing them face to face is titillating, seductive and highly pleasurable.

Fandom is marked by a search for authenticity.[123] In a world filled with virtual celebrities, the authentic presence of the star perpetuates the illusion of intimacy because of a special relationship they believe they have with the star. Furthermore, the live presence provides a stimulating opportunity for the fan audience member to project themselves into the character played by the star or into another character in relationship with the star onstage. Private dreams are projected onto the stage as the audience member lives vicariously through the star. Suspension of disbelief is rearticulated in a new narrative being played out not in the fictional world of the play, but the fictional world of the audience fan that contributes to the electric air.

The spatial relationship to the onstage star is crucial. The convergence of the ekstases radiating from the celebrity presence and those of the audience fan, whether intrinsic or projected, creates the buzz in the air. As Stanislavski observes, "All that is required […] is that [the actor] come out on the stage as frequently and remain as long as possible, so that [her]his audience can see, gaze upon and enjoy its idol."[124] The gaze is fulfilling in itself.

What happens when celebrities are part of the audience? Throughout history, audience celebrities have upstaged onstage actors. Queens, kings, presidents, prime ministers, generals, film stars, television stars and rock stars sitting in the audience receive applause and adulation from their fellow audience members.[125] The close proximity of star actors in the audience and their celebrity magnetism intensifies the electric air at the theatrical event for other audience members and actors alike.

Community

Theatre is a social event. Since the inception of organised theatrical events, people have gone to the theatre not only to see the production but also for social reasons: to see and be seen, to share an experience with others or to be part of a community. While we may not know the audience members sitting to our sides, during the course of the production we are "apart together."[126] We play a communal role – that of audience – and we perform certain rituals such as applauding and laughing as an ensemble.

Theatre is also a community experience for actors. From the commencement of rehearsals to the closing night of the production, actors, directors, stage managers, technical crew and other creatives join together as a community to form an ensemble. Some actors colloquially refer to this ensemble as their theatre family. Theatre also creates audience theatre families. Broadway or West End theatre fans, theatregoing groups, girls-night-out groups and, more recently, celebrity fan groups often form tight-knit communities bonded by a common interest in a star, a production, or theatre itself. These are the obvious community aspects of theatre – the congregating of audiences and actors and the formation of sub-communities within audiences.

There is a transformation that occurs in the meeting of the two larger communities of actors and audience members. The two communities, because of what Fischer-Lichte calls it transformative aesthetics, experience communitas: a collective feeling that the actors and audience are part of something greater than or outside of themselves.[127] We become more than ourselves when we are part of a community. This something more contributes to the electric air. The early-twentieth-century sociologist Émile Durkheim argued that "[t]he very act of congregating is an exceptionally powerful stimulant"[128] which can create what he described as a "collective effervescence." Durkheim's collective effervescence has a number of distinguishing qualities that particularly relate to the theatrical experience: it is experienced as an emotive state, it is ephemeral and it is transformative. In the state of collective effervescence,

> the vital energies become hyper-excited, the passions more intense, the sensations more powerful; there are indeed some that are produced only at this moment. [Wo]Man does not recognize [her]himself; [s]he feels somehow transformed and in consequence transforms [her]his surroundings.[129]

Audience members and actors alike experience moments of positive collective effervescence in the theatre. For the actor it can be experienced as what Stanislavski calls a "tidal wave"[130] that rolls across the footlights touching actors and audience. I would add that while the act of congregating together can create that thrill in the air, it is often the moments of emotional contagion when the audience "catch" the emotions of the actors or each other that create the collective effervescence. A wave of a fear or joy or sadness circulates in the atmosphere. The arousal of excitement and the sensations that tingle effervesce into the atmosphere. Because it is a shared experience, generated collectively among actors and audience members, it is all the more exhilarating and electric. The converse of the collective experience is, of course, the individual experience: one pair of hands clapping, one diaphragm convulsing in a laugh, tears streaming down one person's face. This too can happen in the theatre, yet not as regularly as collective effervescence. These individual audience performances often sever the collective relationship, consequently affecting the electric air.

Durkheim argued that collective effervescence can lead to barbarism just as readily as social cohesion.[131] The riots spanning the hundred or so years in Western theatres from the nineteenth to the early twentieth centuries are testament to this. Emotional contagion so stirred a negative collective effervescence that audience members threw objects at the stage, damaged property and engaged in fist fights. In many ways collective effervescence can just as easily divide as create communities. In the Astor Place Riots in the mid-nineteenth century, particular audience communities stirred up dissent against two star actors. Sixty years later in the Playboy Riots in Dublin, fierce nationalistic sentiment pitted audience communities against each other. In both of these events and numerous other theatre riots, community clashes create a highly charged friction in the air which often changes the theatrical event into a political riot.

Collective effervescence is incited and oftentimes perpetuated by all the socio-logical undercurrents of the electric air I have discussed: community, the celebrity presence of star actors and the collective presence of an audience that are "with" the actors. Since the electric air is ethereal and intangible, I have considered elements that contribute to the electric air: the impact of the play's narrative heightened by the suspension of disbelief and empathy, transferences and projections of the audience members. I have also explored the collective presence of the audience as they encounter the actors − or celebrities among them − in an ephemeral event.

Tennessee Williams mused that a play is not the words on paper but "the quick interplay of live beings, suspended like fitful lightning in a cloud."[132] This depiction, alluding to liveness, electricity and atmosphere, is closely aligned to my description of the electric air of theatre. There is a certain heterogeneity in the elements included in the theatrical, psychological and sociological undercurrents explored in this chapter because the electric air is not made up of one element, but of many. Over the next two chapters, actor and audience member comments expand the concept of the electric air as they share their perspectives from the stage and from the audience.

Notes

1 These comments were taken from interviews for Heim's *Audience as Performer* in 2014/15.
2 Since the eighteenth-century, studies of atmosphere have taken various psychological, phenomenological, aesthetic and cultural geographic perspectives. See Erika Fischer-Lichte, *The Transformative Power of Performance: A New Aesthetics* (London: Routledge, 2008); George Home-Cook, *Theatre and Aural Attention: Stretching Ourselves* (Basingstoke: Palgrave Macmillan, 2015); Stuart Grant, "Performing an Aesthetics of Atmospheres," *Aesthetics* 23, no. 1 (2013), 12–32; Martin Welton, *Feeling Theatre* (Basingstoke: Palgrave Macmillan, 2011); Tonino Griffero, *Atmospheres: Aesthetics of Emotional Spaces*, trans. Sarah di Sanctis (Farnham: Ashgate, 2010).
3 Gernot Böhme, *The Aesthetics of Atmospheres*, ed. Jean-Paul Thibaud (London and New York: Routledge, 2017), 28.
4 Martin Heidegger, *The Fundamental Concepts of Metaphysics: World, Finitude, Solitude* (Bloomington: Indiana UP, 1995), 67.

5 Mikel Dufrenne, *The Phenomenology of Aesthetic Experience*, trans. Edward Casey, Albert Anderson, Willis Domingo and Leon Jacobson (Evanston: Northwestern UP, 1973), 178.

6 Phenomenologists, psychologists, philosophers, aesthetics and cultural geographers tend to all concur on these three principles, some scholars emphasising some principles more than others.

7 Böhme cited in Fischer-Lichte, *Transformative Power of Performance*, 115.

8 Fischer-Lichte, *Transformative Power of Performance*, 114–120.

9 Grant, "Performing an Aesthetics," 21.

10 Ibid., 10.

11 Böhme cited in Fischer-Lichte, *Transformative Power of Performance*, 115.

12 Konstantin Stanislavski, *Building a Character*, trans. Elizabeth Reynolds Hapgood (London: Routledge, 1989), 275.

13 Patrice Pavis, *The Routledge Dictionary of Performance and Contemporary Theatre* (New York and London: Routledge, 2016), 37.

14 Michael Chekhov, *To the Actor: On the Technique of Acting* (New York: Harper and Row, 1953), 50.

15 Ibid., 55–58.

16 Ibid., 50.

17 Ibid., 48.

18 Welton, *Feeling Theatre*, 136.

19 For a full discussion of actors' backstage comments, see Caroline Heim, *Audience as Performer: The Changing Role of Theatre Audiences in the Twenty-First Century* (London and New York: Routledge, 2016), 19–39.

20 Chekhov, *To the Actor*, 51.

21 Friedlind Riedel, "Atmosphere," in *Affective Societies: Key Concepts*, ed. Jan Slaby and Christian von Scheve (Abingdon: Routledge, 2019), 86.

22 Welton, *Feeling Theatre*, 18.

23 Alexis Solokis, "Live Art, Death Threats: The Theatrical Antagonsim of *First Night*," in *Experiencing Liveness in Contemporary Performance Interdisciplinary Perspectives*, ed. Matthew Reason and Anja Mølle Lindelof (New York: Routledge, 2016), 12.

24 Paul Allain and Jen Harvie, *The Routledge Companion to Theatre and Performance Studies*, 2nd ed. (London: Routledge, 2012), 168.

25 Fischer-Lichte, *Transformative Power of Performance*, 59.

26 Matthew Reason and Anja Mølle Lindelof, eds., *Experiencing Liveness in Contemporary Performance Interdisciplinary Perspectives* (New York: Routledge, 2016), 5.

27 Ibid., 23.

28 Patricia Fara, *An Entertainment for Angels: Electricity in the Enlightenment* (New York: Columbia UP, 2003), 74.

29 For an example, see Alice Vincent "'Kanye West Yeezus Tour' Bags of Air Sell on eBay for Thousands," *Sydney Morning Herald*, March 9, 2015, accessed 20 August 2017 www. smh.com.au/entertainment/music/kanye-west-yeezus-tour-bags-of-air-sell-on-ebay-for-thousands-20150309-13ypsw.html.

30 Reason and Lindelof, *Experiencing Liveness*, 29

31 For audience comments on electricity at events, see Heim, *Audience as Performer*, 147.

32 Interestingly, in the eighteenth century, atmosphere was often described as the force field of magnets. See Riedel, "Atmosphere," 86.

33 *Oxford English Dictionary*, accessed 1 September 2018, www-oed-com.ezp01.library.qut. edu.au/.

34 Jane Goodall, *Stage Presence* (London: Routledge, 2008), 78.

35 Cited in Goodall, *Stage Presence*, 73.
36 Ibid., 79.
37 Tracy Davis, "Reading Shakespeare by Flashes of Lightning: Challenging the Foundations of Romantic Acting Theory," *ELH* 62, no. 4 (1995): 937.
38 Eleanor Rugles, *Prince of Players: Edwin Booth* (New York: Norton, 1953), 164, 165.
39 Clement Scott, *The Drama of Yesterday & Today* (London: Macmillan, 1899), 139.
40 Ibid., 139.
41 Ibid., 116.
42 For a full discussion of the performative role of audiences, see Heim, *Audience as Performer*.
43 Harry A. Saintsbury, ed., *We Saw Him Act: A Symposium on the Art of Sir Henry Irving* (London: Hurst and Blackett, 1939), 260.
44 Samuel Taylor Coleridge, *Biographica Literatia*, Chapter XIV (1817), 42, www.gutenberg. org/files/6081/6081-h/6081-h.htm.
45 Michael Tomko, *Beyond the Willing Suspension of Disbelief* (London: Bloomsbury, 2015), 4. The introduction to this text gives an excellent overview of the critical thought on Coleridge's phrase.
46 Ibid., 6, 7.
47 Ibid.
48 Roger Grainger, *Suspending Disbelief: Theatre as a Context for Sharing* (Brighton: Sussex, 2010), 18.
49 Lawrence Levine cites several of these humorous ad libs in *Highbrow Lowbrow: The Emergence of Cultural Hierarchy in America* (Cambridge: Harvard UP, 1994), 30.
50 Grainger, *Suspending Disbelief*, 64.
51 Ibid.
52 Cited in Jean Benedetti, *Stanislavski: An Introduction* (New York: Routledge, 2004), 48.
53 Konstantin Stanislavski, *An Actor Prepares*, trans. Elizabeth Reynolds Hapgood (London: Bloomsbury, 2013), 142.
54 Ibid., 170.
55 Although Robert Jauss introduced this term to apply to the reception of literary texts in *Toward an Aesthetic of Reception*, trans. Timothy Bahti (Minneapolis: Minnesota UP: 1982), 39, it has been applied to the reception of any art form, including theatre. Patrice Pavis, *Dictionnaire du Theatre: Termes et Concepts de L'analyse Theatrale* (Paris: Editions Sociales, 1980), 132, particularly points to the range of social framings audiences bring in with them to the theatre.
56 Cited in Fischer-Lichte, *Transformative Power of Performance*, 43.
57 Heim, *Audience as Performer*.
58 Joseph Chaikin, *The Presence of the Actor* (New York: Theatre Communications Group, 1993), 21.
59 Fischer-Lichte, *Transformative Power of Performance*, 38.
60 What Grotowski predominantly refers to, however, is the actor's encounter with the text, other creatives and him/herself, not the audience. There is surprising little material written about the actor–audience encounter. Jerzy Grotowski and Eugenio Barba, *Towards a Poor Theatre*, ed. Eugenio Barba (New York: Routledge, 2002), 57, 58.
61 Ibid.
62 For a comprehensive overview of performance scholars' discourses on the ephemerality of transience, see Matthew Reason, *Documentation, Disappearance and the Representation of Live Performance* (London: Palgrave Macmillan, 2006), 8–20.
63 Artaud cited in Reason, *Documentation, Disappearance and the Representation*, 11.

64 Actors are taught to "raise the stakes" of their character's situation in order to make their performances more dramatic and vital. See Robert Barton, *Acting Off Stage and On* (Boston: Cengage, 2015).

65 Reason and Lindelof, *Experiencing Liveness in Contemporary Performance*, 7.

66 Jill Dolan, *Utopia in Performance: Finding Hope at the Theatre* (Ann Arbor: Michigan UP 2005), 9; and Marvin Carlson, "The Theatre Journal Auto/Archive," *Theatre Journal* 55, no. 1 (2003): 211.

67 Since the invitation for audiences to sing and dance in the auditorium issued in Mamma Mia in London in 1999, audience performance is now showing signs of becoming more gregarious and participatory. See Heim, *Audience as Performer*.

68 *Oxford English Dictionary*.

69 Wolfgang Iser, "The Reading Process: A Phenomenological Approach," in *Reader Response Criticism*, ed. Jane P. Tompkins (Baltimore: Johns Hopkins UP, 1980), 55.

70 Jacques Rancière, *The Emancipated Spectator*, trans. Gregory Elliott (London and New York: Verso, 2009), 13.

71 And, of course, the other creatives working on the production.

72 Iser, "Reading Process," 284, 288.

73 Creating characters from the imagination is best explained in Stanislavski's "magic if." Stanislavski, *An Actor Prepares*, 51.

74 Jean-Paul Sartre, *Sartre on Theatre*, ed. Michel Contat and Michel Rybalka, trans. Frank Jellinek (New York: Pantheon, 1973), 68.

75 Peggy Phelan, *Unmarked: The Politics of Performance* (London: Routledge, 1993), 146.

76 Sigmund Freud, *Case Histories I: "Dora" and "Little Hans,"* ed. Angela Richards, trans. Alix and James Strachey (Harmondsworth: Penguin, 1977), 157.

77 Ibid., 157–158.

78 Sigmund Freud, *An Autobiographical Study* (London: Hogarth Press, 1959), 42.

79 Eric J. Nuetzel, "Psychoanalysis and Dramatic Art," *Journal of Applied Psychanalytical Studies* 2, no. 1 (2000): 55, 56. While some psychoanalysts and theatre scholars have discussed transference in the theatre, rarely do they consider audience member/actor transference.

80 Maria Grazia Turri, *Acting, Spectating and the Unconscious: A Psychoanalytic Perspective on Unconscious Mechanisms of Identification in Spectating and Acting in the Theatre* (New York and London: Routledge, 2016), 38.

81 Ibid.

82 Sharon Marie Carnicke, *Stanislavsky in Focus: An Acting Master for the Twenty-First Century*, 2nd ed. (New York: Routledge: 2009), 217.

83 Uta Hagen, *Respect for Acting* (New York: Macmillan, 1973), 35, 36.

84 Joseph Sandler, *Projection, Identification, Projective Identification* (London: Karnac, 1989), 2.

85 Sigmund Freud, *Totem and Taboo: Resemblances between the Mental Lives of Savages and Neurotics*, trans. James Strachey (New York: Routledge, 2001), 64.

86 Patrick Tucker, *Secrets of Screen Acting*, 2nd ed. (New York: Routledge, 2003), 17.

87 Quoted in Turri, *Acting, Spectating and the Unconscious*, 9.

88 Jean Laplanche and Jean-Bertrand Pontalis, "The Language of Psycho-Analysis," trans. Donald Nicholson-Smith, *International Psycho-Analytical Library* 94: 350.

89 Turri makes connections between transference and catharsis. Turri, *Acting, Spectating and the Unconscious*, 17.

90 Pavis, *Dictionnaire du Theatre*, 176.

91 Edward Bullough, "'Psychical Distance' as a Factor in Art and an Aesthetic Principle," *British Journal of Psychology* 5, no. 2 (1912): 93.

92 Jean-Paul Sartre, *Sartre on Theatre*, ed. Michel Contat and Michel Rybalka, trans. Frank Jellinek (New York: Pantheon, 1973), 62.

93 Bertolt Brecht, *Brecht on Theatre: The Development of an Aesthetic*, ed. and trans. John Willett (New York: Hill and Wang, 1964).

94 Dolan, *Utopia in Performance*.

95 Elin Diamond, "The Violence of 'We': Politicizing Identification," in *Critical Theory and Performance*, ed. Janelle G. Reinelt and Joseph R. Roach (Ann Arbor: University of Michigan Press, 2007).

96 Henri Schoenmakers, "To Be, Wanting to Be, Forced to Be. Identification Processes in Theatrical Situations," in *New Directions in Audience Research: Advances in Reception and Audience Research 2*, ed. Willmar Sauter (Utrecht: Tijdschrift voor Theaterwetenschap, 1988), 138–163.

97 Elly Konijn, *Acting Emotions Shaping Emotions on Stage* (Amsterdam: Amsterdam UP, 2000), 86.

98 Patsy Rodenburg gives the most accessible discussion of this introspection in her lecture on the three circles of acting; see Patsy Rodenburg, "The Second Circle," Michael Howard Studios, New York City, accessed 2 July 2018, www.youtube.com/watch?v=Ub27yeXKUTY.

99 Pavis, *Dictionnaire du Theatre*, 176; Kent Cartwright, *Shakespearean Tragedy and Its Double: The Rhythms of Audience Response* (University Park: Pennsylvania UP, 1991), 13.

100 For a comprehensive history of empathy, see George Pigman, "Freud and the History of Empathy," *International Journal of Psycho-Analysis* 76 (1995): 237–256.

101 For some discussions, see Bruce McConachie, *Engaging Audiences: A Cognitive Approach to Spectating at the Theatre* (New York: Palgrave Macmillan, 2008); and Matthew Reason and Dee Reynolds, eds., *Kinesthetic Empathy in Creative and Cultural Practices* (Bristol: Intellect, 2012).

102 For a discussion on how complex the workings of empathy in the theatre are, see David Krasner, "Empathy and Theatre," in *Staging Philosophy: Intersections of Theater, Performance and Philosophy*, ed. David Krasner and David Saltz (Anne Arbor: Michigan UP, 2006), 257; and John Muse, "Performance and the Pace of Empathy," *Journal of Dramatic Theory and Criticism* 26, no.2 (2012): 177.

103 Theodor Lipps, "Empathy and Aesthetic Pleasure," in *Aesthetic Theories: Studies in the Philosophy of Art*, ed. and trans. Karl Aschenbrenner, ed. Arnold Isenberg (Englewood Cliffs, NJ: Prentice-Hall, 1965), 377, 411.

104 Lindsay B. Cummings, *Empathy as Dialogue in Theatre and Performance* (London: Palgrave Macmillan, 2016).

105 Hagen, *Respect for Acting*, 98.

106 Bullough, "'Psychical Distance'," 99.

107 Stanislavski, *Building a Character*, 320.

108 *Oxford English Dictionary*.

109 Joseph Roach, *It* (Ann Arbor: Michigan UP, 2007).

110 Stanislavski, *Building a Character*, 271.

111 Dolan, *Utopia in Performance*, 30, 31.

112 These and the subsequent audience comments are taken from interviews with actors worldwide that were part of my empirical research for *Audience as Performer* in 2014/15. I gathered a total of 18 commonly used comments actors used to describe audiences.

113 Herbert Blau, *The Audience* (Baltimore: Johns Hopkins UP, 1990), 5.

114 Chris Rojek, *Celebrity* (London: Reaktion, 2001), 9.

115 Sean Redmond and Su Holmes provide one of the most useful differences between celebrity and star:

> While the celebrity category may flourish on inconsistent behaviour in the personal sphere and contradictions between public and private selves, the professional star depends on a consistent sense of self and the willingness of the industry to franchise a role.
>
> *Sean Redmond and Su Holmes, Stardom and Celebrity a Reader*
> *(Los Angeles: Sage, 2007), 107.*

116 There are many assumptions and exclusions that lie within and behind this term that are outside the scope of this book to examine. The "Hollywood star" is a film industry and mediatised construction. For a closer interrogation of the term "Hollywood star," see Thomas Austin and Martin Barker, eds., *Contemporary Hollywood Stardom* (London: Arnold, 2003).
117 "Gwyneth Paltrow" cited in Karen Hollinger, *The Actress: Hollywood Acting and the Female* Star (New York: Routledge, 2006): 214; Elisabeth Vincentelli, "Orlando Bloom," *New York Post*, 20 September 2013, accessed 11 October 2017, www.newyork.com/articles/broadway/review-roundup-romeo-and-juliet-04406/.
118 Ben Brantley, NYT Critic's Pick, "Review: 'Wakey, Wakey' Stars Life and Death," *New York Times*, 27 February 2017, www.nytimes.com/2017/02/27/theater/wakey-wakey-review-will-eno.html.
119 Michael Quinn, "Celebrity and the Semiotics of Acting," *New Theatre Quarterly* 22 (1990): 155.
120 Stanislavski, *Building a Character*, 271.
121 Sean Redmond and Su Holmes, *Framing Celebrity: New Directions in Celebrity Culture* (London: Routledge, 2006), 37, 38.
122 Ibid., 3.
123 Ibid., 4.
124 Stanislavski, *Building a Character*, 271.
125 For further discussion of celebrities in the audience in the nineteenth and early twentieth centuries, see Heim, *Audience as Performer*, 74, 75.
126 Jacques Rancière, *The Emancipated Spectator*, trans. Gregory Elliott (London and New York: Verso, 2009), 59.
127 See Richard Schechner, *Performance Studies: An Introduction*, 3rd ed. (London: Routledge, 2013), 87.
128 Émile Durkheim, *The Elementary Forms of Religious Life*, trans. Karen E. Fields (New York: Free Press, 1995), 217.
129 Ibid., 424.
130 Stanislavski, *Building a Character*, 332.
131 Durkheim, *Elementary Forms of Religious Life*, 213.
132 Tennessee Williams, *Camino Real Afterword* (New York: Dramatists Play Service, 1994), x.

2

THE VIEW FROM THE STAGE

When any two human beings encounter each other there are two points of view, two sets of emotions, two histories that meet. In the theatre, encounters are sometimes realised in verbal conversations, emotion conversations and body conversations. Relationships are formed, sometimes brief and other times lasting. These can occur backstage among actors, in the auditorium among audience members and between actors and audiences during the production. They all form part of the electric air. Chapters 2 and 3 explore these relationships asking the questions: who is the actor, who is the audience member and what do they see. This chapter considers the actors. I have written elsewhere about actor's backstage conversations.[1] These too ignite the electric air as the actors invariably discuss the audience.

The comments cited are from in-depth interviews I undertook with 22 highly accomplished and respected British, American, French and German actors.[2] The majority of the actors are veterans of the stage and screen and their biographies are included in the Appendix. The purpose of my interviews was to explore the actors' views of their audiences. What emerged was a much more nuanced and perspicacious reading of not only their relationship with the audience, but also their relationship with each other. Importantly, their relationship with the audience was coloured by their own sense of self-worth. Issues of actor security and insecurity surfaced regularly. The candour with which the actors spoke about their fears and their brushes with stage fright was unanticipated, revelatory and much appreciated. The actors' discussion of stage fright during the interviews was so cogent that stage fright emerged as another undercurrent of the electric air for the actors in their view from the stage. Preliminary analyses of stage fright and another important concept that emerged, double consciousness, are included in this chapter to gain a clearer illustration of who the actor is.

The chapter commences with security and concludes with insecurity. It follows the journey of an actor backstage to the encounter with an audience. As we finished with community in the theatre in the previous chapter, we commence with a discussion of the actor's backstage community, followed by an exploration of the actor's understanding of presence. A discussion of double consciousness and stage fright follows. The chapter concludes with an exploration of the actor's often precarious relationship with their audiences realised in the encounter. An epilogue considers how the curtain call is also an important part of the conversation between actors and their audiences.

Who is the actor?

Backstage

The world outside the theatre is a dangerous place for many actors. It is filled with casting agents that bite, relatives that think they should get a real job and people working on computers in little offices that seem to live on an entirely different planet. As Broadway actor Catherine Brunell laments, "So much of this business is being told 'no', and facing lots of walls."[3] There are many hazards: empty promises of "we'll call you," unfulfilled dreams, the exhausting treadmill of having to keep up appearances, the endless rejections that eat away at the actor's sense of selfhood and esteem, and the deathly silence of an empty apartment after closing night of a production. Shutting the door on all of this and entering into the warm glow of a backstage sanctuary is a sigh of relief. The ritual of entering into the haven of a backstage area during a rehearsal or run of a production is akin to entering into another world as West End actor Abigail McKern elucidates: "The great thing about the theatre is, as soon as you walk through the stage door you leave everything in your life behind you."[4] For Ian Bartholomew, veteran of the London stage, the theatre is a place where "you are protected from the outside world."[5] There is, however, what McKern calls an "unwritten law" regarding what passes across the threshold of the stage door: "Never, ever, bring your shit in through the door."[6] Bartholomew describes it as baggage which he leaves outside.[7] Broadway and film actor Keith Randolph Smith finds leaving this baggage at the stage door liberating:

> When there are emotional ills or spiritual ills [in your outside life] it's like a bag. You can either have a clutch purse, a shoulder bag, a hand bag, a tote, a backpack, a roller bag or a trunk, we all have baggage. What I do before I come into the theatre is I leave my baggage at the door. And it's an opportunity that I can leave it at the door, a privilege. [...] I pick it up when I leave.[8]

This unwritten law or ritual of leaving the hazards and the baggage behind produces a safe environment in which actors are able to create unimpeded. Nearly every actor I interviewed described being in a theatre as a safe place:

> Its feels like, it feels safe. It feels like I'm where I should be.
>
> *Chuck Cooper*

I've always found performing in the theatre a very secure place to be, a safe place to be.

Edward Hibbert

I feel like I've got room. I feel like I've got space and I feel safe [...] a bit like being in a womb.

Ian Bartholomew

New York stage and television actor Edward Hibbert regularly discusses the security and safety that actors feel working in the theatre with his colleagues describing it as a "warm-like feeling."[9] The theatre, the physical place and the community therein, is a place of acceptance, of purpose, of security for many actors.[10]

It is also a place where actors can discover the community they do not always find in the "outside world." Hibbert and Bartholomew emphasised how important the sense of community was and also the "family feeling"[11] among the cast of a production. Many of the actors went so far as to describe the theatre environment as a "home" or a "second home." Jay O. Sanders and Maryann Plunkett, two much acclaimed Broadway, off-Broadway and film actors, have worked for many years to create a "home space" in their on-going theatre productions.[12] As Tony Award winner Plunkett described, "When it's a performance, it's you coming into your home."[13] Berlin actor Linda Pöppel described the way she feels onstage as "home. Sometimes I like it a lot. Sometimes I don't feel I am doing a good job. But when I cut all of that off, I feel home."[14]

The "family feeling" is, however, a contentious issue among actors. It is often as ephemeral as the fleeting two hours of identifying with the fictitious world of a play that audiences experience. The wider acting community that sits outside of the individual cast communities is, perhaps, more substantial and dependable and is one of the reasons why Complicité's Simon McBurney states, "within the profession of actors, there has always been a huge political consciousness."[15] Actors are often highly political and unite to support many social causes. In Berlin, for example, Elias Arens described how the Deutsches Theater "did a lot of rallies against the AFD [Alternative for Deutschland] new right-wing party. The whole theatre always has a standing on political subjects. We try and get it into the plays."[16] The political underpinnings embedded in some plays add to the extra charge of tension in the electric air.

In the safe backstage confines, after the rehearsals are finished and the technical aspects have been completed, the stage is illuminated, summoning the actors to "find their light."[17] Although the rehearsal space and the backstage area are comfort zones and safe places, actors accrete most of their energy and sense of worth from performing on the stage in front of an audience

Onstage

The stage is where most actors will say they live. I can say this quite emphatically. It is supported by every actor I interviewed. When asked what it feels like to be

on stage, Parisian actors Edouard Rouland and Stéphane Dauch stated unequivo-
cally: "It's my life" and "It makes me live."[18] Broadway actor Chuck Cooper
emphasised that onstage he felt "like a fish *in* water" (italics in original).[19] Yet it was
a comment made by McKern that revealed the depth of the experience of being
onstage for the actors:

> [You feel] very alive. You feel heightened. Every sense is open and awake.
> The best feeling is relaxed precision. You are absolutely relaxed but you are
> absolutely focused and precise. You're just very, very alive. You are not dead.
> You can see people who are slightly dead, and you can't do that onstage. You
> have to come alive as soon as you walk on. A sort of heightened awareness
> of everything, your ears, your smell, your eyes. More alive than in real life.[20]

McKern's last comment is astonishing. It is even more astonishing when we read
in the next chapter that some audience members also feel this alive in the electric
air of a theatre production. It is the heightened state of being that Thornton Wilder
referred to when he questioned "Do any human beings ever realise life while they
live it? – every, every minute"[21] in *Our Town*. To reach this elevated, sensorially alert
and aware state that McKern describes, Uta Hagen argues that you need to enter
into a conversation with the audience, and an actor can only do this onstage if they
are "*more* vulnerable than in life" (italics in original).[22] This is why the safe backstage
environment is crucial. Vulnerability also places actors in a susceptible position as
explored below. It is a highly risky gamble. It takes an incredible amount of bravado
"for an actor to walk out onto a very dark stage and become somebody else,"[23] and
be believable as that somebody else. Yet, as long-time Broadway and film actor Anita
Gillette goes on to emphasise,

> If you can take it, it is one of the most exciting things you'll ever experience.
> [...] It's almost like ecstasy. That's what it is like. That's the thing. At the end
> of this ecstatic experience you get this. *Anita applauds.*[24]

The ecstatic experience and the "living" onstage is not, however, solipsistic. As Bert
O. States argues, "The egotism of the actor expresses itself categorically in the
simple fact that he risks the stage. [...] If anything, the actor's appearance before the
world is the essence of tact and selflessness."[25] While the overblown ego *does* surface
in what States calls "vain" acting and what is below described as "monstrous" acting,
the "living" onstage of the majority of actors is a kind of "being" onstage that is
not dissimilar to Jean-Paul Sartre's concept of "being for others." It is relational. The
concept that it is only in being aware that we are being watched by others that we
become aware of our own presence; Sartre's perception that "I see myself, because
somebody sees me."[26] As Sartre contends,

> if we happen to appear 'in public' to act in a play or give a lecture, we never
> lose sight of the fact that we are gazed at [...] and we attempt to constitute a
> being [...] *for* this gaze (italics in original).[27]

As Dauch described, acting onstage "is a way of living […] Once I have given emotions and get the [audience] feedback, it gives me life."[28] The audience's feedback is the life force for Dauch, the constitution of his being. Bartholomew describes it symbiotically:

> There is the symbiosis between the audience and the actor. The actor does something and the audience reacts. That's where I live. [It is] frightening, exhilarating, joyous and painful. It's terribly humbling but at the same time incredibly powerful.[29]

Here Bartholomew has described living onstage as relational. It is almost as if he lives in the gaze of the audience. The startling moment of the gaze has, however, the potential to unmask the actor and fuel frightening and painful moments.

It is a bewildering paradox that even though every actor knows that audiences willingly and readily suspend disbelief and have come to the theatre to be caught up in a fictitious world and watch and hear a story told by characters, the actor's greatest fear is of being judged. McBurney suggests that one of the reasons that actors are seen as narcissistic to compensate for this underlying fear of being judged is because the actor fears that s/he is irrelevant:

> You're a siphon on stage. […] Ultimately all actors know that they are irrelevant. They are just tubes through which something comes. They are not the artists, they are the carriers of information, and it comes full circle: you come back to the audience. The audience are making, and the audience remembers performances. They say, "Oh it was a great performance I remember this and this and this" and the actor doesn't remember that feeling ever. But you, you are as ephemeral as somebody's memory of you, and therefore you aren't anybody. And so there is a sense, as an actor, that you are eternally homeless.[30]

Although there are some truths in McBurney's assertions that actors are siphons, I believe that he overstates his case. If actors are not artists we would then have to say musicians are also not artists. McBurney cannot speak for all actors; the vast majority of those I interviewed saw themselves as artists, as shall be seen in the final case study. McBurney's discourse on memory and an actor's homelessness is, however, disturbingly true. Although actors have a strong sense of living in the moment, they sometimes have despair and loneliness that can only be temporarily assuaged by the gelled lights and the slapping of many hands. Bartholomew described one such moment when he had received his first role in a play, *The Merchant of Venice*, and was now embracing the life of an actor. He stood backstage and was overcome by a sense of isolation, loneliness. [He] said to [him]self,

> "This is what you have chosen to do." The idea that you are actually alone, but you're not. It was about being apart. […] You are surrounded by people all the time but some of the time you don't get on with them or you don't really know them.[31]

Actors appear to be leading such glamourous lives, but often stand on the landing and watch others lead happy family, normal lives that they long for. They often consider the choices they have made and other paths that could have been. As Manuel Harder from the Deutsches Theater in Berlin generously disclosed,

> I paid a lot for always going into this world [the theatre world]. I gave a lot away for that. [...] What have I given up? Things in my personal and private life. There are always other contracts, other cities, but it is hard on the private life of course. It's not very fair on family life.

These aspects of an actor's life are rarely divulged. The actor is the master of Erving Goffman's frontstage and backstage faces, even among his/her own colleagues. These choices are also an essential part of who actors are and it too becomes part of an actor's presence onstage.

Presence

The state of "being" onstage is inextricably tied to the concept of an actor's "presence" onstage. As Smith describes it:

> For me the time I'm most present is when I'm in a show and those two hours. Because I'm listening with my eyes, my ears, my nose, my mouth, my tongue, my sense of smell, my heart, my mind, my spirit, my soul. It's hard to live like that. I've met a handful of people in my life who live that way; they are totally present in the moment all the time. [...] it becomes part of my spiritual practice. I practice how to do it in real life by doing it on stage, which is why you're either very wired after a show or very tired. It's because you put that much focus into "being."[32]

Presence is another controversial issue in theatre studies and the theatre industry. The question raised is generally whether an actor has or lacks presence. This is often used as a measure of competency, attraction and magnetism. In her book *Stage Presence*, Jane Goodall concludes that the term presence "can be a way of labelling whatever we most value in performance."[33] The "we" is the audience. Much has been considered about the actor's presence.[34] Yet it is rarely conceived that the audience gaze at the actor affirms and can even be seen to help create that presence. As Sartre argues, "the appearance of the gaze is apprehended as the upsurge of an ecstatic relation of being."[35] It is in this ecstatic realisation of being gazed upon that the actor accepts the relation of being and becomes fully present. This perspective is explored in the next chapter. What, however, is presence to actors?

Every actor that I interviewed stated explicitly "you've either got it or you don't."[36] Broadway stage, film and television actor Lynn Cohen called it "showing up"[37] and was emphatic that some actors just do not show up. Presence was discussed predominantly in terms of a space-filling phenomenon such as is

Böhme's atmosphere. Gillette described presence as "spread[ing] [her]self out into so many different areas."[38] Hibbert argued that it was a persona that can fill a house.[39] Cooper described it as the action of inhabiting "a space with a fullness and a graciousness and a gravity that's palpable."[40] The actors also recognised presence in others. When he was part of the Chichester Theatre Company, Bartholomew would watch Maggie Smith, Joan Plowright, Paul Eddington and Alec Guinness from the wings: "[a] magic happens when they walk on stage. It's indefinable in a way. It just explodes [...] it bursts out."[41] This inimitable way of being onstage appears to augment the persona of the actor as they embody the character so much so that it permeates the atmosphere filling all the in-between spaces with electricity. This emanation is the aspect of presence that works to create that electric air experience for audience members.

Some actors that had worked with box-office names made a clear distinction between what they called "movie-star presence" and stage presence. Smith who understudied Denzel Washington in *Fences* and was in *Salome* with Al Pacino described how

> Movie star is different than actor. Actor is one thing, movie star is another thing. Not all actors are movie stars, not all movie stars are actors. Denzel and Al Pacino both started in theatre; both of them love the theatre. But just the embrace, walking on stage and having the full house ovation and screaming, that's a movie star: "We are thankful for all of your previous performances and we know you are going to be great tonight and we love you."[42]

As discussed in Chapter 1, the audience feel a certain intimacy with onstage celebrity and "embrace" and emanate love towards the star actor who has an already established film presence that seemingly fills the stage regardless of the stage presence of the actor. Smith's observations confirm the distinction already made that actor presence and Hollywood star presence are different forms of presence.

In her comprehensive survey of presence, Goodall explores the many associations of presence as drawing power, charisma, mesmerism and what she calls "dash and flash." It is, however, her discussion of presence as an energy onstage that is pertinent to the current discussion of the electric air.[43] Most actors describe the space-filling phenomenon that explodes from actors and fills the air as "energy." As discussed in Chapter 1, Böhme calls this energy "ekstases" and suggests that presence and atmosphere are interrelated. For him ekstases "determine the atmosphere radiated by things. They are, therefore, the way things are felt present in space." He then goes on to give a further definition of atmospheres based on this premise. Atmospheres are "the felt presence of something or someone in a space."[44]

Here we explore another understanding of presence: presence as being present in a particular time and place. Seven of the interviewed actors discussed this reading of presence in addition to their understanding of presence as a space-filling phenomenon. Theatre and film actor Simon McBurney articulated the sense of living in the moment that is part of presence:

Hidden within the word [presence], is a more important notion of time, and "the present", because presence is about being present. There is nothing with more presence than a seal, or a polar bear, because they're utterly present. If I put a seal into a crowded room, everyone would go "My god, look at that!" But the fact is that the seal is not thinking about the future, though it might be thinking about a way to get out. It's not thinking about the past. It's just in the here and now.[45]

Sanders argued that living in the moment and being and living onstage takes the onus of labour off the audience, so they do not have to work so hard and can just accept. For him presence is a

sureness, clearness, and I think in certain cases a surrender and vulnerability without self-consciousness. That you're so fully at home with being what you are and where you are that people can't take their eyes off you because they recognise life. They recognise themselves in that. And if [an actor] is uncomfortable the audience feel uncomfortable so it's that comfort you need to have with being. [...] It's a release of that border [between stage and audience]. And in a way it creates a crossing to the audience: "it is all fine here don't worry about me, it's all fine, don't worry about you." And the true acceptance of that so that even when [the actor is] standing still and just listening blankly, clearly not showing response but just listening, people go, "oh such presence." Because they feel you're really there, you're not worried about being there, you're not playing at being there, you're not showing people you're there, you're just fully there.[46]

This quote articulates the bridge that is formed between stage and audience when an actor is totally present and authentic onstage. Sanders also associates presence with comfort, an important point that is taken up in the next chapter.

Several of the other interviewed actors emphasised the importance of living in the present moment. Dauch argued that it is only when you live in the present that you exist onstage.[47] Stuttgart actor Wolfgang Michalek discussed how crucial being there, existing in the moment, is: "It's all about presence. [...] You can play like shit, you can play like a sausage, but you've got to be there."[48] Interestingly, Michalek suggested that being present or having presence is not necessarily something that is dependent on good acting. McKern reiterates,

it's very interesting, sometimes you can get an actor or actress who might not be a particularly fantastic actor but they have stage presence, they are watchful. [...] You can't put your finger on it, but they've got it. I don't think it's necessarily about brilliant technique or brilliant acting. It's just something they have got that you can't take your eyes off them. And it's not because they are pulling focus or anything.[49]

This watchfulness is the mesmerism that Goodall also associates with presence.

What is noteworthy about McKern's comment is, however, her emphasis that presence is not a technique you can learn. Goodall states that the production of energy emanating from actors and filling a space commonly associated with presence onstage, is a combination of technique and mystique.[50] This is the contentious area of discussing presence. Some acting theorists and teachers have attempted to teach this filling of a space through a process called radiation. Böhme argues that an atmosphere can only be generated if the ekstases, in this case the energies from the actor, radiate outwards into space.[51]

Konstantin Stanislavski borrowed the term radiation from the late-nineteenth-century French philosopher Théodule Ribot and did, indeed, attempt to teach techniques to his actors on how to radiate in his First Studio and particularly in an experimental production of Ivan Turgenevs' *A Month in the Country* in 1909. Stanislavski directed his actors to radiate their mental states and inner feelings.[52] In many ways, Stanislavski's concept of radiation was not dissimilar to the late-twentieth-century scientific concept of mirror neurons. In 1936, he himself presaged, "What name can we give to these invisible currents, which we use to communicate with one another? Some day this phenomenon will be the subject of scientific research. Until then, let us call them rays."[53] Through radiation, he believed an actor could "fill the entire building of the auditorium with invisible rays and currents of their feeling and captivate the crowd."[54] It was, however, his pupil Michael Chekhov, who most closely associated radiation with atmosphere. Chekhov developed radiation techniques for actors for the purpose of creating an atmosphere that affected both actor and audience:

> Both performer and spectator are unconsciously affected as an atmosphere's unseen waves are absorbed by the actor and Radiated into the audience. Though they cannot be seen, atmospheres can be felt strongly and are a primary means of theatrical communication.[55]

For Chekhov, the actor absorbs the atmosphere of an environment and then radiates this out to an audience. Conversely, Stanislavski taught that the actor's own connection with their inner emotional and mental states created an atmosphere through radiation.[56] Regardless of this distinction, in both Chekhov's and Stanislavski's writings, the association of radiation with atmospheres inhabiting the in-between spaces onstage among actors and between the stage and the audience is prevailing.

The concept of radiation contains mystical and esoteric connotations. Stanislavski was himself significantly influenced by Eastern traditions in his formation of acting techniques.[57] Smith has his own process of building up what he considers to be the spiritual energies required so he can radiate onstage:

> What is the energy? It's very energising, it's very spiritual, it's very dynamic, it's very loving, it's very open. I usually don't eat four to five hours before a performance so I can feel it. It's visceral, it's in my solar-plexus and it radiates

through my body. Usually I warm up vocally and physically, spiritually, mentally and emotionally which makes me very odd to a lot of other actors because mostly they like to talk and laugh and eat and drink coffee. [...] The energy is palpable, it really is. You can almost touch it.[58]

Yana Meerzon argues that Chekhov did not, however, see atmosphere as a transcendental and magical experience, but rather "as a mode of spatial and temporal relationships between actors onstage, and between the stage and the audience."[59] As discussed above, contemporary actors use the word energy to describe exactly the same concept as rays. Brunell goes so far as to call it light and associates it with presence:

> Everyone has a light. Some people are better at owning it and letting it shine. Some people because of circumstances, how they are raised, their humility level, don't have that ability. People who have stage presence are not afraid to let their light shine and have the ability to be fearless.[60]

Brunell goes on to argue, however, that it is only when presence and radiation between actors is aligned that s/he really feels s/he is able to live on stage:

> On those great nights when everything is aligned and you're present and your other actors are giving you so much, it feels like flight. It feels like freedom and flight. It just feels exhilarating.[61]

Returning to Böhme's description of atmospheres that are spheres of presence with ekstases radiating out from them, this is one of the liminal spaces where the electric air is created: the space where presence, ekstases and radiation meet. The actor radiates their presence into the stage space and out into the audience. As Sharon Carnicke argues, Stanislavski considered radiation to be both mystical and psychological:[62] the combination of the actor's presence, constructed by the gaze of the audience, radiating out ekstases.

In essence, for the actor, as argued above by Sanders and McBurney in particular, presence is a lack of self-consciousness. Presence includes, intriguingly, a form of "absence," yet more of a focused absence. McBurney goes on to describe it as such:

> The presence of an actor is about their ability to, curiously, forget about themselves. Or conversely, to think about themselves so much that that is also presence, that kind of monstrousness. But what doesn't work is when you are thinking about the future or remembering the past, when you are distracted into thinking about something else, then your presence reduces.[63]

In his definition of presence, McBurney introduces two important concepts. The first is "monstrousness" acting. A form of such overwhelming mindful presence that results in an actor's preoccupation with themselves is discussed further in Chapter 5. This is a well-recognised pitfall of a Method actor that is so self-absorbed that they shut the audience out. It is equally, however, the monstrousness of the exaggerated actor, States's "vain acting" above, a hallmark of amateurism that Stanislavski referred to as the mechanical acting of the nineteenth century where *cabitonage*, over-the-top playing to an audience, was used. The actor that is able to forget about themselves and "be" onstage has authentic presence.

The second concept is another hazard for an actor, and that is a break in concentration away from the present moment onstage. This is a form of absence that is unfocused. The actor becomes distracted by the future or the past and is not fully there. This is not, however, to be confused with the actor's double consciousness, which is a very focused form of presence.

The actors discussed presence as a space-filling phenomenon, as being present in the moment and described an actor radiating energies: ekstases. Throughout this book, the tenuous balance between what is figurative and what is physical about the electric air has been explored. Similarly, we can ask what of ekstases, radiation and atmospheres is figurative and what is physical. In many ways, science cannot yet fully describe all that our senses are capable of detecting. Actors and audience members likely share a tacit understanding of, perhaps, previously scientifically undescribed phenomena.

Double consciousness

Regardless of how mystical the art of acting can be seen to be, the interviewed actors, and in particular the British actors, were emphatic that at the heart of acting there is a craft or technique to be studied, practiced and developed. In moments of insecurity onstage, some actors explained how they would either anchor themselves in their actor's craft or, conversely, focus on their character. This would centre them and bring them back into the world of the play. What they were describing is essentially what is referred to as a double consciousness, also known as a dual consciousness or split personality. Actors have a consciousness onstage that is split. They are actor and character.

Who is the actor when s/he is performing onstage: the actor, the character or both? Who does the audience see: the actor, the character or both? The former question has been asked since the first staged theatre of Ancient Greece. The latter is a more contemporary question and is addressed in the next chapter.

O. States argues, "the actor [is] a kind of healthy schizophrenic who is living two lives at the same time:"[64] actor and character. To achieve this, the actor is seen to have what has been called a double consciousness. While actors in Ancient Greece did consider the dual role of playing a character and "demonstrator,"[65] debate about the actor's double role intensified in the nineteenth century, a time in which books and manuals on the art of acting proliferated. Denis Diderot's discussion of the actor's double personality[66] in his 1883 book *The Paradox of Acting* evolved into a heated debate over acting styles that still rages today.[67] The basic premise, however, that actors do have a double consciousness on stage and are sometimes actor and at other times character was further elaborated on by actors of the nineteenth century, notably Henry Irving and Tommaso Salvini. Positing an actor's perspective on the art of acting Irving argued,

> It is necessary to this art that the mind should have, as it were, a double consciousness, in which all the emotions proper to the occasion may have full swing, while the actor is all the time on the alert for every detail of his[her] method.[68]

Salvini described it as a double existence:

> An actor lives, laughs, weeps on the stage, but as he weeps and laughs, he observes his own tears and mirth. It is this double existence, this balance between life and acting that makes for art.[69]

Salvini's concept of an actor standing outside of him/herself and observing is taken up by Stanislavski, a great admirer of Salvini, in his letters to actors later in the early twentieth century. Although Stanislavski's system of acting has frequently been associated with complete embodiment of the character, this is more of a perception influenced by Method acting.[70] Stanislavski did indeed argue that "An actor is split into two parts when he is acting"[71] and later expands, "this dividing of oneself does not interfere with inspiration. On the contrary, one helps the other."[72] Stanislavski observed this in his own practice:

> I divided myself, as it were, into two personalities. One continued [as the character], the other was an observer. Strangely enough this duality not only did not impede, it actually promoted my creative work. It encouraged and led impetus to it.[73]

All these explications of the double consciousness paint a portrait of an actor who is highly consciousness of the fact that s/he is an actor/observer on stage while concurrently is abandoned to the "full swing" of emotions experienced by the character. This double consciousness, according to Salvini and Stanislavski, inspires true art.

The interviewed actors were all asked who they were onstage: actor, character or both. Unanimously, the actors stated that they were both, that they had a double consciousness. They were char/actor. Some described their process in which they began as the actor and then were subsumed by the character:

> Early on you'll be getting a lot of Chuck, then later on you'll be getting a lot of what the character is, because it's a slow unveiling, a slow blossoming. It's kind of like watching a flower, only you're being the flower, and you're doing the blooming, and it's never done, it's never finished.
>
> *Chuck Cooper*

Through the rehearsal process, using myself, I find the character within me and the adjustments in the values and the relationships and all of that.

Jay O. Sanders

Early on in a run and during rehearsals, you are fighting to find the person you are presenting and when you relax into it, it becomes more about how do you recreate that person afresh everytime. [...] Its always moving, it's a liquid thing, it's like oilpaint. You put it on the canvas and you can move it around. After a while it sets but if you keep worrying at it, if you keep working at it, it becomes something else.

Ian Bartholomew

There are necessarily many factors that influence the double consciousness: the length of the run of the play, the style of the play, the breaking of the fourth wall, the play's genre. Stuttgart theatre and television actor Lea Ruckpaul emphasised that it depended on the piece of theatre: "Tonight I was Lea who hides herself behind the fact that she is an actor that finds her way into this character so that the audience believes that I am that character on stage."[74] This complex imbrication of character and actor implicating the audience is quite sophisticated. Bartholomew, who was in the middle of a long-running production when interviewed explained:

You become a hybrid. If you've been performing the play a long time, such as this play, over 200 times, you don't go on auto-pilot but [...] you put on the coat, the slippers and you walk out as the character.[75]

Interestingly, the French actors were the only ones to mention the importance of the audience in their explication of double consciousness. As Rouland explained:

We always have a relationship with the audience, we can't forget it. There are many technical things. We have to stay concentrated and at the same time we have to be the character, so we are double.[76]

The audience were perceived as one of their consciousnesses. This is, perhaps, why Robert L. Benedetti argues in film, where the audience is not present, "the actor's awareness must be suppressed [...] in favour of complete involvement in the character's consciousness."[77]

Some of the actors described moments when actor and character conflated arguing that these were rare but sought after and highly prized experiences. Dauch explained:

Sometimes there are "grace" moments. Suddenly we forget ourselves and think only of the character, for the profit of the character. For these small seconds we work and work and repeat and repeat to live and feel these moments and seconds again: because that is the truth.[78]

Michalek described these moments as flying: "It has to come from you. But in the moments when things are flying, I am not myself."[79] Actors often use metaphors such as "flying" or "riding a wave" to describe these heightened moments onstage. There is a certain sense of abandon common in these terms, a release or a surrender. Plunkett describes the transition from actor to character in this way:

> Clearly I'm not another person, I'm who I am. But yes I think I surrender. To me it's about surrender. [...] I'm going to try not to be thinking as Maryann about "oh maybe if I did this" or "oh that was very moving the way I dragged that water" or something. You surrender to just this hour and forty-five minutes or however long the play is.[80]

As alluded to by Plunkett, this doublethinking or standing outside yourself watching can be problematic. McKern explains, "There is a little part of your brain thinking 'oh that didn't work this time.'"[81] For Berlin actor Marcel Kohler, this consciousness is judgemental:

> There's always some part of me describing myself when I am performing and I'm really working on not judging myself too much on stage. I got this from a tennis coach who is teaching players not to judge themselves while they play. In tennis you can see really well there are sometimes phases during the play where you look on yourself and think "oh that's not really good," and then it is not good. I think you have to separate it. You have to look at yourself during different times, but not while you are on the stage. I think it's good to separate that. I'm working on that separation in myself.[82]

In these comments, we see the seeds of the actor insecurity and constant watching that occurs. The actor becomes their own judge, and often their worst enemy. Yet there is another entity that they have to confront night after night who some actors frequently cast as judge: the audience.

These workings in the minds of the actors, their double consciousness, even their judgement become charged with an energy. The conversations they are having with themselves create a tension within the minds of every actor and they bring this tension into every performance. Much of an actor's identity spans the security–insecurity spectrum. The audience benefit, however, from the unpredictability of the precipice that the actors stand on. This tension adds to the electric air and fuels many interesting conversations across the footlights. Yet it also fuels one of the most debilitating aspects of performing in front of an audience for actors: stage fright. What if the audience do not see the character, they see the actor alone. Will they judge? This is the question that haunts many actors.

Stage fright

Stage fright is not only what the actors predominantly discussed in the interviews when asked the question "What does it feel like onstage?" Stage fright at once helps to create and is also a by-product of the electric air. The tightrope that the actors walk is a risk they take. It heightens the stakes and adds to the electricity in the air. Actors have stage fright because they will be judged on both sides of double consciousness: being a person and playing a character. The unsettling, plaguing question for actors is "Will the audience suspend disbelief and not only see, but accept and believe in the character I play rather than the actor I am?" These thoughts may be conscious or subconscious, yet are no less of an anathema because of this. When an actor is wracked with insecurity and anxiety, in their mind's eye, costumes and makeup are often not enough to conceal the naked actor. In many ways, their fate is in the audience's hands. This heightens tension leads to stage fright and helps create the electric air.

Surprisingly, even for the highly experienced actors interviewed, the thought of performing in front of an audience is not merely an insecurity. It is an incapacitating, overwhelming paralysis that can leave them trembling in the wings, nauseous or completely tongue-tied. This is stage fright, also known by its less noxious term Performance Anxiety.

Of the actors I interviewed – the majority of which have been performing on stage in front of West End, Broadway, Parisian, Stuttgart or Berlin audiences for many years – 21 of the 22 had experienced stage fright in varying degrees at some point in their careers. Some so severely that they had to seek professional help or take a break from their careers for several years. Others had milder forms of stage fright that were only temporary. The actors are in good company. Sir Lawrence Olivier was haunted by stage fright all his life. To help relieve his fear before a performance, he would stand in the wings and speak obscenities at the audience.[83] This anecdote clearly illustrates that it is not the actual physical elevated stage that he was afraid of. It is the audience. Actors do not experience stage fright in the close, secure confines of a rehearsal space or in onstage dress rehearsals where the only "audience members" are usually the director, the stage manager and their fellow actors. This syndrome should, perhaps, be more correctly named audience fright. The below discussion of stage fright is actor-led. In the interviews many actors described their onstage experience as "terrifying" or "nerve-wracking," which opened the discussion up for an important exploration of stage fright. They experienced it as a direct consequence of their encounter, or their thoughts of an encounter, with an audience. Their dominant fear was a fear of being judged by the audience.

The majority of writing on stage fright is either in actor's self-help books or in psychological journals. There is limited discussion from theatre scholars and very few of the extant texts actually quote actors' experiences. In addition to the fact that theatre scholars tend to theorise on their own rather than ask actors or audience members their perspectives,[84] there is a more recondite reason for this absence that is endemic to the acting community; what several writers on stage fright call "the conspiracy of silence."[85] Actors tend to eschew any discussion of stage fright. In part because acting is the second most superstitious profession in the Western world,[86] and secondly, because they do not always wish to reveal what many erroneously consider a "weakness" with its attending stigma.[87] As McKern who, we shall see, has battled stage fright all her life disclosed, "I think we should talk about it and I think a lot of actors are very ashamed of it and are very frightened of it. It's almost like if you talk about it, it will happen."[88] Yet none of the interviewed actors hesitated to divulge their experiences of stage fright and their symptoms. Indeed, it was liberating for some to reveal their struggles. There is no attempt in this chapter to analyse the causes or evaluate remedies for this malady. The interviewed actors' own descriptions of stage fright are recorded for the purposes of providing a fuller understanding of the often tremulous encounter of an actor with an audience and the ways that even this insecurity contributes to the electric air experience.

German actors call stage fright *Lampenfieber*: "lamp fever" or a fever caused by fear of the stage lights, and thus the fear of being onstage. In his excellent discussion of stage fright, Nicholas Ridout suggests that the introduction of electric lighting in theatres in London and New York in the 1880s contributed to the actors' stage fright as the actor was "thrust into the glare"[89] of the stage lamps and separated from the audience who sit in the subsequently darkened auditoriums.[90] What he is describing is *Lampenfieber*. Actors used to the natural lighting of gaslights and candles were thrust onto the stage with blaring lights in their faces. Further, auditorium lights on the audience began to be dimmed during this time, focussing the gaze of the audience more intently on the actors. Here the electricity of the stage creates an unhealthy "fever" which may heighten the electric air experience but may also have incapacitating consequences for the actor.

So why do actors get stage fright? Of what are they afraid? Are they afraid of rejection, themselves or that something can go wrong? Or are they afraid of the other? As Sartre argues,

> shame is only the original feeling of having my being outside, engaged in another being [the audience] and as such without defence [...] *recognising myself* [as actor] in this degraded, fixed, dependent being [...] needing the mediation of the Other [the audience] in order to be what I am.[91]

Standing onstage in front of sometimes hundreds of people places actors in a highly vulnerable state. They are in many ways at the mercy of and totally dependent on the approval and acceptance of the other. Will the other suspend disbelief and accept the character, or will they judge the actor for not playing his/her part convincingly?

While the purpose of this discussion of stage fright is not to assess the psychological causes of stage fright in actors, some interesting recurrent findings in the extant stage fright studies pertinent to this research are that "low self-esteem and low self-efficacy were often related to stage fright."[92] The interviewed actors readily disclosed that they were insecure. To be more precise, the actors tended to speak on behalf of their entire profession with comments such as "actors are amazingly insecure human beings." This insecurity is deeply rooted in "wanting to be liked, and wanting what you're doing to be liked."[93] Cohen takes it a step further and argues that it is more than "like": "it all has to do with being loved, needing that love from the audience. And we all need it even though we say we don't. The fear is that they won't like you, they won't think you're wonderful."[94] These often unspoken disclosures are part of the conversations that occur between actors and audience members. This overwhelming need to be liked or loved can sometimes compromise a performance. As Bartholomew explained,

> Actors do what they do because they want to prove something and you want to be liked. I know actors that cannot go onstage and not be liked, and they will subvert the character and try and make it something that the audience likes. I've seen it happen. I might have been guilty of it myself.[95]

The need to be liked or loved comes from

> a huge fear of failing. Lots of people think actors like showing off [...] Most actors are wanting to please, to try and do their best: wanting to please the director, to please the audiences and they beat themselves up when they feel that they haven't done that.[96]

McKern's observation about seemingly "showing off" echoes the narcissism McBurney discussed above. Yet the ostensibly self-consumed actor that is overconfident is sometimes masking what British West End actor Janet Fullerlove called "the crushingly shy individual who is hiding behind what they're doing out there."[97]

Several of the actors revealed that they were "painfully shy as a child"[98] or when they were younger "had problems with under-confidence and [were] very self-critical."[99] In the actor's self-esteem, there is a certain contradiction. As Fullerlove went on to say, as an actor, "you have to have a fucking big ego. You have to have a big ego to be able to go out there and do it."[100] As States emphasises, "How is it possible to be shy when one has so deliberately sought the attention of the world?"[101] Yet at the same time the shy, underconfident individual who is extremely fearful of failure and is constantly judging themselves – "I'm really not that good at all and I shouldn't stay onstage"[102] – is, perhaps, the real person underneath the ego character's facade. Interestingly, this dichotomy mirrors the double consciousness of the actor's onstage persona. Actors, as I have been told often, are complex beings. Yet studies reveal that they are considerably more empathetic and extraverted than the general population.[103] Therefore, when actors are gripped by stage fright, the manifestations are emotive and acute.

The actor stands backstage in the wings ready to go onstage. They have been given their five-minute call and are shaking from head to toe. Their hands are clammy, they are perspiring profusely.

"I can't do it. I can't."[104]

Judgmental thoughts fill their minds.

"They'll hate me."

They start swearing at, and giving the finger to the audience: "You bastards!"

Then they become frozen with fear. Bunny in the headlights.[105]

"I don't remember any word!"[106]

Their faithful bucket sits beside them. In case they throw up.

"Places" cries the stage manager.

They get a sudden urge to go to the bathroom.

"You had half an hour, now you have to pee when I said places? I got to hold the show up for you? Hurry up."[107]

They run.

Once in their place they get a sudden urge to lie down, to sleep, to escape.[108] But the lights come up and they walk onstage and deliver their first line. Seemingly confident. Convincing the audience, if not themselves. They are the character. The pre-performance nerves create a highly charged tension in the air that can be seen to add to the electric air experience for the actors.

While this is a fictitious narrative and no actor would experience all the above-mentioned symptoms of stage fright concurrently, each actor interviewed suffered from at least one, if not two or three of these maladies either regularly or at some point in their career. The most extreme, vomiting and paralysis, was experienced by only two of the actors. Several regularly had onsets of diarrhoea or needed to "pee." One of the most fascinating symptoms was what Deutsches Theater actor Natali Seelig coined as *Fluchtschlaff*: escape sleep. As her colleague Jeremy Mockridge described, "When you are nervous, you instinctively want to sleep."[109] Seelig went on to explain the reasoning: "Sleep. Wake up and it may be over. Sleep away the pain."[110] Elias Arens, another colleague, described his experience of *Fluchtschlaff*:

> I get to the theatre and the stress usually comes five minutes before the show. And I get very tired. My body reacts like that. Before going onstage I could lie down and sleep right away. *Fluchtschlaff*: fleeing sleep. You sleep by fleeing [the situation]. It's a body reaction to escape tension. So I yawn a lot.[111]

Yet so important are the conversations actors have with their audiences that they will endure all of this. All of the actors I interviewed did.

It is difficult to comprehend the intensity of the onset of stage fright for actors. Harder had a very severe bout of stage fright when he was working under one director and had to see a doctor:

> I had some problems because [the work for the play] was totally exhausting and over the edge. So I went to the doctor and said, "I don't know why, I just feel like dying. Maybe I'll fall down onstage." The doctor told me there were studies that examined actors right before their premiere of a play. Adrenaline and rapid heart rate was so high for these actors that it was like watching a tsunami rolling towards you.[112]

This is an apt description and resonated with many actors that I subsequently shared it with. The extreme emotions experienced by an actor, particularly on an opening night, the first moment that they are encountering an audience, can feel like a natural disaster advancing towards you that cannot be averted. This too, however, works to create an electric air experience as the stakes are so high.

Donald Kaplan argues that the audience is an antidote to stage fright. That the reciprocity between actor and audience "banishes stage fright as the performance gets underway."[113] While this may be true for some actors, it is certainly not true for all. Bartholomew described one production when he was playing a police inspector in a crime thriller and experienced stage fright during the play in front of the audience:

> I came on one night and I froze. It was like a black tunnel. There were lights going down to a point in the distance. That point is where I should have been. But I was miles away. Time stood still. Your mind is working furiously [...] it feels forever. We jumped a few pages. But I realised the most important piece of information was two pages before, so we had to go back. Every night after I was so physically ill that I had to have a bucket by the door. As the doorbell rang and I had to go onstage I thought I would throw up. It lasted a few months. I thought "I'm never going to make it as an actor. Because I can't get past this." It's really debilitating.

Many actors discuss how everything goes into slow motion when this curious phenomenon occurs onstage. There is a fear, a paralysis and often a standing outside of yourself watching what is happening. This is also part of the double consciousness. As Kaplan explains, during an episode of stage fright there is a "split between a functioning and observing self."[114]

McKern uses her observing self to get back into a proper and more balanced relationship with the audience:

> When I am nervous I have to give myself a talking to. I have to believe that the audience are a friend out there. It is quite tough. You have to stop trying to impress them, trying to prove yourself. You have to talk yourself into being confident that you have a story to tell that they'll want to listen to. And you hope that they enjoy it and you can't beat yourself up if they don't enjoy it. All you can do is your best.[115]

As Stella Adler argues, "the actor is totally exposed. [S]/he stands on the stage. [S]/he stands in the spotlight. His/[her] every movement is scrutinized. There is no place to hide."[116] It is a perilous venture. Adrenaline flows in response to this. It can, perhaps, even anaesthetise some of the fear.

Yet particular actors are unwilling to take this risk and hide behind the safeguard of their bag of tricks or professionalism. Bags of tricks are the set routines, gestures or ways of delivering a line that actors have honed over the years that may prompt a laugh from an audience or make them appear more convincing in their character. They are often a trap, however, as, forgoing originality, the actor may use their tricks for each character they play or may use them mechanically. They are a temporary but ultimately dissatisfying tool that can become a crutch. Cohen recognises actors that use these crutches immediately: "they just don't show up." She goes on to argue that actors need a little stage fear to be fully present:

What I call "not showing up" means that you've left all your fears so you can be protected. Of course some are great actors. But I can tell the moment they walk on the stage, they don't show up. It's safer, much, much safer. It's like wearing a little iron chest protector. "This is what I do I'm very good at it." And they are. But the audience are not going to see it. You come back tomorrow and you'll see exactly the same thing. It takes the fun out of it.[117]

According to Cohen, taking the fear out of it also takes the fun out of it. Yet it also makes the actor less vulnerable. Mockridge was in a production where "a director has seen it's a bag of tricks and he takes it way. It's interesting when a director takes that away. This is when it can become existential."[118] As an interesting aside, many of the conversations I had with the German actors turned to existentialism. For example, in discussing stage fright with Harder, he explained that even though he had a tsunami rolling towards him at times, it was an existential struggle he was prepared for:

The whole body and the whole human being is built to hold a lot of strength. That's what I like about being an actor. As a body at work onstage you have more of a possibility to feel these fights with existence. I wouldn't do that on the street. I need a room for that.[119]

The room Harder is talking about is the stage, fearful though it may be, because it is there that the actor feels "more alive than in real life." As incapacitating as it can be at times, stage fright often creates an electric air moment as it heightens the stakes.

Acting is a profession of extremes and seeming contradictions. The actor only lives only onstage yet sometimes feels like s/he is dying. To get to the point of being able to encounter an audience, there is often much suffering and self-discovery. The warm confines of the theatre community may be an antidote to the fragmentation of society, but may also be a transient community sometimes involving a competitive undercurrent. Confrontation with an audience becomes a seeming cause of this malady, but it is also the antidote.

The stage fright experienced by the actor fills the in-between space across the footlights with Böhme's emotional tone of feeling that creates an atmosphere that is something emotional and also something spatial. Stage fright is also a conversation; a conversation that an actor has with her/himself as they undertake to solve the double consciousness dilemma. The self-talks above illustrate this. It is the live experience, the fear of being judged in the encounter by hundreds of pairs of eyes, that adds to the electric air. It is also the ephemerality of the experience of stage fright that heightens the stakes: onstage, an actor cannot just "do another take" as they can in front of a camera. What happens if the audience does not suspend disbelief and sees only the naked actor rather than the character? The experience of ensuing stage fright sends tingles through an actor's body, but these same tingles become part of the emotional radiances in the atmosphere, creating electric air experiences.

While considering who the actors are, we can see how vital the audience is. It is the audience who strongly influence how actors perceive themselves. It is the audience who play the key role in the actor–audience relationship: the audience as an antidote to stage fright, the audience as tsunami, the audience as existential *raison d'être*. The ekstases radiating from the actor's presence, the tightrope they walk in the double consciousness between actor and character, the moments they feel they are flying and even the stage fright, can all contribute to an electric air experience.

Whom do they see?

In their view from the stage, more electricity and foreboding fills the mind of an actor than audience members may imagine. The actor has shut out the outside world backstage only to confront it again on the other side of the footlights, the portal into the world they have occluded. They have been nurtured in a safe environment, rehearsed their roles, built their character and are ready to live onstage. Yet now it is time to stand on the precipice, with everyone staring at them, and ask for acceptance. Or so this is how many actors perceive it. Now the actors have to confront the people they shut out when they closed the door of the outside world to enter the safe confines backstage. They have to confront the people who, should they meet them on the streets outside the theatre, often do not understand what they are doing. On the stage the actor is prepared to face the audience. Or are they? That initial encounter with an audience is one of the most exhilarating and terrifying things that actors undertake.

Encounter

After the safety of rehearsals and the "womb" of the backstage sanctuary, the first encounter with an audience is like walking into the unknown. The actor's anticipation of their meeting with the audience and their response to an audience is always intense. It is intense fear of the other, as seen in the above exploration of stage fright, or it is intense thrill – but it is never disinterest, apathy or routine:

> You are scared to death waiting backstage, absolutely frightened out of your being.
>
> *Anita Gillette*

> That first time you go out. [There is a] degree of fear, huge adrenaline. You don't know what you have got in your hand.
>
> *Edward Hibbert*

> I am excited and anxious, a lot depends on me. I have been alone with this text for such a long time and I know if I don't get it I will lose the people.
>
> *Lea Ruckpaul*

> You have no idea what's going to happen and that unknown makes me have a little bit of nerves and anxiety.
>
> *Keith Randolph Smith*

The unknown can be a sobering and frightening entity. To compensate for this, McKern de-personifies the audience: "you know that they are there and they are a big, hopefully friendly, big black monster out there."[120] Similar to McKern, many actors cast their audience. This is, perhaps, their third consciousness. As Gillette argues, "If you are having a conversation on stage with somebody, there is a third party."[121] They are an actor judging themselves, yet, unlike in film where the audience is absent, they are also an actor conscious of the audience, and they often invite them in as a character or player. For Ruckpaul, casting the audience "helps [her] a lot to know who [she is] talking to." She went on to explain, "You can cast the audience as anything. They are my friends, or a doctor [therapist]. Sometimes I cast them as opposite things."[122] Several of the interviewed actors were very specific about productions:

> In *Cyrano de Bergerac* the audience has several forms. In the first act the audience is the Hotel Burgundy audience: *la pièce dans la pièce*. They are friends, we give them gifts.
>
> *Stéphane Dauch*

> Say you are doing the scene at a wake or a cocktail party, one will often [make the audience] guests at that cocktail party. You bring them into your particular position onstage.
>
> *Edward Hibbert*

Actors cast the audience as something specific such as guests at a cocktail party as part of a technique, to build their imaginative world, as something to settle their own nerves or as something particular to them.[123]

For Cooper, the audience is not as defined. It is "the character in the play that [I] have not yet met. And so that's how I greet them: as a wonderful surprise."[124] Sanders often casts the audience as reflections of himself.[125] For Smith casting the audience is deeply personal:

> I make them my family, all the members of my family who I never met. My great grandparents, my great-great grandparents, my great-great-great grandparents, my great-great-great-great grandparents. So the slaves and before the slaves, all those souls are sitting in the audience and they go "This is our relative, he's free, he's on stage and he's acting in a play. We're proud of him. We're dead." So I make the audience my family.[126]

The concept of an extended family in the auditorium was echoed by other actors. Hibbert argued that each of his audiences were "like a family, [sometimes] a dysfunctional family."[127] Personalising the audience or casting them as "friendly" works to alleviate anxiety. The actor is not then encountering the unknown, but a friend, guests or members of their family.

Alleviating anxiety about the audience lessens the actor's association of the encounter as confrontation and elevates the encounter as a conversation. As a conversation it is part of the two-way interchange that happens across the footlights. Through this, a unique, although fictitious, relationship is formed between stage and audience.

Audience presence

Can the audience have presence? The actors certainly create a kind of presence for the audience in casting them. But do they have a presence of their own? If the audience have suspended disbelief and are living from moment to moment in the fictitious world of the play, then they are certainly present in McBurney's understanding of the word "presence." Yet this is not always the case. Sometimes the audience are squirming, and while they are physically sitting there, are not really there emotionally or mentally. Not only do actors sometimes cast their audience, they are highly aware of their presence. Actors invariably discuss the presence or lack thereof of the audience in their dressing rooms during a play. The audience are "dead" or "listening" or "comatose" or "with us" or "alive" or "quiet" or "smart."[128] Actor Smith likes to listen to the audience through the monitor during intermission:

> The audience explodes in chatter: "Oh my god! Did you see that?" You can hear them talking some, and they're excited. When it's really good there's an energy in the house and you can feel it. They're electric because what they're witnessing is so engaging.[129]

The actors can read whether an audience is not only emotionally and mentally "there," they also use descriptors for the type of presence they sense in the audience. The audience may not have charisma, drawing power or magnetism, but in Smith's description, the audience presence is electric.

Catherine Brunell can gauge an audience presence immediately which she describes as a type of alchemy:

> I can tell by my second line in the show the alchemy of the audience. I can tell if they are going to be playful, if they are going to be feisty. And then I gauge things from there. It's in one response from the audience. You can tell right away if the audience is going to be with you. Sometimes I say to the stage manager "oh god, the audience were so tough tonight."[130]

The psychological conversations between actors and audience can be so charged that the audience presence is electric. The "alive" excited presence of an audience, sometimes even before the performance when they are full of anticipation, can create a fertile environment for collective effervescence. In this, the audience presence is collective. The actor presence is singular. When the audience are "with" the actors, fully present, there are ample opportunities for rich conversations across the footlights.

Conversations

With their family/friend/guest audience that is fully present, caught up in the play's diegesis, the actor has a conversation across the footlights because, as Cohen emphasised, a play "isn't a one way street."[131] Michalek described it in terms of a dialogue: "you make a connection with the audience. You speak to them like other people who have to go through these things with you. You get to a place where together, you are celebrating what the author's put together."[132] Once the actor begins to tell the story, the real conversation commences. Like Michalek, Cooper emphasised that that the play is co-created with audience and actors that have agreed to come together:

> Something in us, some primordial thing calls us to the fireplace, to the pit, where something is acted out, and we all become a community in that storytelling. And so I always feel that that is what is going on, that energy from the audience. It can be unwieldy, sometimes quieter than we like, sometimes actually louder than we'd like, but nevertheless it always present and always there, and ultimately always a positive and good thing that we have all come together and agreed to go on a journey together.[133]

Sanders and Plunkett have had audience members return to their plays[134] primarily because theatre is a place where they can have conversations, difficult conversations that they cannot, perhaps, have in their personal lives:

> People come up to us constantly outside of [our] shows, not even the same day, sometimes months later and say "when are you coming back?" Because they miss *the* conversation and they miss *that* conversation. They miss the real conversations [between actors and audience] as well as emotional conversations that they, very few of them, can have with their own families. Or very few of them have a group of friends who you could talk with for an hour and forty five minutes about your questions or fears about the election, your questions about taking care of your mum who is getting older, your questions about paying the mortgage, your questions about why am I doing everything the right way but it doesn't work out.[135]

Here Sanders describes two types of conversations across the footlights: actor–audience conversations – emotion conversations – and societal debates inherent in the discourses and issues in plays which have personal relevance to each audience member. From observation of Sanders's and Plunkett's performances,[136] I have further noted that a powerful empathetic conversation occurs across the footlights. The actors often break the fourth wall and stare at audience members, inviting them to be part of the conversation and share in their character's emotional turmoil. This is an electric air experience for actors and audience alike. For some audience members, when the fourth wall is broken, it can be extreme discomfort. Yet for the audience members I observed at one of their productions, the gaze as an empathic gesture was accepted. It became an embrace across the footlights.

What are actor–audience conversations? They are emotional, psychological, paralingual, verbal and physical. As Chekhov argues, "Actors must have psychological and body impulses."[137] These impulses are not only part of their actor–actor onstage dialogues, they are also an important part of the actor–audience dialogue. As Brunell describes, "you can feel the audience emotions fuelling you, pushing you through the scenes."[138] The audience's emotions are a felt energy, propelling the actor. It is the conversations that actors have with the characters, with the text and with their audience that elicit the emotions. Bartholomew finds the conversation difficult to explain:

> It's a tricky thing to quantify because it's an emotional response. And when you have all that emotion the other side of the lights, it's hard to process it while you are trying to step across those lights with the emotional back of the character you are playing. There has to be a place where you meet. Where the audience meets the actor and goes "okay."[139]

The audience meet in in-between meeting place of audience and stage. For Cooper, the emotion on the other side of the footlights "is helpful, if you just surrender yourself and allow yourself to ride on that effervescence."[140] What Cooper is describing here is a poignant example of Émile Durkheim's collective effervescence which rolls across from the audience immersing actors and audience.

It is not only emotional; however, the physical conversation that occurs is often visceral for actors. Hibbert described the physical conversation in an off-Broadway production of *Gross Indecency*: "That was quite interesting. You could almost feel the audience responding or leaning in, literally. The smallest gasp or the smallest giggle can resonate, which can be very nice."[141] These physical conversations are part of what I have elsewhere described as the audience performance.[142] Just as previously stated intangible emotions can have tangible manifestations – fear, pity, joy – so too tangible physical movements, such as the audience leaning forward in their seat, can create intangible conversations. There is a point in the resonating physical conversation when the actors and audience come together. As Cooper describes,

> Theatre is eyeball for eyeball. In the theatre you can see and feel my breath, you can feel the resonance of my voice. I can feel you rustling in your seat, I can feel you cough. I know when you're not comfortable, and you know when I'm not comfortable, and we know when we're together, the dance that we're doing. It's a level of intimacy that only the theatre has.[143]

Sanders emphasises that although the conversation in theatre is intimate, there are some actors that can sabotage the intimacy:

> Even when I am doing outdoor Shakespeare where it's eighteen hundred people and it wraps around you, I find ways to bring [the audience] in for me. I guess it's a very technical way of reaching to the very back corners and down front and sort of bringing them forward and talking to them closely as though [...] But I think theatre is an intimate experience. And when it's not it becomes too much about showing off. And that's not what I do it for.[144]

Actors are highly intuitive and can read what an audience is saying in their emotional and physical conversations. For actors, the audience dialogue is often very specific. They speak through their laughter, energy, tears, silence, applause and even hate. As Dauch explains, "we are very sensitive to the audience reaction: if they laugh, or they don't laugh. They feed us."[145] Laughter also works to "release the border"[146] between stage and audience. Audience and actors often meet in the effervescent joy of mirth. Laughter is one of the most rewarding, difficult to time and addictive audience response, and yet, as Brunell so insightfully shared, it is, in its essence, vacuous:

> Laughter is like a drug. It fills you in a way that nothing else does. Feeling that love from a group of people you don't even know. It's infectious, you just want more of it. It's hollow and empty, but that's why you fill your life with other things that are tangible and real.[147]

Brunell's final comment alludes to the despair of the temporary fix that performing onstage can sometimes be for actors.

Hibbert argues how, particularly in long runs of shows on Broadway, the actors know precisely the moment when the audience laughter is spent: "[the audience] will be howling and screaming like a child, and then they get exhausted round 8:45: there'll be tears before bedtime. They've laughed themselves out."[148] From this comment, it can be seen that the energy of the audience itself can be read by the actors. The audience also radiate, and the rays they emit or fail to emit can be sensed by the actors. This too emerges as a conversation:

> Sometimes the audience are lit. They're just on fire. I was going to say it was a powerful feeling but that's the wrong adjective; it's more of an energising feeling. And the audience energy helps you focus, it tells you where the lows are in the play.[149]

The concept of the "lit" audience that are on fire is a pertinent illustration of the electricity that the audience gives the actors to feed their performance. They do not always need to laugh or cry or gasp, their energy creates its own tension and excitement.

Silence can also be a conversation. Through their silence, the audience may be speaking volumes. Actors are highly skilled interpreters of silence. Cooper "get[s] off on the silences":

> There are different kinds of silences. There are silences that go "What is this bullshit? I have never seen something so horrible in my life and I'm wasting two hours of my life on this crap that I'll never get back," and they just sit there in disbelief. That's a certain kind of silence. Then there's another kind of silence: something's happening on stage, you don't hardly want to breathe loud because it's so wrenching or focused.[150]

The content of the play can be so wrenching and disturbing that actors feel actual detestation coming from the audience towards their characters, or in reaction to the circumstances the play is exploring. As Cohen bluntly commented, "You sometimes feel like they are hating you."[151] Yet more often than not, it is the content of the play that has aroused the aversion. Ruckpaul described a production in which she sensed fiery darts from the German audience:

> There was a political play I was part of. There was something going on in Dresden at the time and you could even feel hate and anger coming from the audience.[152]

Michalek described his experience of a play performed on 9/11:

> It's wonderful when you can feel an audience. On the day of 9/11 we were performing *The Three Penny Opera*. It was a completely different performance that night. Everyone was there, everyone was aware. I didn't care if people walked out, I didn't care if I got booed. Because the audience are making their statement as well, and I would rather have that![153]

In this instance, the booing and the walk-out become an integral and important statement that forms part of the conversation as explored in the Deutsches Theater *Hunger. Peer Gynt* case study. It is important to note, however, that not all actors respond as well to walk-outs and booing as Michalek in his above account. Having interviewed actors from various cultures I have found that German actors, particularly, rarely take the walk-out personally,[154] while for Western, English-speaking actors, the walk-out tends to exacerbate their insecurity.[155] The reciprocity in the many and varied conversations between actors and audience members builds a rhythm that can be seen to create Böhme's "tuned spaces."[156]

No electric air

Conversations across the footlights, be they hostile, affable or otherwise, help create the electric air. It is when there is no conversation at all that the production can wilt. As Hibbert described it, "there are some houses that are not having it. You just sit there and you go, 'what's it all about Alfie' because they're not having it! They'll sit there absolutely, seemingly, in contemptuous silence."[157] McKern was very pragmatic: "That's when you're earning your living. You can't expect the magic to be there eight times a week when you are in a show for a year."[158] Many of the actors were deeply affected when the magic and electricity was absent. They felt "lonely,"[159] "like you're beating your head against the wall,"[160] "horrible."[161] Theatre is a two-way conversation, and when the audience become complacent and do not participate, the onus is on the actor to take the load. As Cooper explains,

> you're trying to carry something that is too heavy. If everyone does their work, I can carry my load, you can carry your load, and together we can carry the play. But if you haven't done your work, I have to carry your load and my load, and it's too much.[162]

Many actors attempt to compensate for this by trying harder to create a spark, but as Hibbert emphasises, "the worst thing you can do is strive to get the audience to come to you. You just have to sit there and play it as honestly as you can."[163] Honesty and truthfulness in performing is the hallmark of a seasoned actor that does not take the lack of energy personally. Michalek "used to panic about those moments but now [he has] learnt to just be truthful in that moment. To just pull back a little bit and to start getting into relationship with the audience again and build something up."[164]

Interestingly, Smith, who feels incredibly lonely when there is no conversation with the audience, creates his own dialogue which goes something like this:

> "Y'all don't like it do you?" "Not much." (They don't say that but that's the unspoken communication that you're having.) "You're not into this are you?" "It's a weird play." "Yeah, I guess you don't like Brecht do you?" "No. I hate Beckett too." "Okay you're not going to like this play then." "But I don't understand, it doesn't make sense." "What's the metaphor?" "But the metaphor doesn't make sense!" "I can't help you explain that, I can't explain the play to you. You've got to witness and see the play and hear the play."[165]

Many actors invariably take the dead feeling in the house personally. Even highly experienced actors can take it personally. It is very difficult, especially for young actors, not to. Brunell describes her reasoning in her inner dialogue which differs considerably from Smith's:

> It's tough not to take it personally. Tough not to feel that that performance defines you. You really are only as good as your last performance. I find those times hard to stomach. You walk out and say "oh crap I wish I had landed that better. I didn't feel like they were very responsive, I must not have been very good. Oh, they hated me."[166]

This is a veracious example of the inner monologue that haunts many actors when there is no actor–audience conversation onstage. Its roots lie in the deep echoing chasm of actor insecurity.

Whom do the audience see when they perform on stage? As the lights blind actors in most productions, they can only see a dark void. The void is, however, saturated with an emotional presence. It is Böhme's felt presence of something or someone in the atmosphere. As explored, the encounter with this felt presence – the audience – can be extremely intimidating for some actors. Some use techniques to help them overcome their insecurities such as casting the audience. The audience are not a dark, frightening void, but a friendly monster, guests or co-creators. Sometimes the audience presence is so electric that there is no need for techniques as the audience are living in the world of the play with the actors through their psychological conversations. There are other times where there are no electric air experiences and there is a deep chasm between the stage and the audience that is filled with dead air. There is no conversation. Regardless of whether the actors and audience members have experienced an electric air experience, there is one concluding conversation that occurs during all theatrical events. This conversation takes place during the curtain call.

The curtain call

The actors' final view from the stage occurs during the curtain calls. The final word in the actor–audience conversation is with the audience. After the theatrical event, lights fade to darkness, there is a soft drumming of slapping hands in the auditorium that often escalates into a heavy thunderstorm of applause. In the nineteenth century, the dialogue of applause would occur throughout performances: after moving monologues, when good won over evil, when the protagonist was saved from a life of evil or when a star actor made their entrance onstage.[167] We have seen a revival of the latter in this twenty-first century on Broadway and West End stages.

The curtain call is the signal for the unveiling of the actor behind the mask. Given the acute anxiety experienced before and sometimes during a performance, it is reasonable to assume that this expose would also cause disquiet. Yet, with the exception of one actor I interviewed that felt "profoundly vulnerable,"[168] there is predominantly no fear for the actors in this reveal. Kaplan is, perhaps, correct in surmising that the reciprocity of the conversation between actor and audience during the performance has actually banished the stage fright. It is more likely, however, that the performance, the test, the time of judgement and reckoning is over. As seen in the next chapter, the audience rarely withhold their applause if the actor's performance was not deemed worthy, as was the custom in the nineteenth century.[169]

Yet some actors still perceive the curtain call as a competitive event. Cohen finds curtain calls problematic: "I prefer a whole company bow. In single bows I think 'oh God no', that's when competition happens and I don't like that."[170] The competitive urge feeds the actor's ego as explained by Bartholomew:

> There is always still the bow that is: "look at me." The ego plays out at the curtain call. Especially if the [audience] loved the show and they are giving you a big cheer. "Yes I know [says the egocentric actor] aren't I marvellous."[171]

Fullerlove argues that it is vital that the actor strikes a balance: "for me there is a balance between what is tasteful and what is milking it. What is right and what is self-indulgent."[172] Just as it is important for actors to leave their baggage at the stage door, Cohen argued that it is imperative to "leave your vanity in your dressing room."[173] Sanders was quick to state, however, that the feeding of the ego in the curtain call is often an audience misconception:

> The curtain call is talked about by many audience members as "oh you're so hungry for applause" and I say "no I'm not, I'm ready to leave" but instead I acknowledge that we were here together. It's like "thank you for being here with us, thank you for letting us do this, thank you for joining us."[174]

Some actors deplore curtain calls and just desire to go home. Due to her childhood shyness, Plunkett use to "hate curtain calls" but has come to the realisation that the curtain call was one vehicle for her to thank the audience: "we applaud them, we applaud the audience."[175] McKern, who also acknowledged that bowing can become self-indulgent for actors, goes so far as to state that "the curtain call is for the audience. 'Thank you for coming. Thank you for being there.'"[176] This seeming inversion of approbation becomes interesting when we explore why the audience applaud the actors in the next chapter.

But who do the actors think the audience is applauding? Are the actors character or actor when they bow? Now that they are no longer a character in a fictitious world, who is this apparition, someone who has seemingly come back from the dead, that is bending their body or their leg at the front of the stage? The interviewed actors were all asked who they are when they bow and most stated that they were the actor rather than the character. Yet, for a select few, the double consciousness lingered. For Sanders the curtain call is "a transition period. I'm the actor, but I'm the actor with the character on my shoulder."[177] Bartholomew argued that the audience are not ready to see, or do not actually desire to see, the actor during the curtain call:

> I'm always me. It's a version of me. It's not me, me. The graft that you put into a character, the audience don't want to see. But I'm more me than the character at that point. Ultimately, it's not about you. They are not really cheering you. They are cheering the construct that you've made for them to watch.[178]

Here the third consciousness emerges again. The consciousness that is for the audience. More actor than character in this iteration, but a "version" or, perhaps, a simulacrum of the actor. Or are the audience, as Bartholomew hints at, applauding the embodied artwork that the actor has constructed? Broadway actor Denis Arndt echoed Bartholomew's discerning perspective: "It's not me taking the bow, nor is it [the character]. I am an actor, I'm taking my bow. I am. And it is not [the character] nor is it me. It is this thing that I do that wants you to be fulfilled in your appreciation."[179] Arndt returns the onus to the audience.

During the curtain call, the actor's view from the stage shifts entirely from the play's diegesis to the audience. It is, perhaps, the first time they actually see the audience as people rather than a hideous monster. They have journeyed from the safe confines of their backstage space to overcome the insecurities of the encounter and finally stand in front of their seeming nemesis, companion journeyer and co-creator. They smile. Or they "may have died in the last five minutes of the play" and they are "trying to smile."[180] The conversation which has been emotional and physical, but covert, suddenly becomes overt as the actors stare directly into the faces of the audience members. The applause deeply affects the actors' view of the audience from the stage. The actor's stage fright, their fear of being judged as being a person playing a character, is no longer of issue. The transformation from character to actor occurs in the unmasking at the curtain call. At the curtain call, for the first time, they are fully present as the actor wholly, receiving accolades or judgement, while the character fades away. They may perceive judgement in the applause, but the time of reckoning, the performance, the trial, has finished. What seemed like a huge ordeal has passed. Until the next performance. The audience hit their hands together, the actors bend over from the waist. This curious ritual continues until the audience are spent. This time, the audience controls the conversation.

Notes

1 Caroline Heim, *Audience as Performer: The Changing Role of Theatre Audiences in the Twenty-First Century* (London and New York: Routledge, 2016), 19–43.
2 Comments from some of the actors in the case studies were relevant for this chapter, so have been included here also. Five of the German actors, one American actor and one British actor are also cited in the case studies in Part II.
3 Catherine Brunell, personal interview, 1 November 2016.
4 Abigail McKern, personal interview, 6 July 2017.
5 Ian Bartholomew, personal interview, 11 July 2017.
6 Abigail McKern, personal interview, 6 July 2017.
7 Ian Bartholomew, personal interview, 11 July 2017.
8 Keith Randolph Smith, personal interview, 7 November 2018.
9 Edward Hibbert, personal interview, 21 September 2016.
10 Not only is the theatre a safe space, it is also a sacred space to many actors.
11 Edward Hibbert, personal interview, 21 September 2016.
12 Particularly in their performances in the Apple Family Plays. See Sanders's and Plunkett's biographies for details on these. It should be noted that their productions work actively to create a sense of home for the audience as well: often set in kitchens and sharing a meal. One of their productions, *Uncle Vanya* mentioned below, was the warmest most homely (in the positive sense) productions I have ever witnessed.
13 Maryann Plunkett, personal interview, 5 November 2018.
14 Linda Pöppel, personal interview, 28 October 2018.

15 Simon McBurney, personal interview, 28 October 2016.

16 Elias Arens, personal interview, 24 October 2018.

17 A phrase used colloquially in the theatre by actors is directors.

18 Comment 1: Edouard Rouland, personal interview, 20 October 2016. Comment 2: Stéphane Dauch, personal interview, 20 October 2016.

19 Chuck Cooper, personal interview, 29 October 2016.

20 Abigail McKern, personal interview, 6 July 2017.

21 Thornton Wilder, *Our Town* (New York: Avon, 1938), 138.

22 Uta Hagen, *Respect for Acting* (Hoboken: Wiley, 1973), 215.

23 Anita Gillette, personal interview, 21 September 2016.

24 Ibid.

25 Bert O. States, *Great Reckonings in Little Rooms: On the Phenomenology of Theater* (Berkeley: California UP, 1985), 122.

26 Jean-Paul Sartre, *Being and Nothingness: An Essay on Phenomenological Ontology*, trans. Hazel E. Barnes (London: Routledge, 2003), 260.

27 Ibid., 281.

28 Stéphane Dauch, personal interview, 20 October 2016.

29 Ian Bartholomew, personal interview, 11 July 2017.

30 Simon McBurney, personal interview, 28 October 2016.

31 Ian Bartholomew, personal interview, 11 July 2017.

32 Keith Randolph Smith, personal interview, 7 November 2018.

33 Jane Goodall, *Stage Presence* (London: Routledge, 2008), 188.

34 See particularly Goodall, *Stage Presence*; and Joseph Roach, *It* (Ann Arbor: Michigan UP, 2007).

35 Sartre, *Being and Nothingness*, 268.

36 Edward Hibbert, personal interview, 21 September 2016 (quoting Mama Rose in *Gypsy*).

37 Lynn Cohen, personal interview, 9 November 2018.

38 Anita Gillette, personal interview, 21 September 2016.

39 Edward Hibbert, personal interview, 21 September 2016.

40 Chuck Cooper, personal interview, 29 October 2016.

41 Ian Bartholomew, personal interview, 11 July 2017.

42 Keith Randolph Smith, personal interview, 7 November 2018.

43 Goodall, *Stage Presence*, 20.

44 Gernot Böhme, *The Aesthetics of Atmospheres*, ed. Jean-Paul Thibaud (London and New York: Routledge, 2017), 32, 33.

45 Simon McBurney, personal interview, 28 October 2016.

46 Jay O. Sanders, personal interview, 5 November 2018.

47 Stéphane Dauch, personal interview, 20 October 2016.

48 Wolfgang Michalek, personal interview, 11 October 2016.

49 Abigail McKern, personal interview, 6 July 2017.

50 Goodall, *Stage Presence*, 20.

51 Böhme, *Aesthetics of Atmospheres*, 32, 33.

52 Gareth White, *Audience Participation in the Theatre: Aesthetics of the Invitation* (New York: Palgrave Macmillan, 2013), 26.

53 Konstantin Stanislavski, *Building a Character*, trans. Elizabeth Reynolds Hapgood (London: Routledge, 1989), 183.

54 Ibid., 31.

55 Mala Powers, a student of Chekhov and a close personal friend, describes Chekhov's concept of objective atmospheres. Cited in R. Andrew White, "Radiation and the

Transmission of Energy: From Stanislavski to Michael Chekhov," *Performance and Spirituality* 1 (2009): 36.

56 Ibid., 37.

57 Eugenio Barba was also fascinated with the "stream of Magic" that he witnessed emanating from Indian and far Eastern actors, and in interviews with them found that they used techniques to create this energy in themselves that then transferred to the audience members: Erika Fischer-Lichte, *The Transformative Power of Performance: A New Aesthetics* (London: Routledge, 2008), 97.

58 Keith Randolph Smith, personal interview, 7 November 2018.

59 Yana Meerzon, "Body and Space: Michael Chekhov's Notion of Atmosphere as the Means of Creating Space in the Theatre," *Semiotica* 155, no. 1–4 (2005): 261.

60 Catherine Brunell, personal interview, 1 November 2016.

61 Ibid.

62 Sharon Carnicke, *Stanislavski in Focus: An Acting Master for the Twenty-First Century*, 2nd ed. (London and New York: Routledge, 2009).

63 Simon McBurney, personal interview, 28 October 2016.

64 States, *Great Reckonings*, 14.

65 Pat Easterling and Edith Hall, eds., *Greek and Roman Actors: Aspects of an Ancient Profession* (Cambridge: Cambridge UP, 2002), 397.

66 Denis Diderot, *The Paradox of Acting: Masks and Faces* (New York: Hill and Wang, 1957), 11.

67 To see a detailed examination of the two acting styles colloquially known as an "inside-out" approach to acting or an "outside-in" approach, see Caroline Heim, "Found in Translation: Debating the Abstract Elements of Cultures through Actor Training Styles," *Theatre, Dance and Performance Training*, 4, no. 3 (2013): 353–367.

68 George Iles, ed., "19th Century Actor Autobiographies: Sir Henry Irving," accessed 29 January 2018, www.authorama.com/19th-century-actor-autobiographies-6.html.

69 Salvini cited in Konstantin Stanislavski, *Building a Character* (New York and London: Routledge, 1987), 189.

70 For a detailed analysis of Stanislavski's perspectives on double consciousness, see Sharon Marie Carnicke, *Stanislavsky in Focus*, 2nd ed. (New York: Routledge, 2009), 142–144.

71 Stanislavski, *Building a Character*, 189.

72 Cited in Carnicke, *Stanislavsky in Focus*, 119.

73 Stanislavski, *Building a Character*, 18.

74 Lea Ruckpaul, personal interview, 11 October 2016.

75 Ian Bartholomew, personal interview, 11 July 2017.

76 Edouard Rouland, personal interview, 20 October 2016.

77 Robert L. Benedetti, *ACTION!: Acting for Film and Television* (Boston, MA: Allyn and Bacon, 2001): 9.

78 Stéphane Dauch, personal interview, 20 October 2016.

79 Wolfgang Michalek, personal interview, 11 October 2016.

80 Maryann Plunkett, personal interview, 5 November 2018.

81 Abigail McKern, personal interview, 6 July 2017.

82 Marcel Kohler, personal interview, 26 October 2018.

83 Robert B. Marchesani and Mark Stern, *Frightful Stages: From the Primitive to the Therapeutic* (London and New York: Routledge, 2014), 8.

84 Kirsty Sedgman addresses this point in "Audience Experience in an Anti-Expert Age: A Survey of Theatre Audience Research," 42, no. 3 (2017): 307–322. I would also argue that this is partly due to what I call "researcher insecurity."

85 See Bella Merlin, *Facing the Fear: An Actor's Guide to Overcoming Stage Fright* (London: Nick Hern, 2016), xxi; and Glen O. Gabbard, "Stage Fright," *International Journal of Psychoanalysis* 60 (1979): 383.

86 Jockeys are more superstitious than actors.

87 For a discussion of this, see Nicholas Ridout, *Stage Fright, Animals, and Other Theatrical Problems* (Cambridge: Cambridge UP, 2006), 53.

88 Abigail McKern, personal interview, 6 July 2017.

89 Ridout, *Stage Fright*, 48.

90 Several psychological analyses of stage fright refer to stage fright as a form of separation anxiety.

91 Sartre, *Being and Nothingness*, 288, 289.

92 Gordon Goodman and James C. Kaufman, "Gremlins in My Head: Predicting Stage Fright in Elite Actors," *Empirical Studies of the Arts* 32, no. 2 (2014): 133–148.

93 Chuck Cooper, personal interview, 29 October 2016.

94 Lynn Cohen, personal interview, 9 November 2018.

95 Ian Bartholomew, personal interview, 11 July 2017.

96 Abigail McKern, personal interview, 6 July 2017.

97 Janet Fullerlove, personal interview, 20 July 2014.

98 Maryann Plunkett, personal interview, 5 November 2018.

99 Abigail McKern, personal interview, 6 July 2017.

100 Janet Fullerlove, personal interview, 20 July 2014.

101 States, *Great Reckonings*, 121.

102 Linda Pöppel, personal interview, 28 October 2018.

103 See Jacqueline Hammond and Robert Edelmann, "The Act of Being: Personality Characteristics of Professional Actors, Amateur Actors, and Non-Actors," in *The Psychology of the Performing Arts*, ed. Glenn Wilson (Amsterdam: Swets and Zeitlinger, 1985); and Daniel Nettle, "Psychological Profiles of Professional Actors," *Personality and Individual Differences* 40, no. 2 (2006): 375–383.

104 Linda Pöppel, personal interview, 28 October 2018.

105 Abigail McKern, personal interview, 6 July 2017.

106 Ibid.

107 As quoted in Keith Randolph Smith, personal interview, 7 November 2018.

108 Elias Arens, personal interview, 24 October 2018.

109 Jeremy Mockridge, personal interview, 24 October 2018.

110 Natali Seelig, personal interview, 24 October 2018.

111 Elias Arens, personal interview, 24 October 2018.

112 Manuel Harder, personal interview, 27 October 2018.

113 Donald Kaplan, "On Stage Fright," *TDR* 14, no. 1 (1969): 82.

114 Ibid., 64.

115 Abigail McKern, personal interview, 6 July 2017.

116 Stella Adler, *The Art of Acting*, ed. Howard Kissel (New York: Applause, 2000), 19.

117 Lynn Cohen, personal interview, 9 November 2018.

118 Jeremy Mockridge, personal interview, 24 October 2018.

119 Manuel Harder, personal interview, 27 October 2018.

120 Abigail McKern, personal interview, 6 July 2017.

121 Anita Gillette, personal interview, 21 September 2016.

122 Lea Ruckpaul, personal interview, 11 October 2016.

123 Not all actors cast their audience.

124 Chuck Cooper, personal interview, 29 October 2016.

125 Jay O. Sanders, personal interview, 5 November 2018.
126 Keith Randolph Smith, personal interview, 7 November 2018.
127 Edward Hibbert, personal interview, 21 September 2016
128 For a comprehensive overview of all these comments, see Heim, *Audience as Performer*, 19–43
129 Keith Randolph Smith, personal interview, 7 November 2018.
130 Catherine Brunell, personal interview, 1 November 2016.
131 Lynn Cohen, personal interview, 9 November 2018.
132 Wolfgang Michalek, personal interview, 11 October 2016.
133 Chuck Cooper, personal interview, 29 October 2016.
134 See Sanders's and Plunkett's biographies for details on their Apple Family plays referred to in this dialogue.
135 Jay O. Sanders, personal interview, 5 November 2018.
136 This was particularly notable at a performance I attended of *Uncle Vanya*. *Uncle Vanya*, Hunter Theater Project, directed by Richard Nelson, 7 September 2018.
137 Michael Chekhov, *To the Actor: On the Technique of Acting* (New York: Harper and Row, 1953), 2.
138 Catherine Brunell, personal interview, 1 November 2016.
139 Ian Bartholomew, personal interview, 11 July 2017.
140 Chuck Cooper, personal interview, 29 October 2016.
141 Edward Hibbert, personal interview, 21 September 2016
142 Heim, *Audience as Performer*.
143 Chuck Cooper, personal interview, 29 October 2016.
144 Jay O. Sanders, personal interview, 5 November 2018.
145 Stéphane Dauch, personal interview, 20 October 2016.
146 Jay O. Sanders, personal interview, 5 November 2018.
147 Catherine Brunell, personal interview, 1 November 2016.
148 Edward Hibbert, personal interview, 21 September 2016
149 Keith Randolph Smith, personal interview, 7 November 2018.
150 Chuck Cooper, personal interview, 29 October 2016.
151 Lynn Cohen, personal interview, 9 November 2018.
152 Lea Ruckpaul, interview, 11 October 2016.
153 Wolfgang Michalek, personal interview, 11 October 2016.
154 This could also be due to the job security that German actors enjoy compared to their English or American fellow actors. The German actors' job security is discussed in the *Hunger. Peer Gynt* case study.
155 Having interviewed a total of 43 actors from five different countries for this book and *Audience as Performer*, my research showed a clear division between European actors being more comfortable with the walk-out. For a longer discourse on the walk-out, see Heim, *Audience as Performer*, 34–36.
156 Böhme, *Aesthetics of Atmospheres*, 32.
157 Edward Hibbert, personal interview, 21 September 2016.
158 Abigail McKern, personal interview, 6 July 2017.
159 Keith Randolph Smith, personal interview, 7 November 2018.
160 Chuck Cooper, personal interview, 29 October 2016.
161 Ian Bartholomew, personal interview, 11 July 2017.
162 Chuck Cooper, personal interview, 29 October 2016.
163 Edward Hibbert, personal interview, 21 September 2016.
164 Wolfgang Michalek, personal interview, 11 October 2016.

165 Keith Randolph Smith, personal interview, 7 November 2018.

166 Catherine Brunell, personal interview, 1 November 2016.

167 For a full discussion of nineteenth-century applause, see Heim, *Audience as Performer*, 54, 55.

168 Chuck Cooper, personal interview, 29 October 2016.

169 Ibid.

170 Lynn Cohen, personal interview, 9 November 2018.

171 Ian Bartholomew, personal interview, 11 July 2017.

172 Janet Fullerlove, personal interview, 20 July 2014.

173 Lynn Cohen, personal interview, 9 November 2018.

174 Jay O. Sanders, personal interview, 5 November 2018.

175 Maryann Plunkett, personal interview, 5 November 2018. Ridout finds it insulting for actors to applaud an audience; however in Plunkett's case, she has a loyal following for her plays; many are known and are part of their extended "family." Ridout, *Stage Fright*, 165.

176 Abigail McKern, personal interview, 6 July 2017.

177 Jay O. Sanders, personal interview, 5 November 2018.

178 Ian Bartholomew, personal interview, 11 July 2017.

179 Denis Arndt, personal interview, 26 October 2016.

180 Keith Randolph Smith, personal interview, 7 November 2018.

3

THE VIEW FROM THE AUDIENCE

Audience members do not consciously go to the theatre to take part in a conversation. Or do they? This chapter considers the types of conversations that occur in the theatre across the footlights from the audience point of view. Inverting the perspective in Chapter 2, it asks the questions: Who are the audience and whom do they see? To inform this chapter, 21 American, British, German and French audience members were interviewed.[1] The majority of which were what I call professional theatregoers, very regular theatregoers that love the theatre. The audience members interviewed were what Helen Freshwater calls "ordinary" audience members[2] rather than "integral" audience members: critics, friends and theatre industry professionals.[3] The professional theatregoers interviewed had all seen so much theatre and held strong opinions on the merit of the productions they saw, the acting and many other features, that it was often difficult in the interviews to remain focussed on the experience of attending the theatre in general rather than to discuss their treatise on certain productions or actors. They all held actors in very high esteem and felt much endearment towards and attachment to the theatre. For some it was "like you are in your living room at home and [the actors] came to do a show just for you."[4] For obvious reasons, the audience members did not gain the same kind of security or safety from the theatre as the actors, yet the theatre was not merely a place of entertainment, but a familiar, warm, almost "home" environment.

In this inviting, warm environment, many conversations occur across the footlights. All of the audience members interviewed were able to describe in detail the issues raised in the plays they saw and were eager to share their responses to those issues, even when unprompted. Yet many were also highly suspicious of any theatre conversation that could be construed as didactic or agenda driven and abhorred being lectured to from the other side of the footlights. New York theatregoer Maureen Pascal was adamant on this point:

I do not go to the theatre to be preached to. I can think on my own. I can pick up what you're saying. I understand your point, but don't preach. I might even agree with you, but don't preach it.[5]

This kind of theatre is a one-way conversation and it is not tolerated. As Anton Chekhov the father of Modern theatre admonished a journalist: "You are right in demanding that an artist take an intelligent attitude to his work, but you confuse two things: solving a problem and stating a problem correctly. It is only the second that is obligatory for the artist."[6] Maureen was not saying that the issues explored in plays should not be vital, contemporary and reflect the debates going on in society, she was arguing that they be fairly and accurately presented, not preached from a particular point of view or agenda. Furthermore, she wanted to be part of the conversation and credited for her intelligent role in deciding the answers herself: filling in the gaps in the narrative with her own understandings. As Chekhov goes on to state: "It is the business of the judge to put the right questions, the answers must be given by the jury, according to their own lights."[7] Audiences have a clear sense of right and wrong. Theatre, although Bertolt Brecht at times suggested otherwise, is the place for the audience to answer the questions asked from the stage. The audience come to the theatre to engage in these conversations about societal issues embedded in the plays they see.

There is also a conversation that occurs in the encounter between audience and actors. While much audience research considers the audience's conversations with the artwork – the play and the issues therein – this chapter explores the audience–actor conversations and does so from the audience point of view. In engaging in these conversations, sometimes the audience members journey from security to insecurity. Yet unlike the actors, theirs is not a performance-initiated form of insecurity. They arrive at the theatre secure in their role as audience member enthused at seeing a production. Then the issues in the play or the transference or projection that occurs in the encounter with the characters – as explored more in the next chapter – can be unnerving. They are challenged by issues in the play or have a strong aversion to a character.

This chapter follows the audience from their entrance into the theatre auditorium to the curtain call. A discussion of their first moments in the auditorium, the important role of proximity in the audience–actor relationship and the electricity in the atmosphere is followed by the specifics of the encounter, double consciousness and what audience members perceive as the actor's presence. As in the previous chapter, the curtain call concludes the view from the audience.

Who is the audience member?

In the house

The theatre is an enchanting space for most audience members and for all of the audience members interviewed. Leaving their everyday lives behind, they enter into the theatre auditorium expectant, motivated and full of anticipation. Peter

York from the United Kingdom explained the transition: "I think you're sort of stepping off the world because you are wanting to experience something outside the normal experience. [...] You are entering a live situation."[8] This "stepping off" the quotidian to enter a "live" situation in which audience members suspend disbelief is intriguing. The theatre experience is a heightened form of liveness. It is the magnetic pull across the footlights described in Chapter 1 that draws audiences into an experience that is extraordinary.

Yet for some audience members, the mood they are in and other extraneous circumstances can impede their step out of the quotidian and delay their suspension of disbelief. As Konstantin Stanislavski argues,

> The spectator as well as the actor is an active participant in a performance and therefore [s]he too needs to be prepared for his[/her] part, [s]he must be put in the proper mood in order to be receptive to the impressions and thoughts the playwright wishes to impart to him[/her].[9]

Like the actors, audience members too have certain baggage that would be good to leave at the door. Baggage often permeates mood. If atmosphere is read as emotions radiating in space, these audience members can be seen to radiate their own ekstases of mood that overwhelm them to the point that they are not able to be infected by the convergence of a larger atmosphere of theatre's enchantment.

For the majority of audience members, the leap off the world into the "live" space is, however, embraced and the audience settles into the warmly lit environment of a theatre "house."[10] For the majority of the audience members interviewed, their immediate response is one of anticipation and excitement:

> That's one of the most exciting moments, it's the anticipation. [...] It's the total experience.
>
> *Betty Cohen*

> I'm in anticipation of what I am going to see and looking forward to it.
>
> *Rachel Strauber*

> I have all kinds of positive feelings and anticipation.
>
> *Frank Lachmann*

> Excitement. I look around. I'm going to be entertained, I'm going to learn something. Anticipation of excitement.
>
> *Rita Haynes*

> I always like it. It is a social event. A lively experience. In cinema, there is a dead feeling. [In the theatre:] anticipation. I look around to see if there is anyone we know. The stage setting increases the anticipation.
>
> *Peter Cotton*

In Peter's comparison of the lively pre-show experience of theatre and the dead experience of film, we see the seduction of the live event with bodies to interact and co-create with rather than a simulacrum. His comment also refers to one of the rituals that audiences engage in. Just as the actors engage in pre-performance rituals to warm-up or overcome their stage fright,[11] audience members engage in various rituals: reading the programme, looking around to see who they know, examining the set, turning off their phones. These reasonably sedate rituals and the excitement and anticipation of the encounter are in stark contrast to the actor who may be concealed only a few metres away vomiting into a bucket or swearing at the audience under their breath. Yet, as explored in the last chapter, it is not actually the audience they are cursing, but fear itself.

Interestingly, Thousten Gilbert from Germany expressed a certain fear of the unknown in that moment before the performance:

> I'm afraid that I won't understand things. I think about how long the whole thing is going to be. It's something very special. I feel very joyful going to the theatre. But it is also a bit anxiety provoking, not knowing what is going to come up.[12]

Peter relishes this uncertainty: "You know its live: the fact that there's no certainty of what will happen because every audience is different as well as every perform-ance being different."[13] The live and ephemeral aspects of theatre heighten the unknown – the uncertainty for audience members – while backstage the actor fears rejection in not playing their role well enough. Are there, perhaps, other audience members that, like Thousten, also fear they will not play their role well enough, the role of understander.

Proximity

The relationship between liveness and proximity in the theatre is noteworthy as it affects and shapes the intensities of the conversations in the theatre. One of the primary concerns for many of the audience members interviewed was where they sat in the auditorium and their distance from the live happenings onstage. As Philip Auslander argues, "The power of the live resides in the tension between our sense of being connected experientially to something while it is happening while also remaining at a distance from it."[14] This is essentially Edward Bullough's psychical distance. Distance, he argues,

> is a *personal* relation, often highly emotionally coloured [...] One of the best known examples is to be found in our attitude towards events and characters of the drama; they appeal to us like persons and incidents of normal experi-ence, except that that side of their appeal, which would usually affect us in a directly personal manner, is held in abeyance (italics in original). [15]

This succinctly articulates the intimacy of distance in the theatre. Following the suspension of disbelief, psychological intimacy – through identification, transference, projection and empathy – can obfuscate the physical distance between stage and audience. Physical and emotional distance are interrelated.

It is, therefore, not surprising that physical proximity to the stage is one of the vital components of the audience's experience of the production, and the distance the audience member chooses to sit from the stage likely reflects certain aspects of personality and social and cultural construction. As Edward Hall argues, "each one of us has a number of learned *situational* personalities. The simplest form of the situational personality is that associated with responses to intimate, social, personal and public transactions" (italics in original).[16]

Hall's allusion to a situational personality is most interesting. A study of the personalities, inhibitions and cultures of audience members would, perhaps, give insight into their seating choices. The audience members interviewed were very direct in stating their preferred proximity in the theatre. London audience member Rita Haynes "doesn't like to sit too close,"[17] and Maureen Pascal always sits in the front row.[18] Isabelle Petiet from Paris returns often to the same production and will "sit in the front row and then in the last"[19] to have different experiences. It was Rachel Strauber from New York that was most emphatic about proximity:

> [Where I sit affects me] so enormously that I can't begin to tell you. Fifth row centre is very important to me. It matters to me a great deal. The intensity of the performance stays with you. If I sat further back I would feel discombobulated. You lose the connection. The connection between you and the characters becomes attenuated. You will miss nuances and you will miss some expressions. When you can really see the nuances in their faces and their reactions, your mind will never wander. Your mind will wander if you sit further back. When I saw *Curious Incident*: I sat further back. I was totally disconnected, disassociated from it.[20]

The importance that Rachel places in her proximity to the actors is remarkable. There is almost a strident authority and understanding of space which illustrates Hall's observations that our "sense of space is closely related to [our] sense of self, which is an intimate transaction with [our] environment."[21]

For Rachel, the connection with the characters was of paramount importance. As Kent Cartwright argues, "Audiences engage not just with character but with the virtuosity of acting. In the rhythm of aesthetic distance, engagement with the actor can alter the spectator's engagement with the character."[22] For New York theatregoer Debbi Baum, engagement with the actors is "powerful. There is that connection and it's important enough to me that if I really can't see the actor's faces, I'd rather not go. I have serious fourth wall issues."[23] Debbi is here referring to the close phase of Hall's public space. Other audience members also sat in the first row for the purpose of connection to the actors:

We go to a lot of theatre and I often choose the first row because I do want to have that experience. There's no audience in front of me: it is just the actors and us. Being in the front row is almost as good as being in a small theatre.

Chris Lincoln

We enjoy close proximity to actors. It's immediate, like they're playing just for you.

Janet Stahl

Sitting in the front row, even of a Broadway theatre in the absence of an orchestra pit, can sometimes fall into Hall's far phase of the social space[24] where many of the finer features of the actor's faces are readily visible and audience members' close proximity to the actors can alter their engagement with the characters as they are caught in the rhythms and atmospheres of the char/actor's world.

In the majority of the audience interviews, there was a strong desire for connection, for intimacy, almost for total immersion. Auslander goes on to argue that the live connection creates in audience members a desire "to abolish distance, but never actually does."[25] Or does it? It obviously does not abolish physical distance, but for those in the close phase, there is a psychological nearness – Bullough's *psychical distance* – as the play's *fabula* spills over the fourth wall and into the worlds of the expectant and receptive audience members. This, for many, is why they return to the theatre time after time. The physical public space soon becomes a version of Hall's intimate space in the minds of audience members who feel the actors are playing just for them. New Yorker Norman Malter likes to sit in the front row because then he is "more in the story."[26] Yet Rita does not like to sit too close because she does "not like to see [the actors'] makeup."[27] Close proximity to the actors naturally deeply affects the possibilities for and types of conversations that can occur between actor and audience during the performance: psychological and physical.

Electricity and atmosphere

The atmosphere that spills from the stage, or even from the actor's own ekstases, naturally works to create an electric air experience for audience members. It can also be produced by the close proximity to other audience members. For the interviewed audience members, the electric air experience was generated by other audience members, the actors and the possibilities of "the story." For Rita, part of the electricity comes from the collaborative opportunities for the audience members: "In a theatre you may look at people and smile. It's a more collaborative atmosphere. Collaborative with the audience members. We are all there because we want to be there. The atmosphere is electric."[28] Broadway theatregoer Betty Cohen finds "the most excitement in seeing the actors: it is electric."[29] Isabelle describes the atmosphere she feels in the house before an opening night performance: "If it is *la première* and I have never seen the actors performing there is an electricity in the room, in the audience. It is very exciting, a delicious moment."[30] Isabelle is drawn to the actors, and the magnetic pull between stage and audience strengthens. New Yorker Frank Lachmann describes it in terms of enchantment of the world to come: "That's part of the magic. When I am going to be introduced to a whole different world. It's an interesting one, hopefully engaging one, and surprising."[31]

Audience members – particularly the "professional" audience members interviewed for this book – are often astute, discerners of good theatre who know exactly what they go to the theatre for. They do not wish to be preached to, know precisely where they want to sit to be in relationship with the char/actors and often enliven the air of the auditorium with excitement and anticipation before the performance commences. The joy, the excitement and the anticipation of the unknown already work to create an electricity in the atmosphere that calls to the play to begin. In one sense, in this anticipatory moment, the audience are emitting ekstases. Using Gernot Böhme's term, they are present in the space radiating ekstases. The actors backstage feel this presence. Listening through the monitor they can hear the buzz and excitement of the audience presence. And then the play begins.

Whom do they see?

For the audience, the world that opens up when the curtain rises or the lights come up is not only extraordinary and full of possibilities, it is, for some, the real life. In the previous chapter, West End actor Abigail McKern stated that on stage she feels "more alive than in real life." Isabelle expressed a similar sentiment from an audience perspective: "I consider that the life we live all day long maybe is not the real life. The real life is when they open the curtains and you see something beautiful. That is the real life."[32] Isabelle, a seasoned audience member who relishes the opportunity to debate the issues in plays with her friends,[33] was emotional as she described the real life of theatre that, in many ways, also makes her feel more alive. She was not describing escapism, or a delusion, she stated it as a fact. Dennis Kennedy, drawing from a Lacanian concept, argues that "in presenting a fiction to an audience the theatre can open up the Real that in daily life is disguised as ordinary reality."[34] From this perspective and from the actors' and audience members' statements above, theatre has the potential to become "more real than real life."

Interestingly, Isabelle then went on to talk about moments of transference, projection and identification that caught her up in that real life, reducing the aesthetic distance between stage and audience:

> There are so many characters that remind me of me and someone else: *L'avare* by Molière. There is a woman who often gets very angry. It reminds me of me. In all the characters you have a lot of positive and negative sides that remind you of what you are if you are honest and think: "that's me when I am angry" or "that's me when […]."[35]

The theatre is the place for Isabelle to confront parts of her personality and celebrate others. The world of the play for some audience members is a place where they can live in the onstage world, as they identify with the struggles, personality traits and emotive truths of the characters. It is also, as explored in the next chapter, a safe place where audience members, as they disclosed to me "can experience emotional responses that [they] actually don't have in 'real life.'"[36] What, after all, is the real life? The imaginative world can be just as real as real life for children. Why not the world of the play? In a world saturated with screen images that are far less real than characters onstage, perhaps the analogue, live, real-time experience of the theatre is a balm for the restless, digitally programmed, anxiety-haunted individuals of the twenty-first century. It is, at the very least, a healthy alternative. There is no known psychiatric diagnosis of theatre addiction. As Peter Brook argues, "Audiences crave for something in the theatre that they can term 'better' than life."[37] This perspective also points to Jacques Rancière's imperative that theatre has the potential to change something of the world we live in.[38] Audience members and actors are having "more real than real life" conversations. Everyday conversations are often mere pleasantries. If Isabelle were to meet one of the actors from *L'avare* in a coffee shop, the conversation would most likely be small talk. In Isabelle's theatrical conversation with the actor across the footlights, however, her psychological conversation with the char/actor is far more personal and invested. The encounter reveals parts of her own psyche, her "negative sides" such as "anger." This revelation, in turn, perhaps teaches her how to express anger, or at the very least, to admit that her anger can be expressed very negatively. We do not always enjoy meeting ourselves across the footlights. The conversation is often confrontational.

For those that return again and again to the theatre, this "real" environment can become something of a home environment. Even, surprisingly, for the weary and seemingly hardened critic. Although no critics were interviewed for this monograph, actor Jay O. Sanders relayed this episode to me during his interview:

> I did an interview here last week with Ben Brantley. And he said "I have to tell you, I'm so connected to the family now that when Maryann comes on to begin setting the stage, I begin to weep because it is 'we're starting.'" He's telling me this personally. He said "I can't even explain it. I just have such a relationship to these families now, and this style, that you're telling me you're home."[39]

The "family" Brantley is referring to are Jay O. Sanders, Maryann Plunkett and their fellow actors who have worked in repertory in various plays at the Public Theatre and other New York theatres over many years.

This emotional connection audience members have with actors they have seen before is not only experienced by critics. Some of the interviewed audience members described the familiarity they feel with actors that they return to see. Thousten returns to see a specific actor "for his acting, because I like his energy. It is special for me. I have a history with this guy. If I've already got a relationship, it already makes a difference."[40] Thousten is drawn to the ekstases of the actor and, interestingly, is in relationship because he has what he calls a "history" with the actor. This speaks to who the audience see on stage: the character or the actor.

It is important to note that this familiarity differs considerably from the celebrity *attachment*. Many of these seasoned audience members were quick to emphasise that they are "not impressed by celebrities. If the celebrity is in the play, [they are] really going to see the play, [not the celebrity]." As Betty continued, she made a clear distinction between actor and celebrity: "If there is an *actor* that I like, I will go and see the play."[41] Indeed, some of the audience members deliberately avoided plays that starred a celebrity and were aware of how celebrity can obfuscate other important elements of the production. As Fran Halper argued, "Some celebrities are too taken up with their own celebrity to get into the character."[42] Many audience members had, however, their favourite veteran theatre actors that they enjoyed seeing regularly. Audience members relish seeing familiar actors

> because you perceive more of a connection. You know a little bit more about them. You know their story a little or at least what you can glean of their story. So I think that adds a personal aspect. [...] because you've connected yourself. You've aligned yourself a little bit more.[43]

Who are the audience aligning themselves with? The actor or the character? These aspects become very important when we consider double consciousness from the view of the audience. While aspects of identification and projection are alluded to in Maureen's above disclosure, it is still the connection between audience and actor that is of most relevance to her.

The encounter

The audience members' encounter with the char/actor onstage is far less fraught and complex than the actors' encounter with the audience. The actors never actually gaze at the audience until the curtain call at the conclusion of the play. As explored, they have a third consciousness that is the audience, but the direct gaze is the audience's alone. The audience are staring at the actors for the entire performance. As Thousten argued, theatre "is very direct. I have direct contact with the actors. It can be very surprising."[44] In this direct contact, the audience inner monologue can be one of craving: "Let me in, let me experience it, let me digest it."[45] Sartre describes how the gaze can unnerve the other by making the other vulnerable.[46] We have explored this vulnerability in the previous chapter. The audience is not in the gaze of the actor. This is a privileged position for the audience. They, in a sense, become voyeurs without the pressure of being in someone else's gaze. The gaze is reasonably intense, and the actor has a good reason to be intimidated by what Bert O. States calls "the weight of [the audiences'] eyes"[47] on them. As Maureen describes from her point of view in the front row, "I've got good eye contact with you because I'm that close now."[48]

According to the interviews, audience members tend to have more of a positive view of actors than actors perceive. It is more one of incredible respect, awe and admiration. In the interviews, the audience members shared their point of view of the audience–actor relationship. It was "pleasurable to be close to the actors,"[49] "a personal experience between who's on the stage and who is in the audience"[50] and "intimate."[51] Two-thirds of the audience members described the relationship as "intimate." New York theatregoer Suzanne Griffin went on to explain:

> I do enjoy that it is a temporary relationship, but it is a very intimate relationship between the audience and the actors, and the audience is very participatory that way. How you respond and the energy the audience gives off is going to affect the performance during the play as well. A very communal, creative experience, which is a lot of fun I think.[52]

The gaze and the psychological conversations work to create this intimacy.

Suzanne's comments also point to the reciprocity that occurs in the audience–actor relationship. Various theatre audience theorists have considered this reciprocity.[53] Iain Mackintosh describes it as an electric air experience:

> Energy flows chiefly from performer to audience, the performer is rendered impotent unless he or she receives in return a charge from the audience.[…] The energy must flow both ways so that the two forces fuse together to create an ecstasy.[54]

The interviews undertaken for this book confirm this perspective. While Mackintosh is here describing what he goes on to call the ecstasy that is found in a religious experience or sex, the fusion of actor energy and audience energy can also work to create Böhme's ekstases in theatre. In many ways the two are interchangeable, as Suzanne's above comments allude to.

Other audience members were acutely aware of this energy exchange:

> There's an exchange of energy, there's an energy from the stage and an energy from the people.
>
> *Thousten Gilbert*

> A play would be a total failure if there was no reaction from the audience. Because drama is a two-way process, because the actors re-act to audience participation.
>
> *Carol York*

Maureen maintains, however, that the obligation for creating Mackintosh's ecstasy, charge or fusion, is on the actors. She argues that it is a sign of good acting "if you can transform me. I started out one way and you moved me. You moved me. Something happened. That's the chemistry."[55] Theatre is always most successful if it moves audiences in some way: to laughter, to tears, to surprise, to anger, even to confusion. If it takes the audience member beyond their everyday gamut of feelings so that they too, like the actors, can experience something that is more real than in real life. For audience members, the encounter between audience member and actor can be pleasurable, intimate and transformative. Transformation is often cited as one of the primary reasons that audiences go to the theatre.[56]

Double consciousness

As Sartre expounds, "The Other's gaze touches me across the world and is not only a transformation of myself, but a total metamorphosis of the world."[57] Through the encounter with the other – the char/actor onstage – the audience member is transformed and so is the world surrounding them. Finally, we consider the core aspect of who the audience see from their view: actor or character. In many ways, the audience's gaze constructs the character. Sartre's concept that "I see *myself* because *somebody* sees me" (italics in original).[58] To explore this fully, we need to continue the discourse on double consciousness begun in the previous chapter where we explored its historical roots and the debates around split personalities in acting.

Contemporary discussion of double consciousness in the theatre has begun to consider spectatorship. Theatre, more than film, is a prime place for double consciousness to occur as audience members see the living body of the actor in front of them. Before the play starts, the audience are aware that the actor is in their dressing room putting on the costume and makeup of their character. During the play audience members have the opportunity to see an actor, or suspend disbelief and see the character. After the play they see the actor "break" their character and bow as the actor. As seen in the case studies later in this book, often the audience alternate between seeing the actor and the character. There is, however, another aspect that needs to be considered.

Gilles Fauconnier and Mark Turner argue that in the theatre, actors and audience members "blend" the actor and the character:

> Dramatic performances are deliberate blends of a living person with an identity. They give us a living person in one input and a different living person, an actor, in another. The person on stage is a blend of these two. The character portrayed may of course be entirely fictional, but there is still a space, a fictional one, in which that person is alive. In the blend, the person sounds and moves like the actor and is where the actor is, but the actor in her performance tries to accept projections from the character portrayed, and so modifies her language, appearance, dress, attitudes, and gestures. For the spectator, the perceived living, moving, and speaking body is a supreme material anchor.[59]

As seen in the case studies, actors and audience members often experience what Fauconnier and Turner describe as "living in the blend"[60] in theatrical events. This is not, of course, necessarily a contemporary concept. Sartre explored this concept in 1948 when he described the experience of seeing a char/actor blend of the actress Franconay and the character Maurice Chevalier which he called a "hybrid." As he contends, in this "synthesis [...] the face and body of the [actor] do not lose their individuality; but the expressive something 'Maurice Chevalier' nevertheless appears on that face, on that female body."[61] Audience members can often see and experience the character and the actor simultaneously. As explored in the previous chapter, actors can also perform in this blend of themselves and the character. The actors described these as grace moments when they feel like they are flying. Fauconnier and Turner's theories of conceptual blending are derived from neuroscience and it is beyond the scope of this research to analyse the work of blending beyond that it is a useful term to describe the fusion of actor and character.[62] Interestingly Lee Strasberg, one of the founders of Method acting in the United States, vehemently rejects the concept of even a double consciousness for actors preferring "a fusion, where there is seemingly no difference between the actor and the character."[63] This is the blend. Yet is it the blend that the interviewed audience saw?

The audience members were all asked, "who do you see onstage: the actor, the character or a combination." "Combination" or sometimes "both" was more useful to describe Fauconnier and Turner's blend, especially in translation to other languages for the German and French interviews. While two audience members alternated between seeing the actor and the character, the majority of the audience members saw the blend. This blend then transitioned into seeing only the character for some. When audience members return frequently to see actors that they admire, the suspension of disbelief is complicated. Watching actors such as Mark Rylance, Joel Grey or Nathan Lane they "still see him, but see his characters as well."[64] This is, perhaps, the split personality, with two distinct halves. Peter and his wife return regularly to see favourite actors, "If we know the actor, we might say: 'He's doing his business with his hand again.'"[65] It is intriguing how audience members read every gesture, every nuance, every vocal inflection. Maureen finds accents often betray actors: "[actors] can go in and out of character, especially if there's accents involved. You realise 'oh you're losing it.' There is this foreign accent, it's foreign to everybody and it changes."[66] The reading and recognition of these signs illustrates the uncanny aesthetic intimacy that is found in the live experience between audience members and actors which is heightened when audience members "know" and interpret the bit of "business" of their favourite actors.

Celebrity naturally shatters the character illusion and adds yet another thorny layer to the consciousness. The audience see the actor, the character and the celebrity, and projection and identification often occur. New Yorker Peg Wendtland argued, however, that after the moment of recognition of the actor "as long as [the celebrity] is doing a good job, you lose the celebrity and you see the character."[67] There were exceptions for Peg when the celebrity mesmerism overwhelmed the production and directed the audience gaze:

We saw a play with Marlo Thomas. That was a situation where I kept looking at her more than getting involved in the play. I couldn't get into the character, maybe towards the end. Mostly I was seeing her.[68]

As discussed in Chapter 1, the infatuated gaze at the celebrity often hijacks a production.

What is more interesting, perhaps, than what the audience see, is their self-directed gaze. Do the audience watch themselves? Do the audience have what Richard Foreman calls a "duo-consciousness," which is "the act of seeing and watching [yourself] seeing."[69] In relaying information to me in the interviews about their viewing habits, it can be seen that at different times during the production some audience members do, indeed, stand outside of themselves and watch their watching. Comments such as "I do tend to be the little director and even the re-writer as I sit there"[70] certainly point to this. These comments can also be seen to reveal the audience sense of their own presence. The previous chapter considered the audience presence. Maureen is very aware of her own presence while watching plays: "you're a part of it. In a stage show more than in cinema, you're more a part of it. Your being is there. It's present at it."[71] It is a subject that is worthy of future research.

The audience gaze does, in one sense, construct the character. The character is only alive if the audience has suspended their disbelief. If they are hypnotised by a celebrity or watching the bit of recognised business or tricks of a familiar actor, the character does not live. Maureen understands that "the perfect show is when you only see the character. And it's not a character, it's the 'being.'"[72] The "being" onstage that this astute comment is referring to is the "being" fully present onstage.

Presence

Much has been considered about the actor's elusive presence. Yet it is rarely conceived that the audience gaze at the actor affirms and can even be seen to contribute to that presence. The actors, as stated in the previous chapter, were able to identify characteristics of presence from their view from the stage. Presence as a space-filling phenomenon was described. In his discussion of presence, Böhme interlaces atmosphere and presence and describes how "from the perspective of the object [the actor], the atmosphere is the sphere of its perceptible presence." He goes on to argue, however, that it is "[o]nly from the perspective of the subject [the audience] is atmosphere perceived as the emotional response to the presence of something or someone else."[73] In the theatre the audience members' own emotional responses to actors work to create their presence.

Up until this point, drawing from theorist and actor comments, this book has considered an actor that has presence as one who fills a space with the ekstases radiating from them. As Walter Benjamin argues, the aura – the ekstases – of an actor is tied to his/her presence, "yet in film, [wo]man has to operate with his[her] whole living person, yet forgoing its aura."[74] Presence is a crucial element of the liveness of theatre. From the actors' perception of presence, we have also considered presence as living fully in the moment onstage: "being" there. If, as Böhme suggests, atmosphere is created through audience emotional response to the presence of actors onstage, an examination of what the audience perceive as presence is important in exploring what presence onstage is. Furthermore, in Böhme's terms, if we conceive presence as a form of atmosphere it will "shift the attention away from 'what' something represents to 'how' something is present."[75] This is, perhaps, a more efficacious way of considering presence. It was from this perspective that the question about presence was asked of audience members: "Have you ever heard anyone say of an actor 'he or she has presence'? What do you think they mean by this? Can you describe presence?" Quite predictably, audience members responded to this question in the affirmative, describing all of Jane Goodall's noted characteristics of presence: charisma, drawing power, mesmerism, personal electricity.[76] Equally predictable is that, similar to the actors, they all stated that either actors have presence or they do not. What is interesting is that the audience members' explications of these attributes of presence were discussed in terms of their relational aspects, how the actor's presence affected them. Even more noteworthy is that the characteristic of presence that was discussed most frequently in the interviews was none of Goodall's elements above and related more to the actor "being" or living in the moment onstage, rather than some kind of magnetism. An overview of the audience members' construction of presence as charisma, drawing power and a space-filling phenomenon is followed by a discussion of this characteristic of "being."

Charisma

Whenever a discussion of presence is undertaken, the term "charisma" is regularly invoked. Charisma is that charm, that light, that turned-on quality that seemingly radiates out of the actor onstage. As Goodall explores, the meaning of the word has changed over time from its Greek origins as a gift such as grace, talent, healing or prophesy bestowed by God, to its twenty-first century denotation as an individual quality often associated with celebrity.[77] As New Yorker Leslie Tucker stated, "I call [presence] charisma. If that charisma is flowing. [...] Even if the actors speak the lines well and they look good for the part, if that charisma is not there, I would look elsewhere." For Leslie, the charisma directs her gaze. She then goes to describe the contagion of charisma: "If you don't have that charisma, it's not going to flow to the audience."[78] From this perspective, charisma is something that spills from the stage into the audience, similar to atmosphere.

It is, however, Leslie's comment about the ineffable quality of charisma, unassociated with looks or talent, that is of interest and was discussed by other audience members. The question "what is an actor's presence" has haunted Isabelle for many years and she grapples with the fact that charisma is seemingly bestowed on the unlikeliest of actors:

> I have been wondering about presence for years. I thought it was a kind of spirit or being intelligent or being beautiful. This has nothing to do with it.

I must confess even with small roles, I know very stupid people who don't understand a word of what they say, who don't even know the author [...] when they come on stage [...] what is presence? Charisma. And you can be an idiot. I keep looking and asking: what is stage presence? It's not the way they move. It's a kind of charisma, I don't know. A kind of charisma. What is charisma? You have very stupid people that have charisma. You have fantastic people, that don't have charisma. It is not beauty, it is not strength, it is not intelligence, it is not sensibility. What is it? A good actor has charisma, that makes a good actor. He can even be very stupid and have a fantastic stage presence. That shocked me. It is a mystery.[79]

Isabelle's conclusions are not dissimilar to McKern's musings in the last chapter. McKern had also experienced seemingly untalented actors who had presence and were "watchful." There are also actors that have charisma onstage, but not offstage. Goodall describes these actors as those who have a "capacity to communicate with a peculiar intimacy to the individuals massed as their audience."[80] In this we see a relational quality to charisma as presence. An intimate conversation between actor and audience or a drawing power that directs the gaze of the audience member and catches them up in the fictitious world of the play.

Drawing power

In Joseph Roach's seminal book *it*, an actor has presence when "we can't take our eyes off It."[81] "It" seduces the eye of the audience member. "It" draws the gaze of the audience in. British audience member Carol York describes "It" as attention: "[Presence is] if the actor or actress holds your attention, really holds your attention and you are not looking at other things on the stage. Often there's a lot going on on the stage."[82] New Yorker Janet Stahl readily identified presence as drawing power:

There is the ability to draw you in, and to get you into the character, to feel the emotions the character is feeling. There are some plays when you are just shattered at the end. That's because they have just been able to touch you on an emotional level.[83]

Here Janet describes an aspect of drawing power that goes beyond the directing of the gaze to touch on aspects of identification, empathy and projection that are again relational. As Roach describes, "inchoate urges, desires *and* identifications [are] stirred in [audience members]"[84] when gazing on the actors. This was confirmed by audience members. One of Thousten's essential aspects of what he saw as presence was the actor "bringing onstage the sensitivity that awakens feelings in me."[85] The drawing power of presence directs the gaze and stirs the emotional response and identifications and empathy of audience members leaving them sometimes shattered, euphoric or in any number of other emotional states at the play's conclusion.

What is important to again note here is that unlike the celebrity presence of Marlo Thomas that distracted Peg from getting involved in the play, drawing power can lure the audience into the world of the character so that audience members can live in the blend or fully identify with the character. Celebrity presence often obscures the play and other characters and blocks identification or empathy for the audience. The audience may be charmed, titillated and thrilled by the celebrity presence, but they do not need to be sitting in a theatre for this to occur. The experience of the drawing power presence of an actor that is serving the character and the play rather than themselves offers the audience the opportunity of journeying with the character. As well as serving the play the actor that serves the audience will be more concerned with giving rather than taking. An actor that serves themselves or are self-consumed are in less of a conversation with the audience. It is a one-way discourse rather than a conversation. There is a significant difference between actors that want to *im*press and those that want to *ex*press. The former compromises the audience–actor conversation, the latter encourages it.

Space-filling ekstases

Erika Fischer-Lichte describes presence as a kind of ekstase: "[The audience] sense the power emanating from the actor that forces them to focus their full attention on him without feeling overwhelmed and perceive it as a source of energy."[86] Audience member Betty describes this in terms of "something about when they step on the stage, just an aura around them, a presence that they have."[87] This is the ekstases that the actors also described as a feature of presence; a space-filling phenomenon which audience members often explained in terms of "taking the stage"[88] and "taking command."[89] A veteran theatregoer, Peter has seen many great actors onstage: Laurence Olivier, John Gielgud, Joyce Grenfell. He described presence as

> a person filling a stage. Talking on their own and completely taking up your mind and your presence so you are not aware of anything else but them talking and being whatever they are being. Quite an experience to watch, to listen to.[90]

What is interesting about Peter's description is that the actor that has presence subsumes the audience member's presence. Furthermore, the audience member is captured up in the "being" of the actor.

"Being": authenticity and comfort

While charisma, drawing power and the actor's radiation of ekstases that filled the space were aspects of presence touched upon by the audience members, the characteristic predominantly described was the actors "being" on stage. In the previous chapter, Sanders described how presence for him was a lack of self-consciousness, comfort and being "fully there" onstage. This was echoed by the majority of the audience members. Presence was seen as comfort, honesty, believability, authenticity and a lack of self-consciousness:

> A lack of self-consciousness. Lack of awkwardness. An ability to take the stage and be comfortable.
>
> *Maureen Pascal*

> They are really inside the part and it is a natural movement and actual projection and everything else. It has to be honesty within the part.
>
> *Peter York*

> They get up there and you know they know what they're doing, they're believable.
>
> *Norman Malter*

> They're vibrant, or believable to the extent that you can see yourself in them. Realism. I want to feel that I know these people, that they are really people.
>
> *Debbi Baum*

> It is comfort. That the actors are comfortable being there in their roles and completely uninhibited in what they are doing.
>
> *David Herz*

Not only did the audience members find authenticity of paramount importance, similar to Sanders, they also regularly used the word "comfort" to describe presence. Indeed, many of the actors spoke of the importance of comfort onstage. Etymologically comfort is often related to soothing of the senses or the body and producing a certain delight and enjoyment.[91] Both actors Sanders and Bartholomew emphasised how important it was for audiences to sense the actor's comfort in their role. As Sanders stated, when the audience see that comfort onstage, they do not need to worry, they can relax and enjoy the production. Bartholomew describes it as a safe feeling for the audience. When the audience recognises an actor as fully embodying a character, "they feel safe. And therefore, they say, 'Ok I'm happy now.'"[92] The actor relaxes, the audience member relaxes, and the conversation can commence or continue. The last thing actors want is uptight and uncomfortable audience members. The last thing audience members want is uptight, uncomfortable actors. In suspending disbelief, audience members crave for fully embodied, believable, uninhibited, honest characters that are fully present. They do not want to, nor should they have to, work too hard or worry if the actor is comfortable in the role. They long to see actors living in the blend.

Presence, from the perspectives of the audience members interviewed, is, therefore, not only charisma, drawing power and an energy that exudes from an actor. It is also an actor that is fully present in the moment on stage: unselfconscious, comfortable and real. It is, perhaps, this perception of presence that makes theatre more real than in real life. As Fischer-Lichte argues, "When spectators sense the performers' presence and simultaneously bring themselves forth as embodied minds, they experience a moment of happiness which cannot be recreated in daily life."[93] What Fischer-Lichte touches on here is the co-presence of the actors and audience. As already stated, audiences play a role in creating the actor's presence. In this they are co-creators of the actors' presence.

It is the actors onstage radiating the ekstases that in turn infect the audience. This energy can be generated by many aspects: the narrative, the subject matter, the emotional turmoil of the characters. Yet I would argue that it can only be generated when actors are fully present – living authentically and comfortably onstage – and serving the play generously. The actors are then conduits for this energy that enlivens and makes the audience fully present in the electric air of a live theatrical event. When this happens, as Betty enthuses, "You just feel like these are people that you know. They light up, they just become shining lights."[94] This concept of presence as light was reiterated by actor Catherine Brunell in the previous chapter.

Who do the interviewed audience members see? They see actors living in the blend: char/actors. Their gaze is drawn not only to actors that have charisma, drawing power and a certain radiation of ekstases, but also equally to actors who are living authentically and comfortably onstage. For some, when the curtains rise or the lights come up, they see and live in the "real" life.

The curtain call

Curtain calls are the moment of transition between character and actor. The audience play a large role in this transition as they applaud. The percussive gesture seemingly extrudes the layers of the character one slap of the hands at a time. As the crescendo of applause reaches a pinnacle,[95] the last vestiges of character have virtually evaporated. The actor is standing in front of the audience receiving the drumming of admiration and thanks with her/his ego fully intact. The actors are unmasked as the character, but not unclothed. As Martin Revermann articulates, the costume "remains intact" for the entire curtain call, "resulting in a perception that the curtain call is a performance that is both new and at the same time a continuation of a previous one."[96] In this transitional stage between old and new performance, or more what I would call a coda, the audience finally make eye contact with the actors.

The curtain call can not only constitute a "new" performance, the gaze between audience and actors can create an electricity in the air of its own. It was during a curtain call that Leslie had the most exhilarating experience of theatre in her life:

> I remember once when I saw Frank Langella in a play. I loved his performance so much. This is one of the most emotive experience I have ever had in the theatre. I loved his performance so much as an actor. I really felt the character he was playing, that at the end of the play I was the first one to jump up and applaud and he looked right at me and smiled. And smiled! Frank

Langella smiled at me. I was just so happy. I made him happy because I know what a tough nut he is to crack. We had a connection, for a moment.[97]

For Leslie, it was the connection that she found thrilling. The potential for connection, non-verbal yet acknowledged, not only creates delight in the curtain call, it is a conversation. The audience applaud, the actors bow, the audience applaud more, the actors bow again and the conversation continues until both parties are spent.

Historically, audience applause spelt the success or demise of performances and of actors.[98] As this is no longer the case, contemporary analysis now concentrates on the more ritual aspects of applause. Baz Kershaw and Nicholas Ridout describe the curtain call and its applause as a transactional ritual, emphasising the exchange and commodification aspects of the tradition.[99] While analysis or framing of the curtain call in economic terms is useful to explain the contractual role the curtain call plays, or what Kershaw calls the "disempowerment" of the audience, this perspective distracts from a closer analysis of what is happening performatively for actors and audience members. Although many conjectures have been made, no one asks the audience what they are applauding. The very act of excluding the audience voice from this discussion disempowers the audience.

In the interviews, audience members were asked "who do you see bowing at the curtain call" and "what are you applauding them for?" Nearly all audience members were quick to relay that they were applauding the actor, not the character. Only one audience member said he saw them as both. Frank asserted that the curtain call was "one of those strange times when they [actors] are both. When they bow as the actors, but they are still in costume. I saw them both." In this statement he refers to the intact costume as a potent signifier of the remains of the character. Frank is a psychotherapist and often uses the analogy of the curtain call with his patients:

> Very often in psychotherapy the symptoms come back. I use the analogy to actors bowing at the end of a play. They come back to say their final farewell, but they are not the same in the course of the treatment.[100]

This is, perhaps, the "character on the shoulder" that Sanders referred to in the last chapter.

What was significant were the audience answers regarding the purpose of their applause. As stated, various theatre scholars have proffered their own explanations of what the audience applaud. These include applauding actors for becoming their character well,[101] thanking actors for the "commodity" they have received[102] and the audience applauding the audience.[103] The majority of the audience members, however, applaud the actors for their skill, art or craft. Janet applauds the actors "for their art. They have to create a character, they have to get into the character."[104] Carol applauds them for their "acting skill"[105] and Rita "applaud[s] them for their craft."[106] Many also applauded the "hard work"[107] and "lots of effort"[108] that went into the performances "because [they] couldn't imagine doing that eight times a week"[109] and it was something they were "incapable of doing"[110] themselves. Each response to why they applaud was heavily laden with admiration, esteem and deep respect for the actors. Some even applauded them for their "versatility,"[111] their "brilliance."[112] Similar to their construction of presence as comfort and authenticity, several audience members also stated that they applauded the actors for their "believability."[113]

Yet these audience critics were also quick to recognise bad acting and were reticent to lavish undeserved applause on an incompetent performance as illustrated in this story relayed by Fran who attended a play with some fellow neighbours:

> The acting was so terrible that [my friend's] husband walked out at intermission. We looked at each other: "we really don't want to watch the rest of this pitiful performance." We [didn't want to leave because] we knew it was going to be embarrassing for the actors. The second act was better. It was really hard to applaud at the end. When [the acting is] bad, I have a hard time trying to be appreciative of the fact that they have worked so hard.[114]

Here the distinction is made between working hard and lack of skill or craft. Actors can work hard yet have no virtuosity. The interviewed audience members know and appreciate artistry in actors when they see it and measure their applause accordingly.

The point of view of the audience often starts with excited anticipation, as the audience are eager to suspend disbelief and enter into a world that is for some the real life. It is also a discerning view that craves to live in the blend but can be disheartened when the actor fails to be comfortable or authentic onstage or when the gaze is distracted from the fictitious world by the seductive lure of the celebrity aura. The audience work to contribute to the presence of the actor through their gaze and assist their transition into the quotidian through their applause. Regardless of whether a connection with the char/actors is achieved or not, the conversation across the footlights with the actors remains a highly prized and sought-after enchantment of theatre that has the potential to manifest in what Leslie describes as a "chemistry" between actors and audience:

> There is no close-up in theatre. So, my God, the chemistry that has to flow from actor to audience is one hundred times more challenging than the chemistry that needs to flow from just a smirk, like a Clint Eastwood smirk on the screen. I feel the chemistry.[115]

It is this chemistry that fills the in-between audience–actor spaces with a liveness unexperienced in other object–subject artistic experiences.[116] There may be no physical close-up in theatre, yet there is a potent emotional close-up that occurs in the psychological undercurrents that pervade theatrical production as explored in the first case study: *Heisenberg.*

Notes

1 Comments from some of the audience members in the *Heisenberg* case studies were relevant for this chapter, so have been included here also.
2 Helen Freshwater, *Theatre & Audience* (Basingstoke: Palgrave Macmillan, 2009), 4.
3 Richard Schechner, *Performance Theory*, 2nd ed. (New York: Routledge, 1988), 220.
4 David Herz, personal interview, 27 October 2016.
5 Maureen Pascal, personal interview, 1 November 2018.
6 This is taken from Letter to Suvorin, 27 October 1888. *Letters of Anton Chekhov*, Project Guttenberg, accessed 11 October 2019, www.gutenberg.org/files/6408/6408-h/6408-h.htm.
    It is often erroneously and awkwardly paraphrased as "The artist asks the questions, it doesn't answer them."
7 Ibid.
8 Peter York, personal interview, 27 July 2017.
9 Konstantin Stanislavski, *Building a Character* (New York and London: Routledge, 1987), 295.
10 For a detailed discussion of the theatre "house," see Heim, *Audience as Performer*, 111–123.
11 Several interviewed actors described rituals they use to overcome stage fright.
12 Thousten Gilbert, personal interview, 11 October 2016.
13 Peter Cotton, personal interview, 27 July 2017.
14 Philip Auslander "So Close and Yet So Far Away," in *Experiencing Liveness in Contemporary Performance Interdisciplinary Perspectives*, ed. Matthew Reason and Anja Mølle Lindelof (New York: Routledge, 2016), 298.
15 Edward Bullough, "'Psychical Distance' as a Factor in Art and an Aesthetic Principle," *British Journal of Psychology* 5, no. 2 (1912): 91.
16 Hall is here referring to his prominent typologies of the distances between people. Theatre is clearly in either the close phase of public space, where there is a distance of 3.5 to 7.5 metres between bodies on stage and in the audience. Or the far phase of public distance: 7.5 metres and up. Edward T. Hall, *The Hidden Dimension* (New York: Anchor Books, 1990), 115.
17 Rita Haynes, personal interview, 27 July 2017.
18 I am not attempting to make cultural judgements here, rather just recording the seating preferences of the interviewed audience's members.
19 Isabelle Petiet, personal interview, 20 October 2016.
20 Rachel Strauber, personal interview, 27 October 2016.
21 Hall, *Hidden Dimension*, 63.
22 Kent Cartwright, *Shakespearean Tragedy and Its Double: The Rhythms of Audience Response* (University Park: Penn State UP, 2010).
23 Debbi Baum, personal interview, 29 October 2016.
24 2.1 to 3.5 metres.
25 Auslander, "So Close," 298.
26 Norman Malter, personal interview, 31 October 2018.
27 Rita Haynes, personal interview, 27 July 2017.
28 Ibid.
29 Betty Cohen, personal interview, 15 September 2016.
30 Isabelle Petiet, personal interview, 20 October 2016.
31 Frank Lachmann, personal interview, 3 November 2016.
32 Isabelle Petiet, personal interview, 20 October 2016.
33 Petiet was actually my translator in Paris and particularly took up the position as she loved theatre so much.

34 Dennis Kennedy, *The Spectator and the Spectacle: Audiences in Modernity and Postmodernity* (Cambridge: Cambridge UP, 2009), 215.

35 Isabelle Petiet, personal interview, 20 October 2016.

36 Michael Reichgott, personal interview, 31 October 2016.

37 Peter Brook, *The Empty Space* (New York: Simon and Schuster, 1997), 11.

38 Jacques Rancière, *The Emancipated Spectator*, trans. Gregory Elliott (London and New York: Verso, 2009), 23.

39 Jay O. Sanders, personal interview, 5 November 2018. Ben Brantley is a critic for the *New York Times*.

40 Thousten Gilbert, personal interview, 11 October 2016.

41 Betty Cohen, personal interview, 15 September, 2016.

42 Fran Halper, personal interview, 26 October 2016.

43 Maureen Pascal, personal interview, 1 November 2018.

44 Thousten Gilbert, personal interview, 11 October 2016.

45 Ibid.

46 Jean-Paul Sartre, *Being and Nothingness: An Essay on Phenomenological Ontology*, trans. Hazel E. Barnes (London: Routledge, 2003): 282.

47 Bert O. States, *Great Reckonings in Little Rooms: On the Phenomenology of Theater* (Berkeley: California UP, 1985), 157.

48 Ibid.

49 Peter Cotton, personal interview, 27 July 2017.

50 Rita Haynes, personal interview, 27 July 2017.

51 Ibid.

52 Suzanne Griffin, personal interview, 23 September 2016.

53 See particularly Erika Fischer-Lichte, *The Transformative Power of Performance: A New Aesthetics* (London: Routledge, 2008).

54 Iain Mackintosh, *Architecture, Actor and Audience* (London: Routledge, 1993), 172.

55 Maureen Pascal, personal interview, 1 November 2018.

56 See particularly Janelle Reinelt (P.I.), David Edgar, Chris Megson, Dan Rebellato, Julie Wilkinson and Jane Woddis, *Critical Mass: Theatre Spectatorship and Value Attribution*, The British Theatre Consortium, Final report (2014), accessed 14 February 2018, http://britishtheatreconference.co.uk/wp-content/uploads/2014/05/Critical-Mass-10.7.pdf.

57 Sartre, *Being and Nothingness*, 269.

58 Ibid., 284.

59 Gilles Fauconnier and Mark Turner, *The Way We Think* (New York: Basic Books, 2003), 226, 227.

60 Ibid., 267.

61 Jean-Paul Sartre, *The Psychology of Imagination* (New York: Philosophical Library, 1948), 40.

62 For a more detailed examination of how blending works in the theatre, see Bruce McConachie, *Engaging Audiences: A Cognitive Approach to Spectating at the Theatre* (New York: Palgrave Macmillan, 2008), 40–47; and Rhonda Blair, "Cognitive Science and Performance," *TDR* 53, no. 4 (Winter 2009): 96.

63 Lee Strasberg cited in Sharon Marie Carnicke, *Stanislavsky in Focus: An Acting Master for the Twenty-First Century* (New York: Routledge, 2004), 146.

64 Betty Cohen, personal interview, 15 September 2016.

65 Peter Cotton, personal interview, 27 July 2017.

66 Maureen Pascal, personal interview, 1 November 2018.

67 Peg Wendlandt, personal interview, 17 September 2016.

68 Ibid.

69 Cited in Herbert Blau, *The Audience* (Baltimore: Johns Hopkins UP, 1990), 116.

70 Maureen Pascal, personal interview, 1 November 2018.

71 Ibid.

72 Ibid.

73 Gernot Böhme, *The Aesthetics of Atmospheres*, ed. Jean-Paul Thibaud (London and New York: Routledge, 2017), 26

74 Walter Benjamin, "The Work of Art in the Age of Mechanical Reproduction," in *Illuminations*, ed. Hannah Arendt, trans. Harry Zohn, from the 1935 essay (New York: Schocken Books, 1969), 56.

75 Ibid.

76 Jane Goodall, *Stage Presence* (London: Routledge, 2008).

77 Ibid., 44, 45.

78 Leslie Tucker, personal interview, 1 November 2016.

79 Isabelle Petiet, personal interview, 20 October 2016.

80 Goodall, *Stage Presence*, 46.

81 Joseph Roach, *It* (Ann Arbor: Michigan UP, 2007), 10.

82 Carol York, personal interview, 27 July 2017.

83 Janet Stahl, personal interview, 27 October 2016.

84 Roach, *It*, 10.

85 Thousten Gilbert, personal interview, 11 October 2016.

86 Fischer-Lichte, *Transformative Power of Performance*, 96.

87 Betty Cohen, personal interview, 15 September 2016.

88 Maureen Pascal, personal interview, 1 November 2018.

89 Frank Lachmann, personal interview, 3 November 2016.

90 Peter Cotton, personal interview, 27 July 2017.

91 *Oxford English Dictionary*, accessed 11 November 2017, www-oed-com.ezp01.library.qut.edu.au/.

92 Ian Bartholomew, personal interview, 11 July 2017.

93 Fischer-Lichte, *Transformative Power of Performance*, 99.

94 Betty Cohen, personal interview, 15 September 2016.

95 For a discussion on the now *de rigueur* standing ovation, see Heim, *Audience as Performer*, 31, 32.

96 Martin Revermann, "The Semiotics of Curtain Calls," *Semiotica* 2008, no. 168(2008): 193.

97 Leslie Tucker, personal interview, 1 November 2016.

98 Heim, *Audience as Performer*, 54, 55.

99 Baz Kershaw, "Oh for Unruly Audiences! Or, Patterns of Participation in Twentieth Century Theatre," *Modern Drama* 42, no. 2 (2001); and Nicholas Ridout, *Stage Fright, Animals, and Other Theatrical Problems* (Cambridge: Cambridge UP, 2006).

100 Frank Lachmann, personal interview, 3 November 2016.

101 States, *Great Reckonings*, 119.

102 Ridout, *Stage Fright, Animals*.

103 Bettina Brandl-Risi, "Getting Together and Falling Apart: Applauding Audiences," *Performance Research* 16, no. 2 (2011): 14.

104 Janet Stahl, personal interview, 27 October 2016.

105 Peter York, personal interview, 27 July 2017.

106 Rita Haynes, personal interview, 27 July 2017.

107 Betty Cohen, personal interview, 15 September 2016.

108 Peter Cotton, personal interview, 27 July 2017; and Leslie Tucker, personal interview, 1 November 2016.
109 David Herz, personal interview, 27 October 2016.
110 Carol York, personal interview, 27 July 2017.
111 Michael Reichgott, personal interview, 31 October 2016.
112 Carol York, personal interview, 27 July 2017.
113 Norman Malter, personal interview, 31 October 2018.
114 Fran Halper, personal interview, 26 October 2016.
115 Leslie Tucker, personal interview, 1 November 2016.
116 With the exception of dance performances.

PART II
Conversations

4

HEISENBERG'S PSYCHOLOGICAL CONVERSATIONS

As audience members, our perception, our perspectives and our purview of each theatre event is shaped by our beliefs, values and life experiences. Similarly, when actors perform, their characterisations and the narrative that reverberates in their minds is often drawn from their individual experiences, observations and perspectives of life. This concept is one of the recurring motifs in Simon Stephen's play *Heisenberg* and is summarised in this line from the play: "We hold very different perspectives on experiences we imagine we're sharing, don't we."[1] Although we may imagine that we are sharing the same experience, we cannot be certain, and we are most often not experiencing the same thing. *Heisenberg* is essentially a relationship narrative that alludes to and embeds Werner Heisenberg's uncertainty principle in its narrative, structure, dialogue and thematic material.

This chapter is a case study of Manhattan Theatre Club's (MTC) 2016 production of *Heisenberg*. The ensuing discussion has been shaped by actor and audience interview discussions of two phenomena that evoked strong emotive and imaginative responses to the production: psychological undercurrents and the suspension of disbelief. The chapter commences with an overview of the project and a synopsis of the play before discussing how transference, identification, projection, empathy and the suspension of disbelief contributed to the conversations in the electric air of *Heisenberg*. I conclude with an overview of the distinctive and creative Heisenberg audience workshops conducted by MTC that are not only a prime example of experiential audiencing, but also extend the conversation between the actors and the audience. The nature of the play, *Heisenberg*, affords an opportunity to demonstrate how psychological undercurrents and the suspension of disbelief contribute to the electric air.

The production and the project

Heisenberg premiered on Broadway[2] in October 2016. After several viewings of the play and attendance at MTC's *Heisenberg* workshops and post-show discussions,

I conducted ten in-depth interviews with audience members and one with one of two actors: Denis Arndt.[3] The audience members, all of whom were recruited from the workshops,[4] were New Yorkers and devoted theatregoers. Of the people I interviewed, many attend the theatre three times a week during the peak seasons and subscribe to up to nine theatre companies both on- and off-Broadway yearly.

During the actor and audience interviews, I soon became aware that my perspectives of the play, and of the conversations about *Heisenberg*, were different from the perceptions of those I interviewed. Questions that I had thought of paramount importance faded into insignificance as the actors and audience members imagined their own narratives, eclipsing some of my preconceptions. The audience members I found to be discerning armchair critics, well versed in what makes a good production and eager to not only share their critical responses to the production but also describe their emotive and empathic responses and relay their meaning-making processes. While their perspectives on the play and the acting were interesting and varied, this chapter concentrates on subjects during the interviews that evoked either strong psychological responses or that the audience members kept returning to in the interviews. Transference, identification, projection, empathy and the suspension of disbelief emerged as major discourses in these interviews. As the interviews progressed, more time was spent probing into these elements. The specific psychological terms were not used in the interviews.[5] Questions such as "Did any of the characters in *Heisenberg* remind you of someone you know, or yourself, or does the situation remind you of something that has happened to you?" and "At what point were you able to shut out the outside world and enter into the story of the play?" prompted discussions on psychological undercurrents and the suspension of disbelief. Some of the most fascinating moments occurred when I interviewed couples where I found that each individual had a different experience of what they imagined they had been sharing. Clearly, different narratives were playing out in their minds as they drew from their own varied experiences. Given their virtually theatre expert status, rich and insightful perspectives were given by these seasoned audience members.

Denis Arndt is a veteran of the New York stage. As the interview with Denis progressed, I found he was quite a philosopher and his responses were considered and thought-provoking. Before I began the questions, he opened our conversation with a pertinent comment: "The play resonates on some levels that are yet to be defined. When you think about the transactions, it requires a participatory investment from the audience. Lots of gaps in the narrative that the audience has to fill."[6] Denis articulated why *Heisenberg* was an apposite play to discuss the meaning-making that occurs in the electric air. Audience members fill in the gaps in the narrative to make meaning, and in doing this there is a connection formed across the footlights which he elaborates on below.

A brief sketch of the play and some production particulars is necessary for a fuller understanding of some of the nuances in the below discussion. Two strangers meet by chance in a London train station: a 75-year-old butcher, Alex Priest, and a 42-year-old receptionist, Georgie Burns. Georgie talks Alex into a date, talks him into a relationship, talks him into sleeping with her and talks him into giving her 15 000 pounds to find her lost son in New Jersey. Both have suffered loss; both have unfulfilled needs. Alone at the beginning of the play, at the end they are together. It is a simple relationship narrative. Yet this random encounter of two individuals sets into motion the cascade of currents which characterise human relationships: transference, identification, projection and empathy.

Heisenberg's uncertainty principle[7] is woven into not only the narrative, but it also pervaded the pre-show atmosphere. During the play we are uncertain if the meeting was chance, we are uncertain who is stalking whom, we are uncertain about professions, we are uncertain if Georgie has a son, we are uncertain if this is a play about uncertainty. Uncertainty appeared to fill the air in the auditorium even before the play commenced. As one audience member, a self-described professional audience watcher observed, "[before the play started] some people didn't even know why they were there. I remember I answered someone who was [...] thinking 'why am I here?'"[8] I am uncertain what she meant by this.

Part of the initial uncertainty experienced by the audience was instigated by the altered audience seating arrangement. The Friedman Theatre, MTC's home theatre on Broadway, was transformed for this production. Approximately one-third of the 660 audience members sat on the stage in erected raked seating for the purposes of creating the same intimate environment as the original off-Broadway production. The onstage seating took people out of their comfort zone. The uncertainty and comments regarding the seating included "What's the deal about being up here anyway?"[9] and "[The on-stage seating created] nervous expectations. There was a sense of what is going to happen now?"[10] Even some of the ushers broadcasted a seemingly ominous, but actually anodyne warning: "I'll be watching you!"[11] It is important to also note, for the discussion of the suspension of disbelief, that there was no fixed set for this production: two very basic chairs and a table were moved by the actors for the purposes of each "scene." There were also frequent blackouts between each scene. The blackouts created the presence of a random void. To balance the absence of a set, it was the psychological undercurrents that filled the space between the stage and the audience in *Heisenberg*. Consequently, psychological undercurrents dominated the discussions in the audience interviews.

Psychological undercurrents

Transference, identification, projection and empathy are, as argued in Chapter 1, some of the main means through which audiences feel connected to actors in the theatre. Feeling states, transformation and the live interaction between actors and audience were the primary reasons that the *Heisenberg* audience members I interviewed attend the theatre. Michael Reichgott attends the theatre regularly because

It's a vicarious, feeling experience. I find myself being able to experience emotional responses that I actually don't have in "real life," that I don't quite experience in quite the same way. I am a crier in the theatre. [...] It's a place where I really feel.[12]

Chris Lincoln is "into [theatre] for the transformation of [his] feelings"[13] and Debbi Baum finds the "connection with the actors [...] powerful."[14] Theatre and the space "in-between" becomes a safe space to explore and express feelings. Significantly, to experience a connection with the actors and the narrative, close proximity to the stage was of vital importance to these avid theatregoers who sat either on the stage in *Heisenberg* or within the first eight rows of the orchestra to "feel it," to experience "immediacy" and "the liveness" of it, to "connect to the actors and the story," and to "emit more emotions."[15]

Transference, identification, projection and empathy are the vehicles for audience members to connect with, feel and experience emotions in the theatre. Some interviewees referred directly to these vehicles. Frank Lachmann emphasised that for a theatre piece to be considered good, he needs to identify with a character: one of "the character[s] has to have something that makes me feel like me."[16] Chris finds "empathy part of the infection of theatre."[17] Some brief definitions will act as a refresher for these reasonably complex psychological concepts. Transference is the transferring of the thoughts and feelings of a previous relationship onto a present relationship. Identification is the process of seeing your identity in something else. Projection is throwing aspects of oneself in the outside world. Empathy is the process of one person "feeling into" the emotional states of another. As discussed in Chapter 1, these psychological mechanisms are interrelated. Expressed in a simple equation, transfer/see/throw/feel equals the psychological undercurrent felt in the theatre that contributes to the electric air. These states were transferred, seen, thrown and felt in *Heisenberg*.

Transference

The question "Did any of the characters in *Heisenberg* remind you of someone you know, or yourself?" evoked strong, emotive responses for two audience members in particular. In both interviews, the transference was so powerful that the audience members kept returning to a discussion of the transference experience or referred back to it when they were asked other, seemingly unrelated, questions.

The first incidence relates to the character of Georgie. Georgie, played by Mary-Louise Parker, has a scattered, neurotic, talkative persona. Part of her personality, and perhaps, part of her charm, is that she does not always tell the truth. She spins stories. Fifteen minutes into the play, audience member Jay Baum "recognised" Georgie. I include his entire dialogue mapping his thought processes here as it is a poignant illustration of how powerful the transference phenomenon can be:

> Everything that was coming out of [Georgie's] mouth was, "no but that's not really true. Oh, what's really true with this one. I've been through this before." Then I realised she was a crazy ex-girlfriend of mine. Realised fifteen

minutes [into it]: the first crazy thing she said that obviously wasn't true. She said she was an assassin. Is she a housewife? Is she a school secretary? Is she a waitress? "No, I'm not going to believe anything she says." Do I care? Does it bother me? Does it bother him? She's feeling more like my ex-girlfriend. I recognised the character.[18]

This is transference. Jay was transferring the thoughts and feelings he had towards a previous girlfriend onto Georgie, a character he was interacting with in the present. In his first disclosure above he explicitly identifies Georgie *as* his ex-girlfriend: "she was a crazy ex-girlfriend of mine." A powerful nexus was formed between Jay and the character that not only strongly informed Jay's reading of the play but also created an "uncomfortable"[19] tension in the atmosphere. It was a tension that I sensed in the interview which occurred over a week after he had seen the play.

Furthermore, there was a re-awakening of the feelings associated with this relationship. In this case, negative emotions. What is of much interest in this transference incidence is that Jay then *projects* – throws – all of this energy, and his own past feelings, onto the character of Alex, Georgie's love interest:

> I felt a little nervous for him. Confused. Uncomfortable. […] Then I felt a little sorry for him. Crazy ex-girlfriend, I know who she is, and I think he thinks he knows who she is. And I think he's okay with that. I don't know that he can control her, manage it.[20]

In this excerpt we not only see projection, but also empathy with Alex. Jay is reliving these moments and is feeling into the anguish that Alex is, or could potentially experience. Jay's empathy can also be seen to include a protective element. He is unsure whether Alex fully realises the situation he has become enmeshed in, and fears that he may not "manage" it. Clearly Jay identifies with Alex. Tracing Jay's meaning-making processes and responses illustrates how transference, projection, identification and empathy are, in a real sense, four different views of the same essential phenomenon.

The second transference incidence discussed in the interviews, is more situational. In pursuing a relationship with Alex in the first half of *Heisenberg*, Georgie's actions can be seen as a form of "stalking." As the play proceeds, the roles reverse somewhat, and Alex can be seen to be pursuing Georgie. During her interview, audience member Leslie Tucker disclosed that she was stalked by an 80-year-old man while she was in her thirties. Leslie became very agitated in the interview when she relayed this past occurrence:

> I met him on a plane and he asked me out to dinner, and I went. So I could barely watch that part of the play. It was awful. Very nice guy, very smart, but "hey you shouldn't be hitting on a thirty-year-old woman. I'm just your friend." The minute they started talking I thought "my God that reminded me of when […]." When they became sexually involved the aversion started.[21]

Again, this is a typical transference incidence. A series of Leslie's psychological experiences from the past are revived and thrown into the narrative of the play. In this dialogue, Leslie's past experience is intertwined with the *Heisenberg* narrative as she alternates between the past and the present in her dialogue.

For Leslie, the revived negative feelings associated with her past experience were so powerful that she found it difficult to watch the bedroom scene. Leslie's response to a later question disclosed her repulsion. In response to the question "What was the most emotive moment in the play for you?," Leslie replied:

> The moment when they were in bed together. And it was a negative emotion. It was so skeevy.[22] It's just something that is so uncomfortable to deal with. So much so that you would rather not be exposed to it. I'm not saying this part of the play should not have happened. [...] I wanted to shut it out, but it kept going. "Just get out of bed, I can't take it anymore," it was just so uncomfortable for me to watch.[23]

This illustrates the magnetism of the situation. Leslie was repelled and even repulsed. In this transference episode, aspects of the past experience were imprinted onto the character–audience relationship between Leslie and Alex. From this dialogue, we can also see that Leslie identified with Georgie, felt empathy for Georgie and projected her feelings onto the narrative. Interestingly, the transference was so overwhelming that Leslie wanted to "shut it out" because it brought up "that horrible experience of an eighty-year-old man that was pursuing [her]."[24] Fortunately, theatre is a safe place to feel, express and re-live emotions, even negative emotions. I observed the discomfort and squirming in the interview as the feelings were reawakened. It was much generosity on the part of Leslie to share this with me and allow it to be included in this monograph.

Alex and Georgie reminded other audience members of friends, colleagues and even relatives. Although transference occurred for many audience members, the strong emotions experienced in Jay's and Leslie's transferences are the most apposite examples of how psychological undercurrents can charge the air with electricity and inform the reading of the play for those experiencing them. Transference is a potent psychological phenomenon adding layers of meaning to productions that can, as exemplified in Jay's and Leslie's cases, raise the stakes of the performance to new personal heights as every word, gesture and glance onstage is invested and loaded with painful or pleasurable meaning.

Identification

Just as audience members transferred aspects of relationships with others onto characters onstage, some also consciously identified with Georgie and Alex. They saw themselves in the characters. Alex is an understated, genuine, endearing character. Denis identified with Alex but was quick to point out the differences. "It's all very recognisable. [...] I know Alex."[25] In this he is delineating between his responsibility to serving the character and his responsibility as an actor serving the audience.

Denis goes on to describe the "that's me" experience of the audience's identification with Alex in *Heisenberg*, in terms of a kind of "possession":

> [It's] the way they want to possess you in some way. It's the royal "me" on stage. They identify with you to a degree. All the old men who snort at all the male jokes in the play. You hear "snort." You hear the old guys. They are out there appreciating the circumstance and living it, genuinely.[26]

He identified with the character. There is one occurrence in the play when Alex talks about crying: random moments when he cries for no particular reason. There is also a moment in the play when Alex cries. In the interview Denis discussed how many audience members identified with this:

> I cannot tell you the number of men have come up to me and said "I had the same problem," I can stand in the frozen department of a meat store and just find myself weeping, [or] the cat food aisle.[27]

This is identification. All of the male audience members I interviewed identified with Alex on some level, David could "identify a little bit with Alex because he is round about my age,"[28] Chris "could certainly see some of Alex in [him]self"[29] and Jay observed that "he's such a guy. I'm kinda like that."[30]

Denis found that the audience members' identification with his character gave him a connection with them: "You feel an intimacy already with them which I feel a great deal of responsibility to not betray. You can feel an emanating kind of warmth, is the only way I could say it."[31] Identification here affects the emotional temperature in the room, creating a warmth of kinship in the liminal space between audience members and actors.

Georgie is a significantly more complex character and evoked different responses from the audience. Most of the women I interviewed who identified with Georgie would only concede to identifying with some aspects of Georgie's personality:

> I mean in a sense she is very vivacious and talkative and expressive, and I'm a little bit like that, so that would really be about the level of it. But I don't think I'm really quite as absurdist.
>
> *Janet Stahl*

> Well Mary-Louise Parker, she's a person that is very eccentric and I have a little bit of that in me.
>
> *Leslie Tucker*

Janet's comment shows that she did identify with an absurdist quality of Georgie but not to the degree portrayed onstage. The recurring "little bit" of Janet and Leslie found in Georgie was also the little bit that was likeable about her personality. Few audience members are going to share how conniving, dishonest or crazy they actually are in an interview.

Mary-Louise Parker's celebrity status changed the relationship between actor and audience member and also influenced the degree of identification either positively or negatively. In the above comment, Leslie referred to the character of Georgie as Mary-Louise Parker. This slippage often occurs when the actor is a celebrity. The familiarity of the actor contracts the space between actor and character. Or is this slippage? There is identification with the character and identification with an actor. You can identify with a fictitious character onstage. You cannot identify with an actor that you do not know. When an actor is a celebrity, however, an audience member may think they know enough about an actor to identify with them, even if they do not. In this case, the slippage occurred not only because of blending, but also because Leslie had on one occasion previously met and had a personal conversation with Mary-Louise Parker. I discuss the additional layer of celebrity presence in this production further below, but it is important to note that identification becomes much more complex when the onstage actor is a celebrity. Identification worked to create a visceral connection and even a verbal and paralingual conversation between actors and audience members in *Heisenberg* which manifested in a congenial "snort" of laughter at Alex's foibles, an audible "oh-ahhh" when Alex cried or an embarrassed and incredulous "oh!"[32] when Georgie asked Alex for 15 000 pounds.

Projection

Projection in the theatre is difficult to capture as – differing from positive identification – it is largely unconscious and predominantly concerns negative aspects of our personalities. Furthermore, since it is a defence mechanism, audience members are far less likely to share moments of projection in an interview. They may not even be aware of its occurrence. I use three examples of projection here. The first two are taken directly from the interviews and the second is a hypothetical case that could well have occurred during audience members' meaning-making processes during the *Heisenberg* performances.

For Chris, the experience of the climax of the play was so cogent that when Georgie asks Alex for 15 000 pounds, Chris felt as if he were betrayed: "Oh my God he's feeling betrayed. I'm feeling betrayed because I am inside him. What's going on here?"[33] Chris's "inside him" is a compelling example of projection. He has thrown himself up onstage and is psychologically inhabiting the character of Alex.

When I asked Rachel Strauber the transference question detailed above, she replied with the following referring to the character of Georgie:

> Do I know people who are so manipulative? Who set out in one way or another to use another human being? She did that. [...] I don't think of myself as manipulative, but we all are in a certain way.[34]

Rachel is of course right: it is likely that we are all manipulative in some way and most of us would feel very uncomfortable about this. It is possible that being in touch with the manipulative side of herself, and feeling uncomfortable about this, she projected this onto the character of Georgie. This is all aside from the character of Georgie being, in fact, a manipulative person. Rachel's comments could possibly be an example of projection: the defensive attribution of mental states onto some other person. Through the catalyst of the theatrical event, Rachel pondered what could possibly have been a real insight into a, perhaps, previously hidden aspect of her character.

A hypothetical example may be more useful. Imagine if I had interviewed a male audience member who had a strong negative reaction to Alex when he said "Sometimes I burst out crying for no real reason."[35] The audience member becomes disdainful towards Alex for admitting to crying because it exposes weakness in him. It could be seen that this person is projecting negative aspects of his own personality because he himself believes he is being weak if he were to cry. Becoming defensive – "I would never do that" – is often an indication of projection. Strong, negative reactions – "I really can't stand that character, he's so [...]" – towards a character may also denote projection. We largely do not want to own negative aspects of our personalities. Seeing aspects of ourselves in the narrative played in front of us onstage can be confronting but restorative. Again, theatre becomes a safe environment to express, and perhaps, work through, strong emotions.

Empathy

Empathetic moments in the theatre are shared, relational experiences between character and audience member. When asked "Did you ever feel something for one of the characters in *Heisenberg*? Why?" nearly all audience members discussed the character's predicaments, "I felt for her/him because [...]." Most empathised with loss in the play: loss of a son, loss of a girlfriend, loss of a sister, lost love. Empathetic moments are also those shared between character and character. Alex experienced loss. Georgie experienced loss. Audience member Frank identified loss as the empathetic connection between the characters: "A loss, who hasn't experienced that? That was a connection. And [Alex and Georgie] both responded to loss profoundly."[36] On the other side of the footlights, Denis made a similar observation,

> It's really not a profound play on the surface in any way. But what happens between these two entities in the play? That's where all the action is. It is in the story between the two of them that the empathetic participation occurs.[37]

In *Heisenberg* empathy between the characters imbricates with empathy between the stage and the audience. Denis argues that this phenomenon can only happen in live theatre in the connection between actor and audience member because the moment is "happening in the room just as you [the actor] are happening. It is happening with a living breathing, beating being, just like you, with these empathic neurons or synaptic neural resonances that we all share."[38]

Empathetic connection is one of the primary reasons that Chris goes to the theatre. Chris drew from his own experiences, personality and imagination while watching *Heisenberg* to feel into the emotions of the characters:

> I'm empathetic towards [Georgie's] situation where she's lost her son. I have a son. This would just rip me to shreds. It might make me do what she's done if I could find no other way. That's why I'm in the theatre, I want to know how other people feel. Maybe it is the autistic part of me. Vicariously feeling the way I probably normally would not.[39]

Chris's remark underscores the close connection between empathy and identification. Like Michael above, Chris finds theatre a safe place to not only emit feelings but also experience new feelings that life does not always offer or allow him a space to express.

Feeling into a character on stage can be so powerful a state that it provokes a somatic response. Rachel expressed that during the play when she empathised with Alex, she felt she "just want[ed] to hug that man."[40] When asked what was the most emotional moment in the play, Chris described how he empathised with Alex when Georgie asked him for the money to find her son: "At that point you are on pins and needles. [...] Not knowing how you feel. Not knowing where this is going. That's an emotional moment."[41]

Empathy can also link with transference. Debbi discussed how Alex "felt like someone [she] would know." She went on to explain, "[Alex was] the recluse, accepting a simple life. I have a great uncle that was sort of like that. [Alex] felt really real. I felt empathy for him throughout. I think more from his looks."[42] Transference can also have an alienating effect. For Jay "the crazy ex-girlfriend aspect made it difficult for [him] to feel sorry for [Georgie]."[43] In light of his past experiences, Jay could not feel into Georgie's emotions.

The abrogation of the empathetic connection does not make the character–audience member connection any less potent. The transference relationship, although negative, is strong. If, as Theodor Lipps argues, empathy is an echo across the footlights, then transference is a scream across the footlights that can make the heart pound and the mind race.

The interview discussions revealed a natural thirst in the audience members for emotional experiences: a desire to feel, to express and to, perhaps, be transformed through those feelings. For some, the emotional states that were evoked were repulsive and unwanted. For others they were joyfully welcomed. For actors, the emotions experienced while performing on stage are almost sacrosanct. Denis revealed that his most emotive moment in *Heisenberg* is when Alex cries. When asked to describe the moment in the interview, Denis did not want to elaborate arguing, "it's so complex. I don't want to queer the moment by putting it into words. Once you start to describe something and you hear what you've said, you fuck it up."[44] Just like the unconscious emotional states of the audience members, the actors have their own emotions that grip the body when in unchartered territory. The unspoken, the uncanny, the unconscious fills the air with what Hermann Schmitz calls an emotional radiance in space.[45] In *Heisenberg*, the psychological undercurrents experienced onstage, in the audience and in the divide in-between created a highly charged connection between the characters and the audience members. To use Denis's words, the "emotional terrain" that he "skates with the audience" is a "two-way conduit" that is a "collective resonance"[46] creating the magic of theatre.

The suspension of disbelief

As discussed, audience members expressed a desire to experience real emotions and for the actors to emit and evoke real emotions. As Michael described, he had a need for "what you see on the stage [to be] emotionally real, even though you know they are actors and you know that it isn't, but it feels like it is."[47] As also quoted in the last chapter, Debbi highly prizes realism and identification: "[the characters need to be] believable to the extent that you can see yourself in them. Realism. I want to feel that I know these people, that they are really people."[48] Concurrently, there was also an expressed desire among the audience members for the imaginative realm, that the play transport the audience member into a different world:

> [I love] the magic of theatre. It transports me into someone else's world. It's an interesting world, it engages me, makes me think, makes me laugh, or whatever. It's a moment that can never be repeated.
>
> *Frank Lachmann*

> It's magic to watch somebody produce this marvellous illusion on stage of being somewhere else or being someone else and introducing you to a world you never would have met before.
>
> *Rachel Strauber*

These two elements, emotions and imagination, are not mutually exclusive but interconnected. Imagination and emotions are psychological processes. This is where the suspension of disbelief becomes so potent as emotions and imagination are imbricated. As argued in Chapter 1, imaginative truth can stir real emotions. Furthermore, if there are gaps in the narrative – of which there are many in *Heisenberg* – then there is much more space for audience members to fill these gaps with their own imaginative truths. This section considers the audience members' suspension of disbelief in *Heisenberg*.

A starting point for a discussion is Samuel Coleridge's often overlooked "willing." An actor willingly suspends her/his belief that the story they are playing is not real, that the character they are playing is not themselves, that the room they are performing in is not in a real house. An audience member willingly consents to suspend their belief that the story played in front of them is not real, that the characters onstage are actors, that what they see is a set not a real living room. Following observations of consent, the audience's and actors' suspension of disbelief in *Heisenberg* is considered. Discussion of the imaginative realm in the interviews was prompted by three questions which also referred to the double consciousness explored in the Part I. At what point were you able to shut out the world and enter into the story of the play? The play had basically no set. What was your response to this? When you watched her perform, did you see Mary-Louise or her character Georgie, or both? The last question was repeated regarding Denis Arndt and his character Alex. Denis was asked the first two questions and the following: Who are you when you are acting? Alex, Denis or both? Interestingly, consent became an integral part of the actor's and audience members' responses to all these questions.

Consent

The concept of consent to make a willing decision to suspend disbelief in the theatre is intriguing. Is it a letting go, a conscious decision, or does the realm of imagination so sweep us off our feet that we are thrown into it? Is it intertwined with the actor's imaginative truth? Can the actors' suspension of disbelief throw us into the imaginative realm, or can the fictitious world of the play suspend us in that realm and hold us there? Does it depend on personality types? There are so many unanswered questions about the suspension of disbelief that it is difficult to know where to begin.

Suspension of disbelief is a voluntary act. As August Schlegel argues, "the theatrical as well as every other poetical illusion is a waking dream, to which we voluntarily surrender ourselves."[49] Chris described his consent moment in theatrical terms: "A curtain goes up in my mind because I am invested in this, I am not resistant. A curtain comes up in my brain, I am here, now."[50] Chris makes a deliberate choice, he is not "resistant."

I argue that there is, however, another vehicle unique to theatre that facilitates this leap into the imaginative realm: the actors. The actors, in many ways, issue an invitation from the stage to the audience to believe in the fiction of their characters and the story. They have already taken the first step into the world of imagination. In choosing to be an actor in the first place, they have already consented. An actor does not show up and say "I refuse to play this story as if it were real or this character as if s/he were real." As Konstantin Stanislavski argues, it is only through the actors' belief in the character and the play's premise that the audience can be caught up into the world onstage. The actor's belief aids the audience suspension of disbelief. Some actors are more adept at this than others. Denis describes it in terms of a wilful act: "The unrehearsed player [audience member] comes in not quite knowing what to expect [...] but they come willing to have the experience, and they are compelled to play along, to play with you." This is a consensual, unspoken contract and it strengthens the ties between the actors and the audience. As Denis elaborates, "there is that moment where we collectively [...] agree on something that hasn't happened yet. [...] It's mysterious."[51] As Roger Grainger argues, consent is a game we agree to play.[52] Once the audience have taken a leap of faith and taken a step out of the quotidian in suspending disbelief, it is not too great a step to project themselves onstage into the world of the play through projection.

Shutting out the world

Willing or otherwise, as many of the *Heisenberg* interviewees testified, it is a difficult activity for the audience members and actors to shut out the clamouring world of thoughts that permeate our minds, to enter into the realm of the imagination. Although half of the audience members I interviewed said that they were able to shut out the outside world "when the lights went down,"[53] for the remaining, it was more problematic. Michael felt that the episodic form of the way the play was presented interrupted his imaginative flow:

> The structure of the way it is presented works against [entering into the world of the play]. The separating of the scenes with lights down [...] breaks the flow for me. The artificiality removes you from the process. That kept it stage bound to me. Every time you start to get into it [...].

David "got into it in stages as the relationship built up"[54] and Jay came in and out of the fictitious world. Two audience members only began to shut out the outside world during the bedroom scene which occurs around halfway through the play. Understandably for Leslie, because of transference, the bedroom scene was so disturbing that the time when she "basically shut out the world, or maybe wanted to run away from the world was when they were in bed together."[55] Conversely for Janet, the bed scene was a way into the imaginative world. She was submerged in the play's diegesis at that point because "it was that intimate moment where [Alex] was kind of admitting that this was something he had not had for a very long time."[56] One audience member "wasn't able to fully shut out the world" at any point as she "felt like [she] was watching a play."[57] Interestingly, she accredited this to her lack of belief in one of the characters. This is a prime example of how the actor's belief can facilitate or abrogate a suspension of disbelief.

The acting, the staging, transference and even the absence of a convincing relationship onstage occluded the imaginative realm for some of these audience members. When the play is "stage bound" or when the audience members "feel like [they] are watching a play"[58] is a great disappointment for the *Heisenberg* interviewees who go to the theatre to be transported into another world. There is a craving for belief: belief in the imaginative realm. When the magical happens, when belief is suspended and the audience member or actor takes a leap off the precipice of belief, it is a consolation to the overactive, world-weary, information-saturated twenty-first-century mind.

Filling in the gaps

Once the *Heisenberg* audience members and actors consented to suspend disbelief and the outside world was shut out, they were able to be transported into another world. Yet in this play, another leap into the imaginative world needed to be undertaken due to the absence of a permanent set. During the interviews, unprompted, some of the audience members and Denis spoke in detail about this absence[59] and how this impelled them to fill in the gaps of the visual by envisioning an imaginative world. Denis found this very stimulating:

> What more could you ask in terms of theatre? [*Heisenberg* is] the Peter Brook empty space: nothing but the actors and the spoken word and worthy ideas. That's when you get to participate, you get to invent the costumes, you get to see them naked on the table, you get to invest all this. The idea of its barebonedness. It's just the spoken word and two people without distraction and worthy ideas.[60]

The audience members predominantly found the absence of a set either heightened their theatrical experience or added to the uncertainty aspects of the play. Michael, Frank and Chris concurred with Denis that if there were a set, actors and audience members "would have been robbed of the experience"[61] of investing in the play through filling in the gaps by using their imaginations. Michael found the Brooksian empty stage provocative:

> It was compelling. Having to envision that locus, to see the shop that really was sketched very briefly. I could see him in an apron behind the counter. Again in the bedroom scene. It is only a cartoon, barely a sketch. But it's interesting to be able to visualise. In fact, sometimes I wish they would get rid of the director and the set designer.[62]

Frank and Chris argued that a set would have been a diversion:

> It was mainly an "interior of the characters play" and a real stage set, I think in retrospect, would have distracted from that.[63]
> No set is indeed a set. There is value in peeling away the world around us, so that we can concentrate on a finer point.[64]

Theatre professionals often underestimate the creative intelligence of their audience members who, as seen in the above comments, often crave for an opportunity to co-create the play's *mise en scene* by filling in the gaps.

Conversely, for two audience members the absence of the set was an impediment to their engagement. Leslie found it "a highly cerebral use of a set. Pretty brilliant, but not engaging."[65] Debbi asserted that

In general, a set that spare has to be extremely clever for me to find it compelling. I did not feel this was so in this case. Having the actors move the few set pieces around eliminated the distraction of crew members but made it more difficult to lose myself in the play.[66]

Some of the most perceptive observations regarded the uncertainty element that the barebones set provoked. Janet commented that the set's absence

in a way heightens the feeling of being off balance and keeps the audience having to work to construct meaning about what is going on. To have sets [...] would possibly have set up preconceived notions on the part of the audience. *Heisenberg* is named after the uncertainty principle and [the lack of a set] does contribute to the audience's uncertainty about just what is going on at a given time or where it is occurring.[67]

Jay, although he did not appreciate the barebones set pieces, also alluded to the uncertainty it incited:

So, *Heisenberg*'s austere set? Not my preference. It doesn't support the theme of the play, that you can't be sure what's real. Or perhaps it does, because you are forced to create your own reality from blocks you are given, and how well you convince others is all on you. And, therefore, you can start the narrative over with a simple "nope [...] that's not what it is. It's really *x*."

The uncertainty principle in the play and the uncertainty of the set exacerbated, perhaps, Jay's own uncertainty in this comment.

Double consciousness

While uncertainty was seemingly imposed on the play's setting and its narrative, uncertainty about seeing the characters as Georgie and Alex rather than Mary-Louise and Denis pervaded the interview discussions on the characters in *Heisenberg*. The question that provoked these discussions asked audience members if they saw the actor, the character or both on stage. All those interviewed saw Denis as the character and the character alone. Three audience members saw Mary-Louise as the character, two as the actor and five as a blend. Mary-Louise Parker is a celebrity. Most of these connoisseur audience members were adamant that celebrities were not a drawing card for them when choosing a play. The celebrity construction did, however, cloud to some extent, the natural transition from seeing an actor to suspending disbelief and seeing a character for some audience members. What is most significant is the reasons the audience members gave for seeing the actor, the character or the blend. A brief discussion of the audience's experience of audience double consciousness while sitting in a theatre auditorium is followed by an exploration of these reasons: familiarity, celebrity and identification.

There are several layers of consciousness for audience members watching a play. Audience members have an auditorium life and a stage life. In their auditorium life, there is a double consciousness of the individual playing the role of audience watching a play and also the consciousness of being an individual. Their audience role is consolidated when there is a moment of emotional contagion and the audience, laughing as one, become a collective. This is the moment, perhaps, when they become fully audience. Mark Fortier argues that audience members can also blend their stage life and auditorium life[68] such as when there is a distraction in the audience – a walk-out – and the audience's imaginative stage world consciousness is momentarily broken and focuses on the audience member in the auditorium or their own reaction to the walk-out. A significant moment such as this occurred during the original MTC production of *Heisenberg* off-Broadway when there was a medical emergency in the auditorium. The play was stopped, and a very concerned Mary-Louise Parker came into the auditorium and helped attend to the unwell audience member. The audience members attending this performance were able to gain further insight onto the actor Mary-Louise Parker and some gained more respect for her.[69] This occurrence is, however, an anomaly. Having elsewhere discussed in detail the audience's auditorium life or "performance,"[70] this research is predominantly concerned with the audience's stage life. Their stage life is directed by their gaze, psychological undercurrents and occurs after the willing suspension of disbelief. As already discussed, audience members direct their gaze towards live bodies of actors onstage, or suspend disbelief and see the character, or gaze at the blend. There is, naturally, slippage between these three consciousnesses for many reasons, such as when an actor "corpses"[71] and moves out of character to become actor.

Some audience members I interviewed stood outside themselves watching their conscious observations of characters and actors. Fran described her thought processes while watching actors onstage: "I sometimes have a feeling, or I wonder, what are they really like? What sort of people are they?"[72] In a moment in *Heisenberg*, Michael alternated between seeing Mary-Louise the actor and Georgie the character. He described a few similar moments in *Heisenberg* when he watched himself watching Mary-Louise the actor: "especially when she had a couple of her longer monologues. I was watching the way she was doing it, thinking, 'It's interesting the way she is doing that.'"[73] Michael was consciously observing Mary-Louise the actor, playing Georgie the character.

One of the most interesting explanations that audience members gave for seeing the character rather than the actor was familiarity. The majority of audience members expressed that unfamiliarity with the actor made it easier for them to accept the character onstage while familiarity with the actor impeded their perception of character:

> I was not familiar with [Denis] other than Heisenberg, therefore for me he was strictly the character.
>
> *David Herz*

I wasn't familiar with [Denis]. One of my constant questions is the difference between good acting and good directing. [...] He was the character immediately and throughout.

Debbi Baum

Though I met her, I don't really know Mary-Louise Parker. So I could only see Georgie.

Chris Lincoln

From these accounts and others not included here, it can be seen that an actor's personal anonymity appears to be an important aspect in the audience members' suspension of disbelief. Familiarity seemingly draws the audience member closer to the actor across the footlights, but hinders the leap into the imaginative fiction of the character. The last comment above is most revealing. Chris had met Mary-Louise in public on a previous occasion, but expressed that he did not really "know" her. Knowing emerges as an important aspect in the stage–audience relationship particularly when a celebrity is onstage.

As discussed in Chapter 1, celebrities can become like close friends standing in for real friends. This creates an intimacy in the theatre across the footlights with the actor, but can also act as a barrier to the suspension of disbelief and the transition from seeing the actor to seeing the character. As Michael observed of Mary-Louise, "It was harder to appreciate her 'self' and separate her from the performance."[74] Transitions into the suspension of disbelief were also longer:

I think it was sometimes Mary-Louise Parker at the beginning and then more Mary-Louise Parker at the end.

Rachel Strauber

She comes out on stage and I see the actress, she is not the character yet.

Jay Baum

For others, the celebrity presence overwhelmed the character:

She is too much of a presence. It identified her as Mary-Louise Parker for all the flaky characters she has played. And I love all the flaky characters she has played in movies and on TV. But this kind of flakiness, this eccentric, I didn't buy it.

Leslie Tucker

This comment is a pertinent illustration of how high audience expectations are when the onstage actor is a screen celebrity. Other audience members had what they identified as a "bias" either in favour of Mary-Louise the actor or against her, and this in turn coloured their perception of her performance and acceptance of her character. Debbi admitted, "I have a bias, I don't particularly care for her. [...] She was Mary-Louise Parker for the entire thing." Conversely, Fran emphasised,

> Mary-Louise Parker is one of my favourites, seeing her so up close was just wonderful. Her energy is just unbelievable. It was great to see her up close. Not all celebrities should come back on stage. Some of them are too taken up with their own celebrity to get into the character. Mary-Louise Parker is certainly well known enough that she could do that. But she doesn't. She gets into her character and she plays it.[75]

Fran mentioned her spatial relationship to Mary-Louise five times in the interview. Close proximity to a celebrity plays an important role in heightening the feeling of intimacy and familiarity. Fran was "sitting on the stage, practically on top of the actors"[76] for this production, and the spatial intimacy became an important aspect of the relationship with the actors and particularly Mary-Louise.

Although half of the audience members stated that they saw the blend of Mary-Louise and the character, only one could describe it: "You knew it was Mary-Louise Parker but she was the character, she was obviously not playing herself. You are aware that she is an actress playing a role but you get into the role."[77] Whether seeing Mary-Louise Parker, Georgie or the blend of both, the *Heisenberg* audience members expressed much stronger opinions about Mary-Louise and her character than Denis or his character. This heightened, either negatively or positively, the relationship between the stage and the audience. MTC, well aware that celebrity presence can alter the play's dynamics, staged a distraction at Mary-Louise's entrance to prevent the now *de rigueur* applause on a star entrance. Mary-Louise and Denis entered the stage during the stage manager's mobile phone discourse and began to set up the stage as two actors rather than characters.[78] Regardless of these measures, pre-established familiarity with the celebrity onstage in *Heisenberg* made the transitions into belief in the character longer, more disjointed or non-existent. Audience members seemingly scrutinised Mary-Louise's performance more rigorously than Denis's and those favourable to Mary-Louise enjoyed the close proximity that this particular production afforded them.

Is there a clear delineation between actors and characters and stage life and auditorium life when identifying with a character or experiencing transference or projection? Interestingly, Denis's identification with being an actor was seemingly stronger than his identification with the character of Alex. Having a penchant for philosophising, when Denis was asked the question "Who are you when you are acting: Alex, Denis or both?," he responded with the following:

> I don't know what acting is, when I am there doing that. When you asked me am I Denis or Alex, I don't know, I am doing exactly what I am supposed to have been doing as an actor, there's been a huge circle completed in my life. This is what I am supposed to have done on earth. I feel totally and utterly fulfilled in terms of "bliss" doing something that you love so deeply, that you are not doing it at all you're being it.[79]

For Denis, the question was irrelevant. What was relevant was that he identified with being an actor. It is his love, his passion, what he is meant to be doing on earth. As noted above in the discussion of psychological undercurrents, Denis stated that he "knew" Alex, but his discourse on "being" an actor was of far more consequence.

In regard to the audience members, there are many conclusions that can be drawn concerning identification, transference and projection and if the audience were seeing character or actor or the blend at different moments throughout the play. It would seem that when experiencing these psychological phenomena, audience members were seeing the character rather than the actor, or perhaps even a version of themselves or their transference phantom onstage. Michael's identification with Alex facilitated the suspension of disbelief. When asked if he saw Denis as the actor, the character or both, Michael emphasised, "I think for Alex – more because I could relate to him personally – I think I was more connected to the character. I don't think I saw the actor there."[80] The connection across the footlights arises as the most vital part of the relationship between char/actor and audience. In Edward Bullough's terms, the psychological undercurrents work to significantly decrease the distance without its disappearance.

Three different relationships between stage and audience emerged during *Heisenberg* that are equally potent and electric but in differing ways. When the audience member is not familiar with the actor and suspends disbelief, the audience–character relationship is powerful. When a celebrity is onstage and the audience member sees the actor, the audience–actor magnetism is highly charged, either positively or negatively. When an audience member identifies with a character, substitutes a character with someone else from their lives, projects their unwanted feelings onto a character or empathises with a character, the audience member is, as Stanislavski describes, drawn into the thick of the life they see onstage.[81]

I conclude with a concept that Denis used to describe the connection between actors and audience members that he feels onstage. When asked "Can you describe what you feel in the air between actors and audience?," Denis replied,

> There's a collective present that is created. [...] There is a definite collective resonance that is almost kind of limbic. If you go into theoretical physics, it would be "spooky action at a distance." This thing that we share that is an empathetic set of neurons in our brains that resonate when we get together to participate in these conceits. I think it's this sacramental participation in this human thing [called theatre] that defines who we are.[82]

In very basic terms, action at a distance refers to the concept in quantum mechanics that, during what is now known as entanglement, one particle influences another particle, regardless of the distance between them.[83] Objects can be influenced by other objects without being touched. The epithet "spooky" was added by Albert Einstein, a contemporary of Heisenberg, in a letter to Max Born in 1947.[84] In his comments about spooky action at a distance, Denis was inferring that in the theatre, actors and audience members influence each other without touching, creating a collective resonance in the air. "Collective resonance" is, perhaps, similar in many ways to Émile Durkheim's collective effervescence. What is significant is that for Denis, actors and audience members co-create this collective resonance. The concept of distance again emerges as an importance issue in the actor–audience conversation.

In this chapter, I posited that emotions stirred by transference, identification, projection and empathy pour out spatially in between actors and audience members, influencing each collective. Furthermore, the consensual suspension of disbelief transports the actors and audience members into Schlegel's waking dream where imaginative truth stirs real emotions. The psychological undercurrents and the suspension of disbelief in *Heisenberg* created an atmosphere that was in Schmitz's terms "dynamically engaging, 'gripping' the felt body in characteristic ways specific to each distinguishable type of emotion."[85] These emotions and connections between actors and audience members were conversations that transformed and electrified the air.

Heisenberg workshops: extending the conversation

Twenty-three people are sitting in an open circle on the seventh floor of a building on 44th Street on an unseasonably warm September evening in Manhattan. A Bach Sonata is playing in the background. A gentleman in a suit and tie warmly greets everyone and says a few introductory words. The people are invited to stand and greet the person next to them verbally, then adding a physicalisation. They are then asked to establish a fictitious relationship with the person and greet them again. One couple are asked by the gentleman to present their greeting to the others in the open circle: two strangers meeting for the first time. The *Heisenberg* audience performance has commenced. The rest of the evening is spent exploring elements of *Heisenberg*: the uncertainty principle, telling lies, the meeting of strangers, unconventional compliments, personal admissions and revelations, expressions of violent ambivalence and outrageous propositions. Audience members do not sit and listen to a lecture on these elements from the director, dramaturg or actors. The gentleman takes on the role of a facilitator and gently guides a series of provocative exercises designed to prompt inquiry, stimulate audience discussion and create a sense of anticipation about the play. None of the play's narrative is discussed. Audience members are invited to write scenes, act out chance meetings, share shocking revelations, inscribe outrageous propositions on butcher papers, write poems and read them to the group. At the conclusion of the evening, two of the people in the circle, invited actors, perform an improvised scene related to all of the elements that were explored during the evening. The audience members leave the room stimulated, changed, and for some who experienced the workshops for the first time: "blown-away by it all."[86] This too is a psychological experience.

MTC's pre-performance audience workshops are unlike any other pre-performance event I, or those that I interviewed, have ever attended. They are experiential. The audience perform. David Shookhoff, manager of education at MTC, has been designing and moderating these practical and compelling workshops for 15 years now.[87] Many of the audience members I interviewed were loyal attendees who are "in awe of what David Shookhoff does"[88] and attend the workshops "religiously."[89] Some enjoy the opportunity in the workshops to exercise their "inner performer."[90] Others find the activities so stimulating that they journal their experiences, have a collection of all the poems or scenes they have written, or keep mementos from the workshops.

The workshops are designed for the audience conversation with the play's narrative, characters, motifs and issues to commence long before the play opens. In the audience members own words, the MTC workshops:

> Enhance my experience. [...] Really give me an appreciation for what the actors have to do in order to convey to the audience non-verbally. The workshops generally increase my enjoyment of plays, of movies of lots of things. It has a generalising effect of looking to see the staging, how playwrights handle certain issues and so on. It's fascinating.
>
> *Frank Lachmann*

> Open my horizons to be a more informed audience member.
>
> *Debbi Baum*

> Add to the understanding of the play.
>
> *David Herz*

> Invite us to go "meta." To see things in a different way, seeing more than I saw when I was watching the play.
>
> *Chris Lincoln*

During the workshops the *Heisenberg* audience members "rehearsed" their perspectives on the elements in the play in preparation for the performance. The workshops enhanced the experience of the play in very different ways for each audience member. While watching the play, having performed in the workshops added extra layers of meaning to the uncertainty principle, the dialogue, details that may have been missed, the music, the language, unusual compliments, intimacy and the "lying" in the play. Actor Denis Arndt would be, perhaps, surprised to find that the workshop attendees who all went on to watch the play once it opened were not indeed his "unrehearsed players" but rehearsed players.

In addition to the workshops, MTC also offers a post-performance "curtain call." Similar to the pre-workshops, the curtain call is experiential. At the commencement of the *Heisenberg* curtain call, David Shookhoff broke everyone into "Alex and Georgie" couples and then gave each couple scenes to read through. Discussions, prompted by questions from David, ensued for the next hour and a half which delved into the thematic importance of the passages. David added his own insights to the discussion which for Leslie "was like being part of a stellar literature class. Each insight of David's was like a creative growth spurt for me."[91] Audience members had many revelations about the play as they debated among many other aspects: the uncertainty elements, character's motivations and the acting. Shared insights into the uncertainty principle were, perhaps, the most revelatory. Leslie summarises her new-found understanding as follows:

> [A revelation for me was] that Georgie can have two mindsets, but not simultaneously. It is possible for Georgie to one, have feelings for Alex plus two, want to exploit him financially, but these two thoughts cannot occur within her mind simultaneously. Per the Heisenberg Principle, one can never know with perfect accuracy both these important factors which determine the movement of the smallest of particles – its position (Georgie's love for Alex maybe?) and its velocity (Georgie's exploitation of Alex maybe?) It is *impossible* to determine accurately both the particle's position and the direction and velocity of the particle *at the same instant.*[92]

These kinds of insights are not normally gained in your average post-show discussion where the director gives a lecture or actors share stories and anecdotes, and audience questions rarely are more sophisticated than "how did you learn all those lines." I posit that Leslie gained these insights, and many others, because she had had an experiential journey through *Heisenberg* which started with the workshops and culminated in a post-performance event in which she embodied the characters by acting out some of the scenes from the play and then engaged in a debate with other audience members. Some audience members were shocked and/or surprised by the different points of view of the play shared in the curtain call. In this, audience members were experiencing one of the central motifs in *Heisenberg* that "We hold very different perspectives on experiences we imagine we're sharing." These different perspectives fill what Denis described as the "gaps in the narrative" in *Heisenberg.* In the workshops, the gaps are all question marks: uncertainty? relationship? deception? In the curtain call, the audience participants attempt to fill in the gaps. Conversations that have commenced in the workshops, continue with extra layers of meaning during the performance and are extended in the curtain call.

Notes

1 Simon Stephens, *Heisenberg* (London and New York: Bloomsbury Methuen, 2015), 47.
2 After a successful MTC off-Broadway run of the play in 2015.
3 Despite repeated efforts, and most likely because of her celebrity status, the other actor, Mary-Louise Parker, was unavailable for an interview.
4 For a full discussion of the workshops, see "Extending the conversation" section below.
5 The term "empathy" was used in an interview question, since it is a readily accessible term. Transference, identification, projection and suspension of disbelief were, however, not used with one exception where I accidentally used the term "transference" after one interviewee had described a transference episode.
6 Denis Arndt, personal interview, 26 October 2016.
7 Werner Heisenberg's uncertainty principle was articulated in 1929.

8 Leslie Tucker, personal interview, 1 November 2016.

9 Anonymous comment notated while I was an audience member.

10 Frank Lachmann, personal interview, 3 November 2016.

11 Ushers in the orchestra playfully shared this with some audience members as they pointed them to their seats on the stage.

12 Michael Reichgott, personal interview, 31 October 2016.

13 Chris Lincoln, personal interview, 1 November 2016.

14 Debbi Baum, personal interview, 29 October 2016.

15 Quotes taken from seven *Heisenberg* audience member's comments.

16 Frank Lachmann, personal interview, 3 November 2016.

17 Chris Lincoln, personal interview, 1 November 2016.

18 Jay Baum, personal interview, 29 October 2016.

19 Ibid.

20 Ibid.

21 Leslie Tucker, personal interview, 1 November 2016.

22 A colloquial American expression meaning unpleasant, squalid or distasteful.

23 Leslie Tucker, personal interview, 1 November 2016.

24 Ibid.

25 Denis Arndt, personal interview, 26 October 2016.

26 Ibid.

27 Ibid.

28 David Herz, personal interview, 27 October 2016.

29 Chris Lincoln, personal interview, 1 November 2016.

30 Jay Baum, personal interview, 29 October 2016.

31 Denis Arndt, personal interview, 26 October 2016.

32 These expressions were audible in the audience at each performance I attended.

33 Jay Baum, personal interview, 29 October 2016.

34 Rachel Strauber, personal interview, 27 October 2016.

35 Simon Stephens, *Heisenberg* (London: Bloomsbury, 2015), 31.

36 Frank Lachmann, personal interview, 3 November 2016.

37 Denis Arndt, personal interview, 26 October 2016.

38 Ibid.

39 Chris Lincoln, personal interview, 1 November 2016.

40 Rachel Strauber, personal interview, 27 October 2016.

41 Chris Lincoln, personal interview, 1 November 2016.

42 Debbi Baum, personal interview, 29 October 2016.

43 Jay Baum, personal interview, 29 October 2016.

44 Denis Arndt, personal interview, 26 October 2016.

45 Hermann Schmitz, Rudolf Müllan and Jan Slaby, "Emotions Outside the Box—The New Phenomenology of Feeling and Corporeality," *Phenomenology and the Cognitive Sciences* 10, no. 2 (2011): 241–259.

46 Denis Arndt, personal interview, 26 October 2016.

47 Michael Reichgott, personal interview, 31 October 2016.

48 Debbi Baum, personal interview, 29 October 2016.

49 Cited in Frederick Burwick, *Illusion and the Drama* (University Park: Penn State UP, 2010), 246.

50 Chris Lincoln, personal interview, 1 November 2016.

51 Denis Arndt, personal interview, 26 October 2016.

52 Roger Grainger, *Suspending Disbelief: Theatre as a Context for Sharing* (Brighton: Sussex, 2010), 18.

53 Fran Halper, personal interview, 26 October 2016.

54 David Herz, personal interview, 27 October 2016.

55 Leslie Tucker, personal interview, 1 November 2016.

56 Janet Stahl, personal interview, 27 October 2016.

57 Debbi Baum, personal interview, 29 October 2016.

58 Ibid.; and Leslie Tucker, personal interview, 1 November 2016.

59 Their insights were so perceptive that I included the "this play has no set [...]" question in subsequent interviews.

60 Denis Arndt, personal interview, 26 October 2016.

61 Ibid.

62 Michael Reichgott, personal interview, 31 October 2016.

63 Frank Lachmann, personal interview, 3 November 2016.

64 Chris Lincoln, personal interview, 1 November 2016.

65 Leslie Tucker, personal interview, 1 November 2016.

66 Debbi Baum, personal interview, 29 October 2016.

67 Janet Stahl, personal interview, 27 October 2016.

68 Mark Fortier, *Theory/Theatre: An Introduction* (London: Routledge, 2016), 195.

69 I am indebted to Leslie for this story.

70 Caroline Heim, *Audience as Performer: The Changing Role of Theatre Audiences in the Twenty-First Century* (London and New York: Routledge, 2016).

71 Actors are seen to corpse when they "break character" for some reason and become the actor onstage during the play.

72 Fran Halper, personal interview, 26 October 2016.

73 Michael Reichgott, personal interview, 31 October 2016.

74 Ibid.

75 Fran Halper, personal interview, 26 October 2016.

76 Ibid.

77 Janet Stahl, personal interview, 27 October 2016.

78 Although this measure stopped the applause for most performances, the star entry applause still occurred in a few performances.

79 Denis Arndt, personal interview, 26 October 2016.

80 Michael Reichgott, personal interview, 31 October 2016.

81 Konstantin Stanislavski, *An Actor Prepares*, trans. Elizabeth Reynolds Hapgood (London: Bloomsbury, 2008), 142.

82 Denis Arndt, personal interview, 26 October 2016.

83 For an accessible understanding of this concept, see Hrvoje Nikolić, "EPR before EPR: A 1930 Einstein-Bohr Thought Experiment Revisited," *European Journal of Physics* 33, no. 5 (2012): 1089.

84 Arkady Plotnitsky, *Epistemology and Probability: Bohr, Heisenberg, Schrödinger and the Nature of Quantum-Theoretical Thinking* (New York: Springer, 2010), 242.

85 Schmitz, Müllan and Slaby, "Emotions Outside the Box," 249.

86 Leslie Tucker, personal interview, 1 November 2016.

87 The Curtain Call (mentioned later) was introduced in the 2011–12 MTC season.

88 Rachel Strauber, personal interview, 27 October 2016.

89 Frank Lachmann, personal interview, 3 November 2016.

90 Jay Baum, personal interview, 29 October 2016.

91 Leslie Tucker, personal interview, 1 November 2016.

92 Ibid.

5

ENCOUNTERS WITH *THE ENCOUNTER*

"It seems empathy and proximity are connected, I could reach out and touch you. I'd like to get closer to you."[1] The single actor onstage speaks these words to the audience. Eight hundred people are invited to put headphones on. The actor whispers in our right ear and then walks from one side of our head to the other. "I'm not ready for an encounter" someone whispers in the dark. No one can hear her. They can only hear him: the actor, Simon McBurney, Loren McIntyre, Simon's daughter and other voices of the past, present and future relating a timeless story for the rest of the 110-minute performance.

In Complicité's *The Encounter*, the actor's proximity to an audience is so visceral that the audience feel "invaded," "mind-blown" and "surprised"[2] by the intimacy experienced. Yet the actor does not leave the stage. This is a very different reading of Edward Bullough's utmost decrease of distance without its disappearance. The production plays with time, narrative, proximity and presence in such a way that it creates a highly charged electric current that exists in a virtual dimension rather than in the air of the theatre. In Chapter 4 we explored the psychological conversations across the footlights in a conventional theatre production. This chapter explores the phenomenological experience of a virtual liminality and virtual conversations for the actor and multiple audience members in a non-conventional theatre production staged in a traditional theatre setting. A description of the production and project is followed by a discussion of actor's and audience's double consciousness in *The Encounter* and an overview of the motifs in the production: narrative, encounter, presence and time from the stage perspective and the audience perspective. *The Encounter* poses new questions about intimacy, atmosphere and sensory experiences in the theatre. It is a theatrical experience which lends itself to many and varied readings. Is *The Encounter* good storytelling or does it cross some terrain in the imagination that disrupts what theatre is?

The production and the project

Created collaboratively by the UK's Complicité and directed and performed by Simon McBurney,[3] *The Encounter* is a multi-voice, intimate, aural experience that disturbs the traditional conventions of theatre. It has the capacity to reach into Autonomous Sensory Meridian Responses.[4] Audience members wear headphones for the entire performance. The narrative is based on Romanian novelist Petru Popescu's account of a photojournalist's unsettling yet revelatory encounter with the Mayoruna tribe of the Brazilian Amazon. The tribe's understanding of time, their approach to material possessions and their wordless "beaming" communication challenge the photojournalist Loren McIntyre's Western perspectives and values as he journeys with them through near-death experiences to "stay still in time."[5]

The Encounter was one of those rare productions that took a giant leap from its beginnings at the Edinburgh Fringe Festival in 2015 onto a Broadway stage in 2016. It toured to 11 different countries over a four-year period. I saw the production in New York in 2016 and at the Adelaide Festival in 2017 and conducted an in-depth interview with Simon McBurney in New York. The interview was so reflective and performative that I include all Simon's Pinteresque pauses in the discourse quoted below. For me, if not for Simon, the interview became a part of the narrative of the play itself and certainly enriched the performance's meaning the next time I saw it. Since *The Encounter* was so sensorial, experiential and immediate for the audience, it was important to conduct short interviews with audience members directly after the production to capture their emotive and psychological states before they transitioned out of the theatrical world into the quotidian. Forty-eight short interviews were conducted in the United States, Australia and the United Kingdom. I interviewed 14 audience members on the New York sidewalks directly after the performance at the Golden Theatre and 22 audience members in the foyer of the Dunstan Playhouse in Adelaide.[6] Two research assistants interviewed 21 audience members in the foyer of the Barbican Theatre in London in 2018. The audience members interviewed were aged 16–64. Half of the interviewees were aged 16–21. Audience members were asked two questions: "What was your encounter with *The Encounter* like?" and "How did you feel when he was in your head?"

Double consciousness

The one-person performance relies heavily on the theatrical and technological skills of the actor. The production exists in the realm of double consciousness for the actor and the audience members. For Simon, the char/actor consciousness is so complex because of the multiple characters and consciousness's explored that a multiple consciousness is needed. When I asked Simon about his double consciousness in *The Encounter*, he described it as a metacharacter experience:

> I play a character who, according to the character, seems to be someone called Simon McBurney. I play a slightly different character who, perhaps, doesn't

have quite the same name, but might be generically called the father. I play a third character who *(pause)* channels the voice of the Romanian writer Petru Popescu and might loosely be called *(pause)* the storyteller, the narrator, or the commentator. Obviously, I play Loren McIntyre. *(pause)* And then I play somebody who is like *(pause)* a sort of eighteenth century silhouetist, who makes things out of paper, who cuts them out, outlines them, in which I attempt to bring things to life through a single gesture or look. *(pause)* I suppose a character you might call a collagist, sticking stuff together. *(long pause)* Yes.[7]

In many ways Simon "*is* the story that he is telling."[8] A rich layering of characters is intricately woven by this highly skilled collagist into a performance text that plays with the conventional perceptions of character and actor for the audience members.

Simon purposefully walks onto the stage while the audience are arriving to prepare the audience for this extra-theatrical experience:

> I try to find someone in the audience who is looking at me, I smile at them, they smile back, I try to normalise relationships, so I'm not *(pause)* the weirdo. So, when I come out I'm somebody, but I'm sort of nobody. I come out and they're like "oh it's fine, it's just him." I want them to know who I am, "Who's this? Who's this? Oh, it's him, oh he's got a daughter, a past, he's got a dad". And all of these things are deliberately placed for people to go "oh I wonder what his dad was like."[9]

This does not compromise the audience suspension of disbelief, but deftly exposes and makes audiences aware of their own double consciousness. They are watching an actor, Simon McBurney, who has a family and lives in an apartment in London who will play many characters. Blending the characters and Simon creates a hyper-reality. Two audience members described how this "anchored"[10] the production for them. However, as soon as the audience settles comfortably into identifying with one of the characters, Simon disrupts the narrative with a parallel universe. At different times in the production, the collagist intentionally switches back into the role of Simon McBurney to include his own narrative in the story-making process. This, according to traditional narrative theatre theory, could work to further alienate the audience, yet in this production, it works rather to personalise the experience. Personalisation is achieved metatheatrically by extending the narrative to include characters from Simon's life, create a story within a story, and inculcate the storytelling genre.

Narrative

One of the distinguishing elements of *The Encounter* is the purposeful manipulation of narrative and the techniques employed to place the narrative firmly in the minds of the audience members. Simon uses the storytelling trope to seemingly interpellate the audience members as "campfire companions."[11] In Complicité's formation of the piece, the creatives battled with how to theatrically transition the story onstage into the minds of the audience: "The opening. What shall we include? How do we get from presence to the narrative to consciousness?"[12] The production commences with Simon sharing the immense responsibility he feels when he reads his children stories and further explores the relationship of the story-teller and "audience." When I asked Simon if he casts his audiences, he responded, "I suppose I do, particularly when you're telling a story you tend to think of them as, *(long pause)* campfire companions, *(pause)* and that you're sharing a ring."[13] Many of *The Encounter* audience members in that ring consequently cast Simon as the storyteller:

> You were in bed and he was telling you a bedtime story.[14]
> He felt like a nice English person, a narrator that introduced us to these other people and took us through the story.[15]
> I felt like he was telling me a story personally.[16]

This more readerly audience role was emphasised by several audience members: "It was a bit like reading a book where you see it in words and it's all in your head, but this was all by sound."[17] An Adelaide audience member "was desperate to know what happened next." For her "it was a page turner."[18]

An invitation by the storyteller to enter into the ring is facilitated by wearing headphones so that the collagist can weave the story into the consciousness of the audience members in a very intimate way. Wolfgang Iser argues that a narrative is the meeting of text and imagination.[19] In traditional theatre productions, this happens more in the liminal physical space between actor and audience. In *The Encounter*, however, the consummation of text and imagination appears to happen in what Iser calls a "virtual dimension,"[20] in the consciousness of the audience members. This distinction is discussed further below. As Simon describes, "it's not even what I'm doing, it's what they're imagining."[21] The theatrical conceit occurs in the imaginations of the audience members. Interestingly, some audience members described the experience as a "theatre of the mind."[22] This is an apt description of the more readerly experience for the audience as they connect with *The Encounter* story in the virtual dimension.

The "theatre of the mind" was extremely potent. Audience members felt they were "there in the jungle" having a "visceral"[23] experience "with the mosquitoes making your skin crawl."[24] Some audience members described how much more authority was given to them as auditors: "Normally good productions try and put you in and get you lost in it, this one threw you in at the start and you had to find your way out."[25] In playing the narrative in the theatre of their minds, the audience's performative role was questioned. Were they also the narrator? During both productions that I attended, I took my headphones off occasionally to listen to the audience text, the whisperings in the dark. Halfway through the Adelaide production someone muttered, "I can't tell if I'm telling the story or the story is telling me." In the theatre of the mind, does the audience member, perhaps, become the storyteller as text and imagination meet? This is not the theatre where we fill Iser's "gaps" in the story drawing from our own imaginations, but one in which we, perhaps, through identification and projection, emerge as storytellers.

From the stage, Simon can sense the audience's storytelling processes. For him, it is intoxicating:

> The audience narrative is a continuous noise in my head, in my ears. It's constantly speaking to me in one way or another. It's not in words, its wordless, you sort of bathe and swim in what you feel is the narrative coming off them collectively, and sometimes individually. You feel continuous with what is being imagined, it's a flow, it's not a sequence of things, you are in a river, just a continuous river.[26]

The collective narrative that Simon alludes to in this discourse is not dissimilar to Arndt's collective resonance in the previous chapter. This narrative sharing or sensing is a conversation that heightens the electricity in the virtual dimension. There are times, however, that there is no electric dimension during a performance for Simon. There is no flow: when "you're not in that [river or flow], as happens some nights you know, you knock things, they drop, you feel as if things are stopping and starting."[27] It is difficult to ascertain whether audience members can sense this disconnect.

The Encounter narrative is multivalent. It is played by many characters and divulged by many storytellers. Popescu, McIntyre, Simon, the collagist and the audience not only are the story's narrators but, as Western narrators, also are complicit in perpetuating what the collagist calls "the savaging of the land" by being the "most materialist and leisure-minded culture in the world."[28] This saddened one audience member profoundly: "I feel sad, because we have stuffed things, us whities."[29] Some were confronted and incensed by the production's discourse on materialism and walked out.[30]

Although the metanarratives of *The Encounter* are challenging for some, the most electric moments occur when the text and imagination collide. The invitation proffered by the collagist to suspend disbelief and enter into the narrative draws the audience "as close to [them] as [he is] to his children. Closer in fact."[31] What the audience experiences when they hear the collagist in their head is unlike any other theatrical encounter.

Encounter

As Erika Fischer-Lichte emphasises, the encounter of actors and audiences in the theatre can be confrontational. In *The Encounter* there are two actor–audience encounters: the actor on the stage and the actor in the mind. These two encounters are, for the majority of the time, experienced concurrently. The first encounter, an actor onstage setting up his props, talking about his daughter and storytelling, was innocuous. The second encounter, when the actor onstage takes a walk from one side of the audience brain to another in complete surround sound, was unnerving and confrontational for many audience members and intimate and felt viscerally for others. Similarly, the actor's experience of the encounter with the audience was invasive, intimate and somatic.

For audience members aged 16–18, the encounter of the collagist in their heads was "Really weird," "Intimidating," "Pretty intense," "Invasive," and "Creepy." For one young lady "It felt literarily like he was really there." She "had to keep looking to make sure he wasn't."[32] Reading their discomfort, the collagist begins a mind conversation that continues throughout the production and spills into the narrative: "You should have the impression that I really am beside you. Now I'm getting a little bit too close, maybe a little too intimate."[33] The uneasiness created a feeling of displacement and surveillance for some:

> You get that feeling of not being in your own in your head, which is very, very odd.
> If I could hear his thoughts, could he hear mine?[34]

Simon was acutely aware of this intrusion and, interestingly, experienced a sense of rejection because of it:

> people can feel, very naturally, an intrusion, and so I have also had the experience of considerable rejection because of it: "Who do you think you are?" Something I've felt, […] people feel almost as if they've been violated, or they kind of go "Well! What makes you so special?" The same way that anybody who gets too close to you responds.[35]

This is a pertinent example of how the actor–audience relationship can become very personal and the audience's emotions can invade the actor's world and feed into his/her insecurities. The actor draws too close, some people feel violated, and they reject the seeming "intruder." In his treatise on distance, Bullough describes two ways of losing psychical distance between the subject and the object: under-distancing and over-distancing. Over-distancing distances the audience through "improbability, artificiality, emptiness or absurdity." Under-distancing draws the audience member too close to its naturalistic subject or subject matter and they can reach their "Distance-limit."[36] While Bullough is here describing the content and subject matter of an artwork, the broader concept of under-distancing can be applied to the virtual proximity of *The Encounter* experience for audience members. Consent is an important issue. The above audience comments illustrate how some audience members were close to reaching their "Distance-limit" when the collagist was perceived as traversing areas they had not necessarily consented to inside their heads. Other audience members, however, saw the mind encounter as "very friendly," "comfortable," and "non-threatening."[37] The theatre of the mind was such an emotional encounter for audience members primarily because of the intimacy of the experience.

Intimate distance

Intimacy, in terms of proximity with actors, is rarely experienced in a Broadway or large West End theatre or even in a festival setting where distance from the stage can sometimes hinder close encounters. Intimacy through identification, projection, transference or empathy can be experienced, but is predominantly psychological. The intimacy experienced in *The Encounter* was overwhelming for audience members accustomed to physical distance in the theatre. For many, the mind encounter had two stages: an initial shock and then an acceptance of the intimate distance that was quite thrilling: "It was a shock. Then there was an incredible intimacy. A little surprise. He was playing with us."[38] When asked what their encounter with *The Encounter* was like, the audience member's answers predominantly related to intimacy:

> The intimacy was tremendous.
> It was incredibly intimate.
> I felt intimacy with the sound.[39]

Interestingly, London audience members all used the term "personal" rather than intimate and discussed at length how Simon entered into their "personal space" which was "disorientating" for some. One audience member was adamant that he "was sharing [the collagist's] experience rather than him being inside [his] head."[40] Proximity was significantly an issue for London audience members. There are many audience responses to theatre such as this that are culturally inscribed and deserve more academic attention.

Intimacy in *The Encounter* is intentional, as Simon argues, "I want the audience necessarily to feel intimate with me. [...] To place yourself inside somebody's head is a very intimate act."[41] To create this, Simon not only becomes the storyteller in the theatre of the mind, but also invites the audience into his own apartment and makes them privy to his relationship with his daughter. Because of the intensity of the intimacy, this almost becomes voyeuristic, as Simon explains:

> I not only put myself in their heads, but I expose myself by placing the head of the audience snooping in my apartment. So, they're there, and they shouldn't be there. They're there going "huh, huh, my god look at that, he's just getting some water." They're seeing things like a kind of peeping tom, so it's working both ways.[42]

As discussed above, in the mind encounter, many audience members feel exposed and invaded as their Distance-limit is reached. Yet as Simon argues, it works both ways, he also feels exposed:

> It's a curious sensation because it feels as if I've taken all my clothes off. I am naked because this is my real relationship with my daughter and you're looking in on it. I'm certainly here, being watched very closely.

As seen in this example, actors also can reach their Distance-limit with an audience. This is, however, also a consent issue. Simon has chosen to undertake this role and is also a co-creator of the script and performance text.

It was not only watching and listening that created the intimacy, several audience members read the intimacy as dialogue: "it felt like it was just you and him having a conversation."[43] What is significant about this comment is that it is more representative of a one-on-one audience experience of an immersive theatre event than a traditional theatre experience. In *The Encounter*, the encounter between actor and audience is individual rather than collective. This is an important point of difference between this production and a conventional theatre experience. Many audience members related that they "shut [their] eyes for a while"[44] to enter into the theatre of the mind. This theatre of the mind takes the encounter between actor and audience member into a different dimension.

Community

A sense of community was compromised by the wearing of the headphones. Although Simon may have felt a collective resonance flowing from the audience as collective, for the audience member sitting in the auditorium there was no opportunity for the experience of collective effervescence. As discussed above, the actor still feels a "narrative coming off [the audience] collectively, and sometimes individually" yet the audience are in their own worlds, and there is little or no opportunity for emotional contagion.[45] A New York audience member felt a sense of loss in the lack of opportunity for audience–audience encounters:

> We went to *Something Rotten* the night before, and whenever there was a good laugh on the stage or a joke you could turn to the person beside you, laugh, or make a little quick comment. But in *The Encounter* that was completely cut off by wearing headphones. You didn't have this freedom to interact with the person next to you (on a very subtle and appropriate basis). You didn't have that at all. It was very much you, his voice in your ears, and what was happening on stage.[46]

Another audience member felt very isolated: "I went cold and I was all alone."[47]

For others, the isolation from the other audience members made it more intimate: "It felt like he was just talking to me, and there was nobody else in the room."[48] *The Encounter*'s encounter is immersive and individual. The one-on-one experience – the actor and the audience member – heightens the intimacy with the actor yet abrogates any collective response or sense of audience communitas.

In one sense, the audience are performing for the actor on stage. Their paralingual sounds, physical gestures and facial expressions are all visible to the actor as the lights remain on in the auditorium for one-third of the performance. Simon explains:

> When I start to speak, and I'm at the desk, and I'm looking at the audience, looking at 500–600 faces, *(pause)* I see these kinds of expressions, you know,

little smiles. Some people, when I catch their eye, they don't want to look at me, it's somehow quite obscene. [...] I hear people laughing, and when the head is on[49] I can hear all the reactions from the audience very intimately because it's so sensitive and it picks it all up.[50]

The audience performance enriched Simon's performance because "the audience are the ones that are doing things; that response of the audience is absolutely key."[51] Their physical gestures and the sounds they made became an essential part of the performance text for Simon.

Although the audience were predominantly unaware of their own physical performance, some audience members commented that the mind encounter with the actor triggered a physical response. They felt "fuzzy," "tingly," and "cold." One audience member said she "had shivers."[52] This was, perhaps, elicited by sensory moments in the performance when the actor blows in the audience ear, or the mosquitos buzz around the Amazon jungle.[53] The atmosphere of the jungle created in the theatre of the mind of cackling monkeys, crunching leaves and the rhythmic dancing of the Mayoruna people, while highly potent, was not as all-consuming as the invasive, intimate and physical encounter with the collagist in the audience members' minds. Simon and every audience member I interviewed had strong opinions about the actor–audience relationship. The theatrical encounter in the virtual dimension was highly charged particularly because it was confronting for the audience members and the actor alike. It was, perhaps, in this actor–audience encounter, that the only sense of community was found in this production.

Presence

In *The Encounter* presence, time and the virtual space are interrelated. As discussed in Chapter 2 and elaborated further here, for Simon, presence is not about the space that an actor fills, it is about time:

> The idea of presence is normally associated with the space that somebody takes up. The presence is to encompass the whole room, the whole stage, wherever they're in. But in fact, hidden within the word, is a more important notion of time, and "the present", because presence is about being present. [...] The presence of an actor is about their ability to, curiously, forget about themselves. Or conversely, to think about themselves so much that that is also presence, that kind of monstrousness.[54]

Simon's perception of presence as living in the present is not dissimilar to Method acting teacher Sanford Meisner's imperative of the actor living in the moment.[55] Taken literally, the kind of presence that Simon describes is a form of mindfulness. One of the primary goals of mindfulness is to focus your attention on the present moment. Being present as the actor or as the audience at the theatre is, however, the antithesis of mindfulness. When we go to the theatre, we consent to enter into a fictitious world. An actor consents to enter into a fictitious character. Being present in Simon's sense of the word is closer to identification; what he describes as "an actor's ability to forget about themselves" and identify with a character. I would argue that there are, however, instances when an actor is mindful. Simon alludes to this when he discusses the monstrosity of actors "thinking about themselves so much." Actors are also mindful when they consciously stand out of themselves onstage and observe what they are doing. This, of course, occurs as part of their double consciousness. Audience members can also be mindful. During the play their attention may be drawn to their surroundings. They start thinking about how uncomfortable the seats are, they observe what the person next to them is wearing, they step away from the fictitious world and consider how much they are enjoying the performance. They are living in this moment of time.

The temporal, yet vital nature of time in the theatrical event distinguishes its aesthetic construction from those of other art forms. The fictional world of the novel is not restricted by a specific time; a piece of visual art is as material as it is enduring: but the theatrical event takes place at a particular point in time, in a particular place, with a particular audience. It exists in specific present moments. Simon invites audience members into the present and to be present with him. To undertake this for *The Encounter*, however, they must suspend more than their disbelief. They are invited to suspend time.

The time discourse in *The Encounter*'s narrative contains, perhaps, one of the production's most enduring, unsettling and challenging messages. In his encounter with the Mayoruna tribe, Loren McIntyre is invited to forgo his Western perception of time and enter "instead [a] space/time/mind continuum"[56] that is part of the past, present and future where time does not, perhaps, exist. Consequently, the narrative challenges the audience to relinquish their Western perception of time by entering into a virtual dimension where time is suspended. A London audience member described this experience like being "in a parallel universe for two hours."[57] Through the narrative and the intermedial experience, Simon invites audience members to have the experience of suspending time.

It can be seen that the narrative and the encounter in the theatre of the mind work simultaneously to encourage an altered state of consciousness for the collagist and the audience members. Simon stated that "it feels like [I am in] a kind of meditation." At times in the production he goes "into a kind of a trance. [...] I'm in a state." Yet he was quick to add that concurrently "as a performer it is incredibly important to be conscious of the moment of the present."[58] Simon's double consciousness is of vital importance throughout the performance. Interestingly, audience members' encounter with the collagist and the story prompted similar trance-like experiences. For many it was: "A bit trippy," "Surreal," "Like I'm dreaming," "A fever,"[59] "Spooky,"[60] and "Some sort of consensual group hallucination."[61] Just as the production changed Simon's state, for one audience member *The Encounter* "changed [his] mind, entered [his] state and left [him] altered."[62] The actor's and some of the audience member's embodied trance-like experiences worked to suspend contemporary understandings of time. Experiencing the performance gave audience members the sense that, as the character of the headman states in the play, "time is falling off."[63]

Several audience members were confronted and insulted by the challenges to "change your mind" about the perception of time. Simon, as McIntyre, performs several of the tribe's rituals in the performance; some of which are for the purposes of going back to the beginning of time, or to even re-write or eradicate time. One of the rituals is the burning of possessions. As the text explains, the Mayoruna people "never think of the future, they don't hoard or store up belongings. Time for them [is] an invisible companion, something comfortable and unseen like the air."[64] In the production, this is brought into sharp contrast with the Western understanding of time where "For the civilizados, time [is] a possession. An increasingly more efficient machine."[65]

During the ritual of the burning of possessions McIntyre reflects, "I stare at the fire and I imagine us in the west, burning our possessions so as not to remain still in time!"[66] As already discussed, some audience members walked out during the discussion of Western materialism.

For others, however, the response was more introspective:

> It made me feel kind of invalid. Afterwards I kept thinking about time and how I spend time and I was like, "wow I feel invalid." A lot of the ways I feel about time seem different now.
> It really questions your morals and ethics, makes me question myself.[67]
> It made you think about a lot of things. It's deep and philosophical. Why do I get so worked up about *things*? (italics in original).[68]

For one audience member, the time motifs in the narrative and the encounter with timelessness seemingly achieved Simon's sense of presence, that of being present in the moment:

> In the moments of the show it changed my relationship to time and how I felt about time. I felt all these times and realities happening at the same time. In this one moment, this big pastiche, there's no forward or backwards: it was all happening at once.[69]

The actor, Simon, is present in the moment. The audience members are present in the moment. Yet they are present in the theatrical rather than a self-conscious moment. Their senses are on full alert in what one audience member described as a "full sensory overload."[70] In this heightened, at times, trance-like state, the actor and audience encounter each other in the virtual dimension rather than the physical. In many ways the experience is so "powerful, like an explosion inside your own head,"[71] that the suspension of time can only occur in the theatre of the mind.

Questions raised

There are two questions that *The Encounter* raises that are related to the concept of a virtual dimension and a theatre of the mind. Firstly, does the use of technology in the production display how intimacy can be used by someone to manipulate and be subversively didactic? As one audience member described, "he just gradually sucks you in so that you become part of it."[72] The actor's under-distanced proximity to the audience can be unnerving in *The Encounter*. As explored above, when the audience members put their headphones on and the collagist entered into their minds, some felt invaded, creepy and shocked. The actor is not on the stage but inside your head. Once accustomed to this intimacy, the characters weave their story, relying on and, perhaps, manipulating the sensory and the imaginary. Simon's use of metatheatrical techniques punctuates the story to constantly remind the audience that they are in a theatre listening to an actor. He prompts them to be mindful. From this perspective, the intimacy, should an audience member take up the invitation, is consensual. Furthermore, the most contested discourse in the production – the questioning of Western materialism – is played out on stage, not in the mind. Simon rips into a table on stage with a hammer. This is a visual, not a cognitive experience. From one perspective, the method of delivery of "whispering into the mind" though a very intimate experience can be seen as didactic and some kind of hegemony. As one young man described, "to have someone actually speaking inside your head like it's your own thoughts is really weird."[73] Yet Simon prepares and always cautions the audience member. Additionally, Simon welcomes contrary opinions. He made it clear in the interview that he was not unhappy that people walked out or were insulted by some of the production's discourses, but rather was encouraged that it made people think and that they responded actively. He believes strongly that without the audience, theatre does not exist:

> Without their collaboration, the thing doesn't exist, they need to actively engage: really actively. Otherwise it doesn't exist anywhere, it doesn't come to life.

Actor and audience collaborate to bring *The Encounter* to life in the virtual dimension.

The virtual dimension can, however, be seen to be problematic theatrically. Is *The Encounter* good storytelling or does it cross some terrain in the imagination that disrupts what theatre is? Why do people close their eyes? Rather than questioning the foundations and purposes of intermedial theatre, this second question is raised to address the central concern in this monograph: the conversations in the electric air. As one audience member described: "You were there, you were there with him constantly. You were meeting all these people and characters and situations just from what he was describing."[74] If the conversations are occurring in the theatre of the mind between the characters and the individual audience member who, it has been established, sometimes feels "all alone," is the atmosphere in the theatre relevant in this production at all? Unlike other theatrical productions, *The Encounter* exists in the theatre of the mind rather than pervading the physical auditorium of the theatre.

When questioned about the atmosphere created in the space of a theatrical production, Simon described it as follows:

> If you can *(pause)* be sensitive to who's there in the room, then that is when what you might call the magic, but what I might call the meaning, is created, as this implied, embodied, set of ideas and vision, emerge in the empty space between you.[75]

For Simon, the magic is in the meaning. While the physical air in the empty space between the actor and the audience members may not be as charged as in a traditional production where community is built in triangulation among the audience members and with the actors, in *The Encounter*, the magic occurs in the meaning-making in the virtual dimension of the theatre of the mind of each individual.

In a traditional theatrical event often, as Böhme argues, a set can create an atmosphere.[76] We feel the sultry, suffocating atmosphere of a cramped apartment in New Orleans as the lights come up in the opening scene of *A Streetcar Named Desire*. Or we sense the bitter, cold austerity of wartime in Germany in a set depicting an historical period in *Mother Courage*.[77] In *The Encounter* there is no set design. As Simon explains,

> It's a bit like going to the middle of Macy's and seeing the whole place stripped out and there's a farmer with boots and mud, offering you some carrots with clay on them. You go "What the fuck is this? Where's my bed linen? Where's my bed and all that sort of stuff? Well I'm not staying here. There's nothing there, it's all gone."[78]

From the commencement of the piece, the audience are aware that this is not a traditional theatre experience. There are no visual clues. The audience will have to contribute from their own meaning-making to create an environment. That, in itself, can be seen to contribute to the atmosphere of the physical theatre. Yet where the visual has disappointed, the aural was quick to gratify.[79] For many if not all, the aural became the theatrical experience: "I'm reverberating from the power of it. Literally the sound of it is reverberating in my mind."[80]

The individual experience of a kind of virtual atmosphere can be seen as much more of a sensory experience than that of traditional theatre. As Böhme argues, atmosphere is always related to a bodily feeling in an environment.[81] In *The Encounter*, the aural and the visual, embodied in the collagist's actions and presence, work together to create the virtual atmosphere. When the collagist blows into the ear of the audience member, their skin prickles, it is a physical sensation. When they hear the mosquito sounds of the Amazon or listen to the crinkling of the leaves as McIntyre runs, they "attune" to the atmosphere of the jungle. The audience's encounter with *The Encounter* is more immersive than it is co-creative, more aural than it is visual and more intimate than it is collective. The conversations between actor and audience occur in the virtual dimension in the theatre of the mind.

Extending the conversation: theatre of the mind

There were two audience members that referred to *The Encounter* as a "theatre of the mind." I explore this interesting concept further here. All theatre is, in a sense, a theatre of the mind. Yet in the absence of many visual stimuli, *The Encounter* predominantly unfurled in the audience members minds. Images of insect-ridden Amazon jungles, lost tribes and treacherous rivers created a dreamscape of images for the audience members to co-create in their minds. *The Encounter* pushed the boundaries of theatre in a direction mainstream theatregoers would seldom have encountered. Something is gained and something is lost in this. Just as Western civilisation has colonised jungles, Simon is colonising new vistas of experience. Simon is colonising our minds. This has the advantage of exploring new vehicles for theatrical experiences but has the danger of invading and perhaps even dismantling our private environments without our consent.[82] This is a step beyond the willing suspension of disbelief in traditional theatre productions. Exploring new vistas needs new theories and brings up consent issues.

If we are successful in creating these new vistas, where encounters do indeed happen in the mind, then the experience has the potential to be an electric virtual air experience for audience members. The following illustrates, perhaps, this potential. One of the interviewed audience members at the London Barbican production was visually impaired.[83] The first comment he proffered was that "it was really good to see a bit of theatre which actually didn't rely on you being able to see it." Due to the reliance on aural storytelling, the other 1157 audience members had no extra visual cues to navigate the piece. When asked the question "what was it like when he was in your head?" the response was predictable: "It was pretty normal for me. Pretty normal to be honest. I mean, that's how I take in my information. So, actually probably no different from my normal day." Since expectations of familiar theatrical generic tropes did not need to be overcome, this audience member lived the experience from the commencement of the performance and described his encounter with *The Encounter* as "jaw dropping." In many ways, his theatrical experience was more intense than those around him. He described one moment during the performance:

> Funnily enough, the person next to me was taking their coat off and put their hand on my shoulder. It was sort of like "Ooh, aww! He's just touched me!" So the panning and the sound of the actor inside my head was utterly convincing.

The theatrical blended with his quotidian. The slippage between the real and the fictitious world was surprising for this audience member but also hyperreal. Simon and the other character's voices inside his head were "very, very, very effective. Very, very plausible." What was most significant about his experience was that the theatre of the mind was described in terms of a soundscape. He described how he lives his life in terms of a soundscape: "I'm trying to make sense out of the soundscape around me." *The Encounter* emerged as another soundscape to experience and make sense of.

I found a new way into the production after hearing these comments. The theatre experienced in *The Encounter* was a soundscape not a landscape. The collision of text and imagination in the minds of the audience members builds that soundscape, but only in the virtual dimension in the theatre of the mind. The magic of theatre in *The Encounter*, as Simon elucidated above, is in the meaning-making, not in being overwhelmed by highly detailed and representative landscape sets or even "clever" minimalist set designs. The audience may have to overcome preconceptions and work a little harder to enter into the soundscape without any visual cues, but the rewards are rich and sensorially acute. Furthermore, just as Simon and Complicité deliberately disrupted the audience's Western sense of time, the absence of the crutch of a perceived landscape heightened the intimacy and revelation of the story and rendered it, and the conversations across the footlights, all the more potent. As one young audience member described, because of the "Intimacy with the sound [...] It felt like just you and him having a conversation."[84]

Notes

1 Complicité, *The Encounter* (London: Nick Hern Books, 2016), 7.
2 Audience responses from *The Encounter* audience interviews at the Broadway production (October 2016) and Adelaide Fringe Festival (March 2017) conducted by the author.
3 Richard Katz is the stand-by performer and performed the play in the Adelaide production that I attended.
4 Known by its acronym ASMR. See Thomas Hostler and Theresa Veltri, "More Than a Feeling: Autonomous Sensory Meridian Response (ASMR) Is Characterized by Reliable Changes in Affect and Physiology," *PLoS One* 13, no. 6 (2018): 1–18.
5 Complicité, *The Encounter*, 47.
6 The interviews were vox-pops interviews which are traditionally short interviews with members of the public. It is for this reason that the audience members are not identified.
7 Simon McBurney, personal interview, 28 October 2016.
8 Bert O. States, *Great Reckonings in Little Rooms: On the Phenomenology of Theater* (Berkeley: California UP, 1985), 123.
9 Ibid.
10 Audience interview from London.
11 Ibid.
12 Simon McBurney, Kirsty Housley, Victoria Gould, Gareth Fry, Helen Skiera, Pete Malkin, Jemima James and Caroline Moores, "Making *The* Encounter," Workshop Notes, 29 September 2014, accessed 19 June 2018, www.complicite.org/encounterresource/map/rehearsal-notes-29-9-14.html.
13 Simon McBurney, personal interview, 28 October 2016.
14 Audience interview from Adelaide.
15 Audience interview from New York.

16 Audience interview from London.

17 Ibid.

18 Audience interview from Adelaide.

19 Wolfgang Iser, "The Reading Process: A Phenomenological Approach," in *Reader Response Criticism*, ed. Jane P. Tompkins (Baltimore: Johns Hopkins UP, 1980), 284, 288.

20 Ibid.

21 Simon McBurney, personal interview, 28 October 2016.

22 Audience interviews from New York.

23 At least six different audience members from both productions that I saw described their "in the jungle" experiences as "visceral."

24 Audience interview from London.

25 Audience interview from Adelaide.

26 Simon McBurney, personal interview, 28 October 2016.

27 Ibid.

28 Complicité, *The Encounter*, 48.

29 Audience interview from New York.

30 Simon McBurney, personal interview, 28 October 2016.

31 Complicité, *The Encounter*, 7.

32 Audience interviews from Adelaide.

33 Complicité, *The Encounter*, 9.

34 Audience interview from Adelaide.

35 Simon McBurney, personal interview, 28 October 2016.

36 Edward Bullough, "'Psychical Distance' as a Factor in Art and an Aesthetic Principle," *British Journal of Psychology* 5, no. 2 (1912): 94, 95.

37 Audience interview from New York.

38 Audience interviews from Adelaide.

39 Audience interviews from New York.

40 Audience interviews from London.

41 Simon McBurney, personal interview, 28 October 2016.

42 Ibid.

43 Ibid.

44 Audience interview from London.

45 For a discussion of emotional contagion, see Caroline Heim, *Audience as Performer: The Changing Role of Theatre Audiences in the Twenty-First Century* (London and New York: Routledge, 2016): 22.

46 Audience interview from New York.

47 Audience interview from Adelaide.

48 Audience interview from London.

49 Simon is referring to the binaural head that he has on stage through which he communicated with the audience.

50 Simon McBurney, personal interview, 28 October 2016.

51 Ibid.

52 Audience interviews from Adelaide.

53 Similar to ASMR. See note 4.

54 Simon McBurney, personal interview, 28 October 2016.

55 Sanford Meisner and Dennis Longwell, *Sanford Meisner on Acting* (New York: Random House, 1987), 98–100.

56 Complicité, *The Encounter*, 61.

57 Audience interview from London.

58 Simon McBurney, personal interview, 28 October 2016.

59 Audience interviews from Adelaide.

60 Audience interview from London.

61 Audience interview from New York.

62 Audience interviews from Adelaide.

63 Complicité, *The Encounter*, 56.

64 Ibid., 25.

65 Ibid.

66 Ibid., 48.

67 Audience interviews from Adelaide.

68 Audience interview from New York.

69 Ibid.

70 Ibid.

71 Audience interview from London.

72 Ibid.

73 Ibid.

74 Ibid.

75 Simon McBurney, personal interview, 28 October 2016.

76 Gernot Böhme, *The Aesthetics of Atmospheres*, ed. Jean-Paul Thibaud (London and New York: Routledge, 2017), 28.

77 There are, of course, many exceptions to detailed set designs depending on the creative's choices as we saw in the *Heisenberg* case study.

78 Simon McBurney, personal interview, 28 October 2016.

79 It is important to note that visual images were added later in the run of the production and consisted of lighting effects projected onto the back wall of the stage. These effects were predominantly abstract images evoking the landscape. I did not see the production with the visuals, but my research assistants at the Barbican production did. Interestingly, no comments were made about the visuals in the London interviews.

80 Audience interview from London.

81 Böhme, *Aesthetics of Atmospheres*, 1.

82 This is one of the aspects that needs further interrogation in the immersive theatre genre.

83 This interview, which took place at the Barbican production in London, was longer than all others and extra questions were asked.

84 Audience interview from Adelaide.

6

HUNGER. PEER GYNT: A THIRST FOR CONVERSATIONS

Deutsches Theater, October 2018. Thick mist suffocates the stage. We make out only the forms of the actors in tulle and tattoos silhouetted against brushstrokes on a massive canvas. The huge canvas overwhelms the stage. The actors are tattooed on nearly every area of their bare skin. There is no colour onstage, only black and white. The mist pours over the *Grenzland*, the borderland between stage and audience. Musical rhythms shake the walls of the theatre: sensuous, blatant, invasive. Light beams are imprisoned in suspended rays, attempting to penetrate the mist. Some bodies on stage contort in a primitive dance. Others speak chunks of Ibsen or Hamsun text. Static and impulse simultaneously drive the piece forward and interrupt its progress. The actors' and audience's senses are overpowered by the intense visual, auditory, oral and felt atmosphere. It can be felt on the skin, it reverberates in the chest and it seduces the eyes. The world of the stage immediately pervades the world of the audience. For the hour and a quarter before interval, the actors and audience are in the same room. By the end of interval, if you can call it that, over one-third of the audience have walked out: why?

This is Sebastian Hartmann's *Hunger. Peer Gynt* which premiered at the Deutsches Theater on the 19 October 2018. In the last chapter, we looked at a production where the actor seemingly crept off the stage and into the "theatre of the mind" of each audience member. The spatial atmosphere onstage was replaced by a virtual atmosphere as a powerful narrative conjured images through the medium of storytelling in Complicité's *The Encounter*. In this chapter, we consider a production where the onstage spatial atmosphere is the protagonist itself. We move from the mind to the sensory, from narrative to non-narrative and from relationship with the actor to little if no relationship. How does this very visceral, corporeal experience change the electric air and the consequent experience for the actors and the audience members?

This case study of *Hunger. Peer Gynt* concludes this book where I started, with a discussion of atmosphere in a production that uses the nebulous element of atmosphere in a thematic way, "tuning" the environment onstage and in the audience. An overview of the production and project is followed by an analysis of atmosphere as *Stimmung* and the production's atmosphere from the actors' and audience's perspectives.

The production and the project

Hunger. Peer Gynt directed by Sebastian Hartmann is based on the texts and, I would argue, atmospheres of Knut Hamsun's 1890 novel *Hunger* and Henrik Ibsen's 1867 play *Peer Gynt*. At the commencement of rehearsals, the ten actors were asked to select texts from the novel or play that resonated intellectually or emotionally with them. Each actor had a suite of excerpts that formed the text of the play and were delivered as monologues randomly throughout the evening's perform-ance. Similarly, around 30 lighting cues were selected in each performance from 100 lighting states by the designer to reflect the onstage mood. Music selection and cues replicated this pattern. A light box onstage projected an artwork by Tilo Baumgärtel onto a colossal canvas which the actors painted, re-painted and ruined at different stages in the evening. The production lasted between three and four hours, depending on the shape of the evening. Nothing was dictated, yet everything was dictated. As Hartmann argued, "the players[1] have to have a concentration that they are not used to in their normal everyday playing life. [...] All players need to be constantly alert to whether or not what they are doing is right or wrong. Or wrong."[2] As the actors I interviewed emphasised, the play was not improvised, the structure was improvised. One of the actors, Natali Seelig, remarked,

> Everybody's acting quite *au Tag*. The great thing is, we all have our texts, that we were supposed to go and say in the moment. You decide to do some-thing – move, or speak your text – but there is always something happening that changes your plan [...] which is actually great because that's life.[3]

Although the actors improvised the structure, there were rules regarding what was right and wrong. A seemingly strange imperative in a play that aims mostly to live "in the moment."[4] Yet even the colour palette of black and white reflected this binary.

In the programme notes Hartmann argued, "I do not need a plot in theatre and no main characters, because when I look around, I realise that life does not have them."[5] One of the most contentious issues regarding the play for the audience was that *Hunger. Peer Gynt* had no narrative. As the production's dramaturg, Claus Caesar explained "Hartmann distrusts narratives. [...] for him this evening shouldn't aim so much into the consciousness, not so much into the mind, but rather into the sub-conscious."[6] The monologues reflected the motifs of *Hunger* and *Peer Gynt* of the struggle with death, with God, with hunger and with meaning.

After opening in October, the production was staged three times that month. I attended two of these performances. As part of the case study, I conducted in-depth interviews with five of the actors. The actors were all part of the Deutsches Theater 41-member ensemble and each had been working as a member of the ensemble from between one and eight years. Two of the actors, Linda Pöppel and Manuel Harder, had worked with Hartmann on many of his previous productions and had been part of his original ensemble in Leipzig. In a seemingly utopic situation, German actors working as part of ensembles in the major German theatres have the luxury of continuous employment[7] and a stable income. As such, many have the daily opportunity of developing not only their craft, but also their artistry. The interviews, almost from their commencement, included conversations about aesthetics, philosophical concepts and ruminations on human nature that are regularly explored in their work. The actors are more than players, they are artists. Especially in a play such as *Hunger. Peer Gynt* which celebrates each actor's vision. As Caesar argues,

> because [the actors] are, so to speak, their texts, they also represent them differently. It's not a character text that someone has written for them, such as a Shakespeare or a Schiller it's, so to speak, their own texts, their own concerns.[8]

In *Hunger. Peer Gynt*, the raw emotions of the actors were exposed, making them all the more vulnerable. Yet they were very secure in their vulnerability and willing to take more risks. The actors I interviewed exuded a unique confidence I had not yet encountered in other actor interviews. Secure in their positions, secure in their contributions as artists, in a seeming oxymoron, they displayed a confident vulnerability.

On the other side of the footlights, I conducted 21 interviews with audience members, 11 of which walked out during the "interval" or before and 10 which stayed for the entire performance. Two of the audience members were recruited from a *Vorbesprechen*, a pre-show talk given before each performance by Caesar. The others I approached as they were leaving the theatre. I also arranged an interval interview with a young man I was sitting next to. He left abruptly during the first act, so I did not get this opportunity.

Berlin theatres do not have subscriptions, so each production, rather than each theatre, competes for an audience. German dramatic theatre dates back to the tenth century. As most theatres in Germany are heavily state subsidised, the Deutsches Theater included, theatregoers are significantly invested in their theatre and have a strong sense of ownership. This can be seen as a different kind of "subscription" yet one that, similar to the New Yorker subscribers interviewed in Chapter 4, produces discerning, astute armchair critics that have much to say about productions and have no qualms about walking out of a production. It should be noted that German ticket prices are also significantly lower than New York productions and this changes the relationship of the audience member to the theatre and the production from consumer to patron.

Hunger. Peer Gynt cannot be discussed without talking about the two largest issues confronting the actors and the audience: atmosphere and the walk-out. Both were the outstanding signifiers of the evening and one informed the other. Both affected the actors and audience and their relationship/conversation. The actors and audience members were asked questions about the atmosphere, how they felt about their relationship with other actors/audience members and how they related to the performance text itself. The actors were asked how they felt about audience members walking out and audience members that walked out were asked why they walked out.

Stimmung

For *Hunger. Peer Gynt*, the word "atmosphere" no longer seems sufficient to describe the mood created onstage or in the audience. For this chapter, I adopt the German word *Stimmung* which in contemporary parlance is translated into English as mood, spirit, atmosphere, feeling.[9] German does not replace *Atmosphäre* with *Stimmung*, both words exist in the language.

The actual etymology of *Stimmung* traces back to its usage as a musical term in the sixteenth century: "tuning." Yet, as Erik Wallrup asserts, the likening of a soul to a stringed instrument "sometimes tuned, sometimes out of tune"[10] can be traced back to the sixth century and it is often seen as a mystical concept.[11] The contemporary understanding, as a mood, atmosphere or feeling, comes from the 1770s.[12] A long history of philosophers, writers and composers – Kant, Schiller, Schubert, Hegel, Strauss, Stockhausen, among many others – explored *Stimmung* through aesthetics, philosophy and psychology. Jean Sebelius in his diary entries highlights the relationship between music, mood and landscape.[13] Martin Heidegger discusses how artworks, landscapes and time "attune" our way of being.[14] William Stern was one of the first philosophers and psychologists to conflate atmosphere and *Stimmung* in 1935. As Friedlind Riedel explains, "Stern argued that a feeling of familiarity, for instance, would be of 'completely "atmospheric" nature; it is a total mood [*Gesamtstimmung*] in which the special affective tonings of people, things, and events are indistinguishably embedded.'"[15]

Of particular note is *Stimmung*'s association with empathy. The dominant aesthetics of the period between 1890 and 1910 was *Einfühlungstheorie*, the theory of empathy. The creation of empathy through tuning with an atmosphere, landscape or even an object or person was seen as a primary element of *Einfühlung*.[16] This approach was not dissimilar to the contemporary theory of limbic resonance, which explains how love and empathy work among humans. The empathic conversation across the footlights, between actors and even – through emotional contagion – among audience members, is one of the greatest sources of pleasure in live theatre. As Michael Chekhov argues, in the theatre two types of atmospheres are created: the atmosphere created by theatrical effects – lights, sets, colours, music – and the *Stimmung* created through empathic conversation, or attunement between actors and between actors and audience.[17] Both are explored in this chapter.

Of interest is the contemporary understanding of the word in common German parlance. I have now asked eight native German speakers, that are fluent in English, how they would translate *Stimmung*.[18] They have all found it impossible and several disagreed with each other most fervently. All understood its musical association. In English translation, *Stimmung* is, perhaps, a conflation of tuning, mood and atmosphere.

Stimmung as tuning is the focus of this chapter. The original musical connotation of tuning is upheld, but in relation to the tuning of moods and spaces. Tuning is used in the Heideggerian sense of "attunement." As he writes, "determining our mood is here to be grasped as something attuning us in such and such a way."[19] In his writings on atmospheres, Gernot Böhme also discusses *Stimmung* as an aspect of atmosphere in reference to tuning. He defines atmosphere as "*tuned space*."[20] Böhme argues that,

> The present dominance of light and sound design [in contemporary theatre] creates an acoustic space which tunes the whole performance. At the same time this has made it possible for the art of the stage set to leave the stage itself and spill over into the auditorium or, or even into space itself [creating] "tuned" spaces, that is to say, atmospheres.[21]

Böhme goes on to give a second definition of atmosphere as "the felt presence of something or someone in space."[22] In the theatre, it is more than a felt presence, but an empathic conversation creating the *Stimmung*. Not only did the *Stimmung*, in a very physical way, spill over into the auditorium in *Hunger. Peer Gynt* but the essential tuning of the atmosphere, physical and emotional, spelt the success and demise of the production itself.

In one sense, the *Stimmung* was electric for the entire performance, but for very different reasons than the psychological electricity of *Heisenberg* or the narrative, plot-driven electricity of *The Encounter*. In *Hunger. Peer Gynt*, the absence of an onstage narrative shifted the focus from the performance to the event itself. Actors and audience alike became more self-conscious and their spatial, interpersonal and aesthetic attunement emerged as a quasi-narrative of its own. Their physical tuning to the atmosphere created by the theatrical effects is followed by a discussion of their tuning to the performance piece and each other, and their discord during the walk-out.

Tuning to the space

In his essay on psychical distance, Edward Bullough commences with a vivid description of a fog at sea. He firstly describes its physical properties and the hazards of encountering a fog at sea. He secondly explores how one can concurrently perceive the "abstract" and aesthetic experience of the fog as a source of "delight." The realisation of the latter experience of the fog, in contrast to the initial anxiety felt, "is like a momentary switching on of some new current."[23] This was the experience of *Hunger. Peer Gynt* for all of the actors and some audience members. Both groups were confronted with the physical properties of the atmosphere of the production while synchronously experiencing its aesthetic delights. Interestingly, however, some of the "hazards" of the production were in its aesthetic delivery, as explored further below.

The initial and overwhelming experience that actors and audience of *Hunger. Peer Gynt* were confronted with, was a very immediate, physical atmosphere.[24] Suffocating fog, pulsating musical rhythms and interplays of light assaulted the actors and audience from the commencement of the performance. The heavy fog, which for one actor had a strong smell of a waterpipe drain mixed with oranges[25] was so thick that the actors initially could not see their fellow actors if they were more than two metres away. As actor Elias Arens stated, "the whole production gets its atmosphere from the hazard."[26]

For the actors, this seething, hazardous space was a gift, a "great relief."[27] Actors often use psychological promptings, costumes, makeup, long warm-ups, music or visual inspirations to enter into the worlds of productions. Some arrive at the theatre a few hours before their call time for this purpose. The atmosphere was so immediate in *Hunger. Peer Gynt* that the actors had no need for these provisional stimuli and attuned to the world almost instantaneously. As two of the actors described:

> You don't have to go into a big dramatic atmosphere before you start the show. I just look at my colleagues and then its starting. All the fog, the lighting, the painting, it all helps because it is so strong. It's like another reality.
>
> *Linda Pöppel*

> It brings me into the world, the music and the fog. The music and the dancing and screaming. For me it's like I am completely somewhere else. I'm outside in my normal life and then enter a door to the world. In one second, or five seconds its like *vooooot shhhhhhhh shhhhhhhh ahhhhhhhh!!!* and then I'm there.
>
> *Marcel Kohler*

On a very practical level, in Chekhov's terms, the actors just need to "receive the atmosphere in which [they] find [them]self in."[28] The actors just needed to tune to the physical and sensory atmosphere, the sounds, the smells and it brought the world into being.

Entering into this hazardous world was very powerful and, for some of the actors, quite "trippy."[29] Linda felt it was "a bit like going on a moon mission together"[30] and Manuel described it as "a very dark planet [...] where the atmosphere is a little more extreme than in a real play."[31] This world was, however, for the actors, much more than a stage filled with theatrical effects. As she tuned to the atmosphere, Linda "Actually ha[d] the feeling that [she] enter[ed] a room without time and without place. And from there the world start[ed] to think."[32] Manuel also found that the physical atmosphere created an "organic room"[33] that had a mind of its own. In many ways, the physical atmosphere, at the commencement of the performance particularly, became the sensuous director of the production for the actors. Although there were certain set rules onstage, the arrangement of the play was improvised: the moments when the texts were spoken, certain music played, the lighting effects all were chosen to go with the flow of what was impulsively happening on the stage at that time to "celebrate the moment."[34] Each actor had a variety of costumes in their dressing room that they could choose from to help create the *mise-en-scène* of the moment. Therefore, the effects, the degree of fog, the type of music, the way the light hit a certain part of the stage, determined much of the actors' movements, choices and performances. The actors had to tune very quickly to the physical atmosphere in order to create the performance text. This is, perhaps, part of what Linda was alluding to when she said, "the world started to think."

If the atmosphere emerged as a director for the actors, then it became the protagonist of overwhelming presence for the audience. The audience response to the physical landscape that unfolded before them onstage and spilled into the auditorium was, for the majority, the most potent experience of the evening. Similar to the actors, they immediately responded to the multitude of "impressions."[35] The atmosphere affected their mood and feelings. If, as Hermann Schmitz argues, feelings are "poured forth atmospheres [...] which visit (haunt) the body which receives them"[36] then the atmosphere of *Hunger. Peer Gynt* had a consciousness of its own that deeply affected the audience:

> I will dream of this tonight: the very impressive pictures. It burns in your brain when you see this.
>
> *JJ*

> You get the feeling that you want to scream.
>
> *Fabian*

> Very depressing, disturbing in a way.
>
> *Felix*

This haunting impression imposed on the audience[37] was made all the more vivid by the music. The music ranged in genre from heavy techno to opera. It was the acoustic atmosphere above all else that impacted the audience deeply or alienated them. Böhme argues that music shapes the way we react in a space and "directly intervenes in our physical economy."[38] Audience member Felix observed the way the music not only shaped the atmosphere, but also how it intervened onstage:

> The music had a huge impact. I think it's very well chosen. It reflects the people around who are screaming. It is all around you. It's shaking from the walls. The actors keep moving towards the walls. They are so helpless. The music adds to the atmosphere, to the intensity.[39]

Conversely, Karin found the music far too confronting and "too difficult to listen to."[40] The acoustic atmosphere created during *Hunger. Peer Gynt*, which made the walls vibrate, and was dissonant to some and captivating to others, was one of the largest contributors to the electric air of the production.

While many audience members found the atmosphere incredibly dark, some enjoyed the visual feast. Lara "found it very interesting, visually." She went on to describe how the visuals affected her emotions even giving the atmosphere a rating:

> It was stunning. It was really dark and mysterious but not too gothic. I was very moved by the stunning lighting and the design, but not by the words. The acting was great. The atmosphere: this was five stars. Visually it was beautiful.[41]

Conversely, other audience members were only affected by the words. Many of the excerpts from *Hunger* and *Peer Gynt* were either heavy with imagery or referred to *Stimmung* such as "The tranquil, pregnant night was starting to affect me."[42] For Paul "it was much more words that were painted than the movement of the actors. I was concentrating on the words. They were like pictures themselves. There were more words than sentences. This was the most intensive part for me."[43] Sensory, acoustic, visual and auditory atmospheres pervaded the space creating the complex, rich and intrusive *Stimmung*. It was, however, the search for meaning that preoccupied the audience for most of the evening. There was a constant struggle occurring between accepting the performance as an artwork in surrendering to the physical atmosphere or trying to make meaning of a non-narrative performance.

Tuning to the artwork

As much has been discussed about the audience empathising with or making meaning of the aesthetic artwork, this section focuses only on the *effort* undertaken by audience members to make meaning of the performance piece as this becomes of particular relevance in the exploration of the walk-out below. The audience members went to great effort to try and make meaning of the production. Henrik expressed that he "wanted to get into the world. I tried to get into it because I knew we would be seeing it for a long time [...] but no."[44] Reiner continued to search for meaning: "There are several parts for me that have no meaning. Sometimes the actors would repeat it to become a meaning, but I could not find it. [...] Some things you find sense in, others not." He finally deduced that "It is just good to look at."[45] It was, however, in this surrender to the *Stimmung* that the performance began to take on new meanings for another audience member, Bruno:

> I was trying to make sense of the whole play. At some point I stopped looking too much for a meaning. I started to enjoy the whole multi-media of the spectacle. Then it gained some aesthetic quality. The acting, the movements, often the synchronicity of three actors, the music, the painting in the background, the lighting. Then I switch off the brain and just enjoyed what I saw and heard and felt. That brings a different quality to it. I think that was the part I enjoyed the most, when I got into a sort of flow. I guess that was when

I was in the most passive state also, the most "left out" state, just sitting there. There's music, there's movement, there's people saying something, but maybe I like taking a few steps back and taking it all in without thinking too much.[46]

Gabe had a similar experience:

I live on my own and I sometimes need some sound to go to sleep, a meditation, and I think this is what it is tonight. To come into a certain state of mind. It's not important what they are saying, the impression is the most important.[47]

For Bruno and Gabe, the surrender to a meditative state or a flow was essential for their enjoyment of the piece. They had to modify their expectations, expand their horizons and tune to the piece that was before them rather than their preconceptions of what theatre "should" be. Preconceptions that have been built over centuries of theatregoing. Others saw the production as far too much work for them as audience members and found the experience of trying to make meaning "exhausting." Almost every audience member interviewed was looking for meaning but could not find it.

Two of the actors interviewed that had worked with Hartmann before, Linda and Manuel, were familiar with performing in a non-narrative piece so they found no difficultly in tuning to the performance piece and the improvised structure. Others initially struggled. Similar to some audience members, Elias found the process "Exhausting. Especially the way to get there to where it is now, which is still on the way." He continued,

I found it very, very disturbing how much it confronts me with myself. As a director Hartmann just leaves you to it. He may say, "there's this subject I'd like you to treat." Then he leaves you on your own. You are confronted a lot with your own boundaries, inner boundaries. I got quite tormented. During rehearsals and performances everything is possible. You pick parts out and it gets difficult to see if they are all relevant parts, because it all just evaporates.

When asked if the process made him feel insecure he replied "Insecure? I felt completely lost. It was rough times to say the least." What he received in the "aftermath" of this very difficult process was, however,

exceptional, because it breaks so much with routine: with the way of working and the way of thinking about theatre. It really feels like a rebirth. Somewhere in between rehearsals and onstage it gave back some belief in the job.[48]

Natali also had this revelation, but straight away. She found the process "exciting. Hartmann said 'Take the parts that you like' to me it was a gift, I was astonished. Take the parts that you like?"[49]

Yet within this freedom, there were rules that had to be observed. As Manuel describes:

> When the world starts it is full of clear regulations and directions and there are some things that cannot happen and are forbidden to do and we are reduced down to the rules. Not everything is possible, for example if the fog comes and the atmosphere comes you can on one hand react ironically if you want to, or act comedically, but that is forbidden. But, if you have, for example, Wagner music that starts when you are on stage then you have to react like Wagner, you cannot just say "oh Wagner" you have to react like Wagner. You react on that high level, or react on a low level, as necessary, depending on the music of the moment.

He was quick to clarify, however, that although "the production is full of decisions [they] are not like strict rules," they are what he called "feeling decisions."[50] These feeling decisions required an intense concentration from the actors. Rather than getting caught up in a prescribed imaginary world as in narrative plays, they had to "always calculate whether this is the moment [to speak or move, or] look for the impulse. And that's the exhausting part. It's always a stop/go tension."[51] The actors had to "listen to the emotion and the text that the other actor is bringing in to the moment [...] and then [they] have to give a counterpart to that: build on it or disturb it."[52] Rather than becoming identified with the character they were playing as they were, as Caesar argued, ostensibly playing themselves, the actors had to have what Böhme calls a mindful physical presence which is essentially "The experience of one's own physical presence" in the atmosphere of a space. In that space there are sensations: "We sense expanse or confines, we sense elation or depression, proximity or distance, we sense openness or entrapment, we sense intimations of motion."[53] These were many of the sensations experienced by the actors of *Hunger. Peer Gynt* as described in the interviews.

In a state of mindful physical presence and tuning to the physical atmosphere, in many ways the actors had no need to tune to the performance artwork as they were the co-creators of that artwork. The actors were very industrious in this. There was always much activity onstage: delivering monologues, changing costumes, creating a new movement or dance, moving the light box projector around the stage, moving ladders, repeating another actor's dance, painting the huge canvas. This labour created its own unique *Stimmung*. Yet, for the actors, this was not meaningless industry, as Natali described,

> If we are painting, it is symbolic, we have something to do. We are working on our life, we are working on cities, we are working on biographies or homes or families: life. We are exploiting the world to build and create.[54]

While tuning to the physical atmosphere was of paramount importance to create the performance artwork, the actors also had to attune to each other as an ensemble.

Tuning to each other

In rehearsals, actors work very closely together as an ensemble. As explored in Chapter 2, some actors feel that the cast become a family or, at least, a temporary community. In the repertory theatres of Germany, some actors have worked together with each other for years, and are very much in tune with each other. As Natali, who has been part of the Deutsches Theater ensemble for nine years, emphasised,

> It takes about three years [to feel like a community]. In the beginning it is the outside part, the surface of the other actors that you see. After three years you trust each other. You can open up more. It's more fun. You have worked with each other. You have built up more. You can go deeper.[55]

And deeper they went in the seven weeks of rehearsals of *Hunger. Peer Gynt*. There was a closeness and almost as Linda described "tenderness" among the group members during rehearsals. As Natali emphasised, "During rehearsals it was very intimate, sensitive, it felt like a present."[56] Linda felt that "if we are quite close as actors, if we are quite sensitive with each other, then the connection is extremely strong."[57] During rehearsals for *Hunger. Peer Gynt*, a kind of communitas was formed between the actors, some of which transferred to the ensemble performance onstage. The rehearsal space had a *Stimmung* of its own.

Since the actors do not play individual characters onstage,[58] the group became what Linda described as "a bigger consciousness that is building itself."[59] The co-creation and group consciousness changed the relationship between the actors entirely. As Marcel Kohler so deftly articulated:

> During the acting of the role onstage there is almost no relationship between single actors, because we are always individuals. It's like a solo play for ten players on the stage. Almost as if we are a gang or a group. I do not mean that in any critical way, I think it's very positive, because it creates a kind of mutual feeling where you support each other and feel responsible and see how you can help each other in the play.[60]

The actors worked as a group by tuning to each other. Elias describes how he tunes to the group:

> I relate to the other actors as bodies onstage. Of course as individuals, of course I know them. But I never see characters. I see impulses[61] and I see relations but very momentous ones. It's very abstract. Another body may be standing two or three metres away and it creates a tension. I respond to that tension.[62]

The kind of tension sensed only when the actors are in a state of mindful physical presence. There was no individual character-to-character relationship, but there was certainly a body-to-body relationship that created a group consciousness that accreted into a form of collective effervescence in some of the more highly charged moments onstage.

In this seemingly ideal communal situation for the actors, what happens when there is an intruder? An entity that has not been present in the safe cocoon of the rehearsal space and is now introduced to the production. The intruder in *Hunger. Peer Gynt* was introduced to the cast at the *Premiere*, the opening night,[63] and was not an individual, but a group: the audience.

The introduction of the audience to the cast of *Hunger. Peer Gynt* changed the dynamics of the piece entirely. It created a friction onstage that was palpable and felt by all the actors. Since it worked more to alienate, this was a different kind of electricity than that co-created between actors and audience, but it sent sparks through the ensemble that would compromise their group consciousness for that performance. The ensemble was out of tune. Linda describes the friction:

> I was quite looking forward to the *Premiere*. But now there is this audience factor and so there are actors who feel [...] the adrenaline does a lot and everybody reacts differently. But then it started and I felt from [some] colleagues this energy. I felt it so strongly that I completely lost the fun. I felt myself being pressed into a narrative. Not for the whole evening, but I had the feeling that [some] colleagues built for themselves a narrative. I was so angry because I felt that was an immense misunderstanding of the whole work. I then came quickly to the conclusion that it is because of the audience. Because there is the audience, and because it is the *Premiere* and then there are all the people from the theatre and from the newspapers. The experiment [of this play] is something else. I was quite disappointed really. [...] Afterwards I was crying for an hour. I was in my dressing room with a colleague and I was so mad. And that's something I think about. Why was I so angry?[64]

Linda's investment in the ensemble and her sense of the artistic integrity of the non-narrativity of the performance piece was so strong that the she almost felt betrayed when group members played to the audience or tried to create a narrative. Linda was not alone. Every other actor interviewed felt some degree of loss at the *Premiere*:

> We lost it a bit on opening night because everyone was confronted by an insecurity. [...] It was very tense onstage, a very tense performance.
>
> *Elias Arens*

> I didn't like the *Premiere*. We didn't have this intimate situation in the group. Every day of rehearsals I loved then because something new happened. It was poetic what happened, it was great. On opening night everyone pretends what happens. You can't be open, it's not possible.
>
> *Natali Seelig*

> It was interesting in the *Premiere* when we first had an audience: it was a completely different show. […] We were no longer free or cosy with each other. We weren't playing or having fun anymore.
>
> *Marcel Kohler*

The presence of the audience seemingly severed the group connection. There were various reasons proffered by the actors for this: the actor's own insecurity, the role of adrenaline, ego, the need to pretend or overact and the need to fulfil or satisfy audience expectations by creating a narrative. This last issue is of most significance to the discussion of the walk-out explored below.

Working as an ensemble builds a strong sense of community *Stimmung* onstage for the actors. As Linda emphasised, "I'm always an ensemble player. I don't really believe in protagonist structures. And that's something why I'm completely freaking out [after the *Premiere*]: this piece is about being ensemble. I lost my faith in community."[65] This began to change for subsequent performances as actors aligned more with the ensemble again to try and recreate the intimacy they had experienced in the rehearsals. For the *Premiere*, however, the actors were not in tune and this discord clearly broke the ensemble community.

Interestingly, on the other side of the footlights, this was largely unnoticed.[66] Certainly by the majority of the *Premiere* critics who found the play to be an extraordinary triumph. The *Daily Level* alluded, perhaps, to some of the strain: "An enormous tension lies in this strong ensemble, which also expends itself physically."[67] What is of more interest, however, is the effect the actors' group consciousness and the *Stimmung* of the entire theatrical event had on the audience members: dividing some, uniting others and creating a group self-consciousness rarely experienced in the theatre. This occurred during both of the performances I attended: the two performances after the *Premiere*. It was clear from the actors' comments that the actors and the audience inhabited two separate worlds.

In this twenty-first century, in most traditional, Western, mainstream theatres, there are unwritten rules for audiences: keep quiet when the actors are speaking; sit in your seat for the entire performance; do not use any technology; when the lights come up halfway through the performance, it is time to leave the theatre for interval; applaud at the end of the performance. All of these rules were broken during *Hunger. Peer Gynt*, and at times, as Bruno described, "some sort of anarchy broke out"[68] in the auditorium. Although audiences customarily tune to each other through their emotional contagion as expressed in laughter, tears and applause, the attunement that manifested in the auditorium of the Deutsches Theater during *Hunger. Peer Gynt,* was altogether different and a form of rebellion in itself.

With the absence of a narrative, exposed to an overwhelming spectacle, and with seemingly little help from the actors who appeared to live only in their world, audience members looked to each other for respite, understanding, answers and meaning. As Henrik argued, "I'm looking for meaning and defending my meaning against other people's impressions."[69] There was a disturbance combined with a fascination that spread from person to person and by "interval" had pervaded the atmosphere. It emerged almost like a collective effervescence or, perhaps, a collective disturbance. This uncanny *Stimmung* created a self-consciousness in the audience. By interval several groups had already left the theatre and as Bruno described,

> The intermission was a situation I have never experienced in the theatre. The audience didn't know what to do. The doors were opening, some light was coming on, so that is a typical sign. Either a break or the end, which also was difficult to determine. But then the action was going on onstage so some people were sitting there while others were going. I found it quite interesting and a little unsettling [...] Some sort of anarchy broke out which I liked. There were people speaking to other people behind them in the rows, people checking their mobiles all while there was still action happening onstage. It was also a bit upsetting: people were saying "what's happening, is it finished?" [...] There were conflicting messages, we were trying to interpret what to do. People were asking "well what do you make of it?"[70]

The confusion about audience etiquette and the seeming abandonment of audience "rules" made some audience members very insecure. They wanted to "do the right thing or behave correctly."[71] They turned to each other for understanding, guidance and camaraderie. In many ways they formed an isolated community of their own.

During the two performances I attended, I sat in one of the two balconies to observe the audience and sense the *Stimmung*. At the commencement of each performance, audience members sat, almost in a stupor: entranced, overwhelmed and mesmerised by the spectacle unfolding before them. From around 45 minutes into the performance, I observed a general agitation. The first audience members walked out after about an hour on both nights. The agitation manifest in a variety of "audience performances":[72] shuffling and fidgeting, whisperings, growing tension in the face, the use of mobile phones. Yet there were also audience members leaning forward, apparently fascinated and transfixed that cast disparaging glances at other audience members who disturbed their enjoyment. These audience performances built to a climax in the "break" described by Bruno above. At this point audience members began talking to each other, some displayed their consternation and walked out, others left silently. There was a kind of anarchy, a hazard. The audience were highly self-conscious and very aware of each other, looking for cues from their fellow audience members as to how to react. Henrik found this the most fascinating part of the event. "It's very, very interesting that people left. [...] The most interesting part for me was seeing how people around me were acting."[73] The audience performance was a narrative in itself. The audience were keenly watching the audience, either for cues, or out of captivation. This heightened self-consciousness created a state of mindful physical presence in the audience. In this group-alienated state, they were acutely tuned to each other, and their consternation, bewilderment and fascination created a highly charged *Stimmung* in the auditorium. As noted above, there were seemingly two separate worlds created: one onstage and the other in the auditorium. A strong physical atmosphere pervaded and, perhaps, united both worlds at times, but the psychological conversations were muted at best.

Tuning to the actors

In *Hunger. Peer Gynt*, there was little evidence that the audience were tuned to the actors in a psychological sense. The disjunction mentioned above meant there was little if no co-creation. There was tension onstage among the actors and tension among the audience members as they tried to negotiate their way through a production that exploded their expectations and took them out of their comfort zone. Through this, the attunement between actors and audience was compromised. Although the physical atmosphere poured over the edge of the stage, beckoning the audience to unite with the play's diegesis, the audience members found it difficult to tune to the actors. The interviewed audience members all proffered conclusions as to why they could not connect. Lisa needed to see "more relationships between actors."[74] Bruno could not connect because he also "noticed that the actors on the stage very rarely interacted with each other. Most of them were making sense of the surroundings for themselves."[75] Felix found the lack of specific characters challenging, which in turn made it "really difficult to connect" with the actors.[76] Claudia could not connect because the atmosphere became not only the protagonist, but an obstacle. The physical atmosphere and the visuals were so overpowering for her that "you don't see the actors a lot. [The play] sucks you out."[77] The only interviewed audience member that felt even remotely connected with the actors was Fabian. He expressed it as "a psychotic feeling. It kind of transfers from the actors to yourself."[78] This was, however, more to do with the *Stimmung* of the production than the direct relationship.

The concept of "sucking the audience out" was, perhaps, the most discussed issue related to actor–audience relationship. The actors above commented that there were seemingly two separate worlds in the theatre: the onstage world and the auditorium world. Gabe, Bruno, Henrik and Serena found the onstage world very insular. As Gabe explained, "The actors have fun, they play on their own. We are not so important to them. [...] It's not for us, it's for the actors on the stage."[79] Bruno also felt a sense of loss in this lack of relationship with the actors: "No, I didn't feel included."[80] Serena found the chosen style of acting solipsistic and this alienated her: "I'm a bit tired of seeing people expressing themselves 'who am I?' And what else?"[81] Interestingly, Henrik found himself questioning his relationship with the actors very early in the performance: "Ten minutes into the play I asked myself: 'am I here for me or for the actors? Is it more for the actors to somehow live out their needs or am I here because of social constraints?'"[82] Henrik's questioning of his tuning to the actors not only made him self-conscious, but he also began to ask ontological questions about his role in the theatre that evening as projected by the actors' behaviour. He actually left the performance and had a drink in the bar, pondering this for some time. This deliberate disengagement reflected his sense of separation from the play. The relationship between the actors and the audience, while it emerged for some as a contentious issue, was an aspect of the production that was questioned far more than in a traditional play where character identification, projection or transference immediately creates an audience–character relationship, rather than an audience–actor relationship.

The audience members were, however, very quick to explain that the distance they felt and the lack of symbiosis was not the fault of the actors. Having no desire to slur the actors, the majority of the audience members went to great lengths to mitigate their seemingly pejorative responses:

> It's not a bad thing that they play on their own. I don't feel [the actors] are egotistical.
>
> *Gabe*

> The words did not move me but the acting was great.
>
> *Lara*

> Overall I felt some connection on an emotional level with the actors, *some* connection, but not at a rational level. Maybe I will feel it more two days after the show.
>
> *Lisa*

> I really liked the setting and also the actors, the atmosphere, so no offense!
>
> *Manuela*

The audience members felt a certain need to protect the actors' reputation and to retain an agreeable and equitable actor–audience relationship on leaving the theatre. All of the interviewed audience members, with the exception of one, sought relationship. This shows how important a psychological relationship is for audience members.

If, as Chekhov argues, "Atmosphere [...] unites the audience with the actor as well as the actors with one another,"[83] then *Hunger. Peer Gynt* can be seen as a direct experiment in the juxtaposition of the effects of the physical atmosphere and the *Stimmung*. The physical atmosphere was captivating. The emotional atmosphere was inimical at times. The audience were not in direct relationship with the actors. This severed the empathic conversation and, for many, compromised their enjoyment of the production. They felt left out because they could not attune to the actors.

Tuning to the audience

Were the actors attuned to or estranged from the audience? The audience are often perceived by actors as the third actor in the play.[84] As such, the audience play a huge co-creative role in performance. As Linda describes, "Connection with the audience is something that I believe in and I also feel quite strongly about. It's like I have antenna during the whole show out to the audience."[85] Elias had a sense that the audience were asking for a "dialogue." And his role as an actor was "To integrate [the audience into the performance]. Not in a way to interact, but in a way to take them along. Not *for* them but *with* them."[86]

At the *Premiere* of *Hunger. Peer Gynt*, the actors were struggling to find a way to invite the audience into the performance. There were several reasons for this. Similar to the audience members, Elias felt they were only playing for themselves:

> I remember telling colleagues 10–15 minutes before the show "I still can't imagine how people are sitting here watching this." I have felt this about other plays as well, but this was different. It was so bizarre because it was like we almost rehearsed it for our own group. It didn't feel like this was meant to go somewhere because the only working process was so much about ourselves.[87]

Elias's candour was matched by others who revealed their insecurity. A very different insecurity than that felt by the audience who did not know what the "rules" were. The actors knew full well what the rules were, but these rules seemingly did not account for the presence of an audience and the effect the audience would have on the performance. As Marcel explained, "we had the feeling as if we had guests during the play."[88] This made some actors feel insecure and fearful of being judged:

> On opening night you suddenly have the perspective of judgement in your head. For the seven weeks before in rehearsals, in a hard way, we tried to get the feeling of judgement out. Stop thinking about what you are doing. Because if you think about what you are doing you censor it. And with a play like this you can't. So suddenly you have an audience, their perspective comes into your mind.[89]

This differs to the insecurity that is a component of stage fright explored in Chapter 2. In one sense, because of the nature of the play, it is more acute as the actors bring so much of themselves onstage.

The prevailing intent among all actors was, however, to find a way to invite the audience in, to be in relationship with them. With their antenna out, and aware that this was a difficult performance to negotiate, they were highly aware that the audience needed to find a way into the play. As Natali emphasised, "I know it's difficult for them to find a way into this world. But I wish that they could find a way because actually it is like a kaleidoscope and everybody can see themself up there."[90] Manuel explained, "This show is like a little dark rustle. How do [the audience] feel? Do we have to move to them? You don't hear reactions." He relied on the rhythm and the *Stimmung* to understand the audience: "It's our feel of the rhythm. How does it feel in the room?" One of Linda's primary initiatives was to ensure the audience were "not lost. 'Okay, it's every cryptic. What's that? Who's that? What is it talking about?' You have to invite them in."[91] As Gareth White argues, permission from the actors to enter into the world of the play is a crucial aspect of theatre.[92]

Just as the audience struggled to read the actors, the actors, who are highly intuitive and have a tacit understanding of audiences during productions, found immense difficulty in reading the audience and playing off their cues in this production. The verbal, paralingual and gestural "cues" of the audience are the essential parts of the actor–audience conversation. If these are subverted, indecipherable or absent, then the conversation is compromised. As Natali disclosed, "I have absolutely no idea what the audience are feeling."[93] Manuel went so far as to state

> You cannot really get to the point of knowing whether they like it or hate it. In this show it is not possible to read the audience. There is always the darkness, the sound, you are always thinking onstage. You always have to be hot in the brain [sharp or mindful][94] to get into the play again.[95]

The rules, the onstage industry expected of the actors and even their necessary heightened awareness of each other's performances jeopardised their relationship with the audience.

It should be noted that the encounter between actors and audience members in *Hunger. Peer Gynt* is precarious. Actors are *more* vulnerable than in traditional theatre as they are playing so much of themselves. The stakes are much higher for them. For Elias the *Hunger. Peer Gynt* encounter was Fischer-Lichte's confrontation: "This play doesn't ask for a track. It asks for a confrontation. A confrontation with yourself, with the subjects and with an audience in the end. That's what was really weird at the *Premiere*."[96]

As some of the above actor comments illustrate, the actors had a very strong desire to build relationship with the audience, to let them into their world. As Linda stressed, "It is not just something they bought a ticket for and that the people onstage don't realise who's there and don't really care. We care."[97] Manuel constantly searched for ways to let the audience in: "You have to work with us otherwise you won't get into the show. And we are aware of that. But without the co-creating audience, we are nothing."[98] This last comment is revealing[99] and alludes to the unsafe nature of the encounter for the actors in *Hunger. Peer Gynt*. The co-creating audience are vital for the construction of the performance text. If the relationship with the actors and audience is compromised, and there is no magnetic pull across the footlights as audience and actors are swept up in the fictive world of the play, then this has ramifications for the actors and audience alike. They are out of tune.

The walk-out

Finally, we discuss the walkout. It is of importance to explain that the Deutsches Theater is what could be described as having more of a traditional or mainstream focus in Berlin. Especially in comparison to the Volksbühne or the Schaubühne which traditionally have staged more cutting edge, radical and non-narrative works. Although many of the stagings, interpretations and issues explored are often very contemporary at the Deutsches Theater, the more traditional reputation of repertoire, classical and narrative offerings obviously construct the audience's horizon of expectations. Before each performance of *Hunger. Peer Gynt*, a *Vorbesprechen*, a pre-show talk, was held during which Caesar introduced the audience to the play. Those that attended were informed that the play had no narrative, and this informed audience expectations. The audience were forewarned, and it was expected that this information would help them engage with the play as it was presented. Not all audience members, however, attend the *Vorbesprechen*. Around one-third of the audience members interviewed had attended the pre-show talk. In spite of this, to reiterate, one-third walked out despite this preparation. The Deutsches Theater main auditorium where *Hunger Peer Gynt* was staged holds 600 people and the auditorium was full at the commencement of each performance I viewed.

Audience and the walk-out

Although half of the 21 audience members interviewed walked out, this was not always because they disliked the production. Commensurably, of the ten interviewed that stayed, not all stayed because they liked the production. Many were ambivalent. Most all of the audience members interviewed were pleased that I approached them and relished the opportunity to discuss their responses. One audience member even approached me and asked if he could be interviewed. What is of much more interest are the reasons for the walk-out, the reasons people stayed until the end of the three or four hours and how this affected the relationship with the actors and the conversations across the footlights. The walk-out is a very powerful statement. Depending on the production, it can have a number of inferences: distaste, boredom, insult, anger. Often single walk-outs are innocuous: the audience member needs to use the amenities or has been called out in an emergency. In Western English-speaking productions, the walk-out and applause[100] are two of the only remaining platforms for audiences to express their genuine critical response, and in these productions, actors nearly always take the walk-out personally.[101]

In most German theatre, with the investment audiences have in the theatre culture, audience members are more outspoken, capricious and forthright in their critical response, even during performances. Some theatres encourage this criticism by providing avenues for audiences to "argue with them."[102] This not only results in a more intense, healthy and egalitarian theatre conversation, it also creates an environment where co-creation can thrive. As seen below, German actors do not always take the walk-out as a personal affront, and are more philosophical about the walk-out than their English-speaking audience cousins that I have interviewed in New York, London, Sydney, Chicago, Toronto and Glasgow.[103]

The dominant reason that people walked out of the performance of *Hunger. Peer Gynt* either during the first act or at interval was, unsurprisingly, because of the absence of a narrative. Seventy percent of those interviewed walked out for this reason, some of which had attended the *Vorbesprechen*:

But it's always repeating the same thing so I miss the clear idea. I left because of the story, there's no story for me. The different scenes don't seem to belong together.

JJ

After 2 hours without any ending or any story, we have seen enough […]
I think I need a final plot.

Manuela

There was really no story, so it was scenes one after the other. No story with a climax.

Joel

I like hearing stories actually, so that's why I had to get out.

Serena

There was a prodigious need for a narrative. Although many had read Hamsun's *Hunger* and/or Ibsen's *Peer Gynt*, the fictive world of these two texts that was created in the atmosphere, the fragments of text from them, the allusions to the characters and the motifs, were not enough to sustain these audience members. Interestingly, as discussed above, at the *Premiere* the actors seemingly sensed this need for a narrative and, as Linda asserted, some actors broke community with the group to try and create a narrative for the audience.

Many others struggled to make meaning or tried to create a narrative. There was a plethora of Wolfgang Iser's gaps in this narrative. Actually it was full of gaps. Rather than drawing from his own experiences to fill in the gaps of a narrative, Paul found his own experiences imbricated with those in the *Stimmung*: "I mixed my own things, my own experiences today and last week with the feelings onstage. So for me it was very intensive."[104] The *Stimmung* overwhelmed the production. Interestingly, one audience member, Richard, delighted in the non-narrativity:

The radicalism of this play is lasting. It poses the right questions, what are words? What is action? What is narrative? Castorf[105] used to do this but he always stuck to the text, but now it is broken up, it's fantastic![106]

These are the questions, by his own admission, Hartmann asks in *Hunger. Peer Gynt*. Yet, when some audience members knew the play did not have a narrative and others take pleasure in post-dramatic theatre, why did audience members, even those that enjoyed many aspects of the production, abandon it at interval?

The second most common reason for the walk-out was the length of the piece. Anne, Felix and Manuela said that had had "enough for today," and JJ and Reiner felt that if they stayed they "wouldn't see anything new." The content was also too "dark," "depressing," "disturbing," "strong," and "sucking" for Anne, Felix and Claudia. There were various other autonomous explanations: Karin left because she felt it was too loud; Paul because he found it too intense; Felix because it was very confusing and Claudia because it utterly exhausted her. Manuela, who "really liked" the production not only needed a narrative, but she also wanted "involvement," with the actors or with the production. Attempting to make a connection, she exerted much effort in trying to find "certain stories behind the personalities onstage."[107] By interval, however, this was not realised, so she left.

If, as in *Hunger. Peer Gynt*, we are left with no narrative, then the relationship with the actors is ultimately compromised. They are interesting beings to watch and play the role of people depicted on a canvas, but the audience are not invited in. As explored in the *Heisenberg* case study, identification with a character onstage creates an immediate nexus with the actors and begins a psychological conversation. In *Hunger. Peer Gynt*, there were not only no characters, but because of the ensemble imperatives, there were no individuals. This entirely changed the perception and tuning of the event for the audience. As Fabian explained, "I saw the whole picture, not individuals. Because if there was someone on one part of the stage acting the others were still there."[108] This was also, however, one of the strengths of the production: the *Stimmung* became the protagonist.

The physical atmosphere and the *Stimmung* was the dominant reason why audience members either liked the production or stayed for its entirety. Audience members were intrigued, immersed and stimulated by the *Stimmung*. Two young men who declined an interview during interval asked me to query their thoughts at the conclusion of the production. They sat transfixed for at least five minutes after the conclusion of the three-and-a-half-hour performance, still staring at the now ruined painting on the stage. As I approached them, one commented, "I have only one word: 'astonished.'" The other also only proffered one word: "speechless."[109] The production affected them deeply in some way. It would seem that they needed to remain immersed in the *Stimmung*. Böhme argues that "[t]he need to feel one's own mindful physical presence also reveals the need to feel one's own vibrancy, vitality."[110] These two audience members were clearly swept up in the vibrant vitality of their experience of the piece. One-third of the audience left, two-thirds stayed. Some of those left were enthralled. A production such as this stimulates a much wider range of responses from the audience than a traditional narrative production.

Actors and the walk-out

Since the actors were also swept up in the vibrancy and vitality of their experience of the performance work, some of the actors "couldn't understand that the audience didn't like it."[111] Walking out was clearly read as intense dislike of the piece. Furthermore, over half of the actors felt the audience walked out because they were angry. There were few expressions of anger, no resentments, no bitter responses in any of the audience members I approached.

While their understanding of the walk-out was somewhat clouded, none of the actors minded that the audience walked out:

Yesterday a lot of people were leaving. If you don't like it you are more than welcome to leave. I really don't mind. I have no problem at all when I see people walk out.

Elias Arens

It's their decision.

Natali Seelig

That's normal.

Manuel Harder

It's always a bit strange, but I'm used to it actually.[112] It happens a lot in other plays. It's okay.

Linda Pöppel

As Linda alluded, the walk-out does occur more frequently in German theatres than English-speaking Western theatres for the reasons mentioned above. At the particular time that I conducted the interviews, the actors were seemingly far more tense about their relationships with each other, especially given the happenings at the *Premiere*, than they were about the walk-out.

The actors continued to question, however, and make assumptions about the reasons for the walk-out. In this production the actors have, perhaps, more investment in audience response as they are co-creators and sometimes onstage directors. The walk-out, or any audience response, leaves lingering questions in their minds. In one of the performances, there was an audience member who booed very loudly and repetitively in the curtain call. His response confused Linda:

He seemed quite angry. Why did he stay? Maybe it was important for him to express in the end or maybe he said "I bought the ticket." But this is also okay. If you have the strength to do the "boo" in the end, then it's also okay.[113]

The actors strongly desired to stay in relationship with the audience so Marcel felt a "little bit sad"[114] at the walk-out. Their desire to not offend, blame or estrange the audience was commensurable with the audience's aspirations. Although some of the actors felt confused about the reasons or saddened by the walk-out, they too went to great pains to try and justify the audience's rights and retain relationship with them. Manuel did not want them to "feel compelled to stay" and Linda "didn't want them to feel that [the actors] mind if they are angry" and "walk out."[115] They understood how the material of the performance work could be too cumbersome and exhausting for the audience. The actors knew that the audience were their greatest allies and their fellow co-creators and wanted to maintain relationship even in the midst of what they perceived as anger.

Marcel, who had been preoccupied in the past about walk-outs and had sought advice from directors, had reached some conclusions about the *Hunger. Peer Gynt* walk-out:

> I was a little bit sad, because it is indeed important to reach everyone. But maybe you have to reject some [audience members] to reach the others even more. And then it would be a good calculation if one third went out, but we reached the others more. Maybe it was not possible to reach the other third. So then it's okay when they go and you work with the others. Maybe it's worth that loss, and maybe it's the best result. [...] I talked with some directors that don't have anything against it, because they think that sorted the audience out. So if all the people went out who are not so interested or don't listen or aren't involved, afterwards the play can really begin. So it's damage control.

Marcel was not the only actor to consider that it is best if the audience that stay choose to stay because they want to and not, as with audience members above, out of social constraint, because they wanted to boo at the end or even because they do not wish to offend the actors. During interval in one of the performances, one of the actors directly addressed the audience: "Everyone who doesn't belong here, leave!"[116] This, understandably, led to mass confusion in the auditorium, but it did, however, work as a form of "damage control." It also worked, however, to further alienate some audience members. Marcel was quick to add,

> The best scenario would be, of course, if all of the audience members would stay in the theatre. The other option would be that we stage something that everybody is interested in. That is very honourable, but that is not the task of the theatre.[117]

Although it is not the purpose of this book to debate what the task of theatre is, this last comment provokes a discourse on theatre's purpose in different cultures. Berlin itself has a long history of different approaches to the audience such as Bertolt Brecht's *Verfremdunseffekt* and Heiner Müller's incredibly long post-performance audience discussions that extended the audience conversation well beyond the end of the performance. German theatre also tends to be more provocative and adventurous in presenting different forms and approaches than theatre in other theatre capitals such as New York and London. It can afford to be, and it is. When plays are in repertory in German theatre, there is not a performance every night.[118] When I questioned what determined the length of the run of *Hunger. Peer Gynt*, Caesar explained that it could run for as long as two to three years. "Dependant on ticket sales and the audience and critics response to the production" would be the standard measure of longevity in New York and London. Caesar explained that in the Deutsches Theater

It depends on the audience but it also depends what we as a theatre think about the play [...] If we really like the performance and think it is important then [even if the audience numbers drop] we would continue to play it[119]

for its aesthetic merit. This could be the case for *Hunger. Peer Gynt.*

Ultimately, the walk-out is an important part of the conversation. Manuel recognised it as such: "The walk-out is part of the discussion. Don't feel oppressed to stay in your seat for the full three and a half hours. You can leave, you can stay. You are of course, a part of this event."[120] The walk-out became a vital part of the *Stimmung*. It caused confusion, tension, consternation, sadness, discouragement and fascination. All of these states filled the in-between spaces and tuned the atmosphere of the auditorium and the stage. Confusion, exhaustion and disappointment followed some audience members as they walked out of the play and chased them out of the theatre. Fascination and tension lingered in the foyer during interval. Sadness, joy and confusion flowed off the stage and into the brightly lit dressing rooms. The audience as "generators of atmospheres"[121] added to the atmosphere with their confusion and/or absorption. The walkout *Stimmung* emerged as one of the most crucial aspects of the *Hunger. Peer Gynt* actor–audience conversation. It was electric and possibly contagious.

Atonality and tuned space

For many of the interviewed audience members, *Hunger. Peer Gynt* was atonal. Linda believes that the way into the production was to "sit with open hearts, then the audience can realise what it means."[122] When Bruno stopped intellectualising, seeking meaning and surrendered to the flow of the piece, he had great pleasure. When Gabe recognised the piece as a meditation rather than a story to be told, she found the piece had "a lot of honour."[123] Although she predominantly found the piece "confusing" she bought another ticket for four weeks' time as she was excited by the prospect of seeing a different version of the production. Bruno and Gabe surrendered disbelief and accepted the performance as an aesthetic conversation. They both sat there with open hearts and yielded to the flow or meditative aspects of the evening, embracing the production as a *Gesamtkunstwerk*.

Despite the atonality of *Hunger. Peer Gynt*, as explored in this chapter, there were many aspects in the production that the audience and actors did tune to. Actors tuned to the space and, with the exception of the *Premiere*, tuned to each other. The world they created onstage was captivating and enigmatic at the same time. Audience members were not tuned to the actors but were tuned to each other and to the atmosphere. New alliances were formed in the audience as some form of anarchy broke out in the audience and a collective effervescence swept through the auditorium. In the audience there were either dissenters or fanatics. There was no apathy. The atmosphere as protagonist was confronting, challenging and stimulating.

In some ways, the lack of narrative and the fog itself created a fourth wall on the stage that obfuscated and impeded the actor–audience relationship. Tuning to the physical atmosphere – and this includes the visual, acoustic and sensorial atmosphere – was the most successful and immersive aspect of the production for actors and audience alike. In Böhme's tuned space – the atmosphere – the audience were spellbound by the *Stimmung* for at least the first half hour of the production. The actors were enveloped in both the physical atmosphere and the *Stimmung* for the entire three to four hours. The first walkout after one hour awakened some audience members from their reverie and others were ignorant of it. The walkout confused some actors, yet they all accepted it and some perceptively understood that it was an important part of the conversation. The actors even had empathy for the audience, knowing that the production was "hard work for the audience as well."[124] This was a new empathic connection that emerged across the footlights. Although actors and audience were not attuned, both troupes worked hard to find a way to connect across the footlights. In spite of the walkout and in spite of the lack of a narrative, the actors and audience members evidently still cared for each other. In the final analysis, the *Stimmung* – as a combination of the physical atmosphere and the mood, feelings and temperament of the actors and audience – emerged as not only the protagonist and director in *Hunger. Peer Gynt* but also the honour of the work.

Extending the conversation: reaching out from the border

Manuel sat on the edge of the stage. He sat there for quite some time observing the audience, observing the onstage actions, in a state of mindful physical presence. This was the third performance of *Hunger. Peer Gynt* and Manuel was attempting to find a way to connect with the audience, to invite them in. This *Grenzland*, this border, is a place that Manuel finds compelling:

> I try to play with the border of the stage. I want to feel the audience. I love the feeling of the little edge because it's only one step […]. It could be one step and then it would be something totally different. For me it's being sure of what you don't do. A little border for me, myself. I find it very interesting to play with that.[125]

I was fortunate enough to observe Manuel playing on the *Grenzland*, in *Hunger. Peer Gynt*. He would dip his toe into the vast sea of the audience and circle it there. Testing the waters. He never lost involvement in the world of the play on stage. He was playing with the border. He was playing on the border. The little edge. This created an electric air experience for him: the tension that with one step "it would be something totally different." Occasionally he would notice some action on the stage. His very presence emanating ekstases seemed to summon, challenge and compel the audience to enter the world of the play. He was the conduit through which they could read the indecipherable.

For Manuel, this border is enticing but can also be treacherous. He later proffered some thoughts he has about this border quoting Jean Genet: "The stage and death are the closest of neighbours."[126] In the interviews Manuel and other German actors had alluded to the feelings or fear of dying onstage. Yet here Manuel was relating it to the *Grenzland*. Suggesting, perhaps, that the step off the stage is the most terrifying of all, yet an actor has to take that risk to invite the audience in. Manuel's presence certainly connected the two rooms, the two worlds.

Other actors from the ensemble also acknowledged the border and attempted to reach out from or across the border to find a way to invite the audience in. Marcel recognised that the production was closed to the audience: "It is a kind of closed world with borders."[127] For him there was a clear delineation between the stage world and the auditorium world. From an antithetical perspective, Linda saw no border between stage and audience:

> [In *Hunger. Peer Gynt*] I hope that [the audience] feel in a different way invited to share an evening with us. And that there is the possibility to understand that there is no clear border between audience and stage, but it is a complete room where everybody is sharing time.[128]

Sharing time, in one room, in a powerful atmosphere when both actors and audience are sharing the same *Stimmung* is the objective of theatre. It is also what Jacques Rancière argued for in *The Emancipated Spectator*: "That is what the word 'emancipation' means; the blurring of the boundary between those who act and those who look; between individuals and those of a collective body."[129] Rancière goes on to argue that only when this boundary is blurred can actors and audience become "an emancipated community […] of narrators and translators."[130] In *Hunger. Peer Gynt* narration and translation were compromised. Yet Manuel and Linda were both in their own way attempting a blurring of this boundary as a means for the audience to find a way into *Hunger. Peer Gynt*.

Other ensemble members reached out across the border. Natali did "not [want] to lose the thin thread between everyone in the room,"[131] so in the third performance she tried to wake one audience member up by clicking her fingers and clapping. Two other actors[132] improvised a humorous dialogue. The audience laughed and were engaged. This small conversation of mirth briefly bridged the gulf between stage and audience.

As can be seen from these attempts to reach across the border and include the audience, the actors of *Hunger. Peer Gynt* were not completely fulfilled living and performing in their very intense onstage world. They did not like being cut off from the audience and sought ways to invite them in. You may be able to destroy the engagement between actor and audience, but you cannot destroy the *need* for engagement or conversation. If you attempt to break the relationship between actor and audience, both troupes will scream louder. Audience members will scream louder by walking out and booing at the end. Actors will scream louder by working within the constraints they have to draw in the audience by playing at the border of the stage in the timelessness of the physical space, or by snapping their fingers so that the audience wake up. All in an attempt to restore or even create relationship.

The actors "want to feel the audience" they want to "invite them in." The audience want to be included and, in this play, found it "really difficult to connect" as they "didn't feel included." As has been illustrated in this chapter, audience and actors crave the magnetic pull or push across the footlights. They thirst for a conversation. They desire relationship. The reciprocity of the conversation is an essential element of theatre that reaches across the *Grenzland* to blur the boundaries and emancipate not only the audience, but also the actors.

Notes

1 German actors are no longer referred to as "actors" but "players."
2 Sebastian Hartmann in Conversation, "I'm Interested in the Celebration of the Moment," accessed 2 January 2019, www.deutschestheater.de/programm/aktuelles/spielzeit_18_19/sebastian_hartmann_im_gespraech/.
3 Natali Seelig, personal interview, 24 October 2018.
4 Ibid.
5 *Hunger. Peer Gynt* programme notes.
6 Claus Caesar, personal interview, 26 October 2018.
7 Most are under two year contracts which invariably are renewed or they move into another ensemble.
8 Claus Caesar, personal interview, 26 October 2018.
9 *Oxford English Dictionary*, https://www-oed-com.ezp01.library.qut.edu.au/.
10 Erik Wallrup, *Being Musically Attuned: The Act of Listening to Music* (London: Routledge, 2016), 17.
11 Ibid., 15.
12 Jacob Grimm and Wilhelm Grimm, "Stimmen," *Deutsches Wörterbuch* 10, no. 2 (1960): 3129–3130.
13 Wallrup, *Being Musically Attuned*, 19.
14 Ibid., 78, 79
15 Jan Slaby and Christian von Scheve, eds., *Affective Societies: Key Concepts* (Abingdon: Routledge, 2019), 87.
16 Ibid., 51.
17 Although Chekhov does not use the term *Stimmung*, his descriptions in these two excerpts essentially describe *Stimmung*. Michael Chekhov, *To the Actor: On the Technique of Acting* (New York: Harper and Row, 1953), 53, 48.
18 One described the experience of being in a bar in Southern Germany where the crowd collectively chanted *Stimmung! Stimmung! Stimmung!*
19 Martin Heidegger, *Theorie der Befindlichkeit: Sein Denken zwischen 1927 und 1933* (Freiburg and Munich: Alber, 1996), 289–293.
20 Gernot Böhme, *The Aesthetics of Atmospheres*, ed. Jean-Paul Thibaud (London and New York: Routledge, 2017), 2.
21 Ibid., 32.
22 Ibid., 33.
23 Edward Bullough, "'Psychical Distance' as a Factor in Art and an Aesthetic Principle," *British Journal of Psychology* 5, no. 2 (1912): 88, 89.
24 As German has both words, *Stimmung* and *Atmosphäre*, atmosphere is used here as it describes the physical atmosphere of the space created by the fog, lighting, music and other visual effects.

25 Elias Arens, personal interview, 24 October 2018.

26 Ibid.

27 Ibid.

28 Chekhov, *To the Actor*, 19.

29 Elias Arens, personal interview, 24 October 2018.

30 Linda Pöppel, personal interview, 28 October 2018.

31 Manuel Harder, personal interview, 27 October 2018.

32 Linda Pöppel, personal interview, 28 October 2018.

33 Manuel Harder, personal interview, 27 October 2018.

34 Sebastian Hartmann in Conversation, "I'm Interested."

35 Half of the audience members used this word several times to describe the atmosphere.

36 Cited in Böhme, *Aesthetics of Atmospheres*, 17.

37 This response, particularly with impressions that last for days, was something that the dramaturg Caesar argued was one of the responses to the production that would have been welcomed by Sebastian Hartmann. Claus Caesar, personal interview, 26 October 2018.

38 Böhme, *Aesthetics of Atmospheres*, 171.

39 Felix, personal interview, 23 October 2018.

40 Karin, personal interview, 23 October 2018.

41 Lara, personal interview, 23 October 2018.

42 Text from one monologue in *Hunger. Peer Gynt* directed by Sebastian Hartmann, Deutsches Theater, October 2018.

43 Paul, personal interview, 23 October 2018.

44 Henrik, personal interview, 23 October 2018.

45 Reiner, personal interview, 26 October 2018.

46 Bruno, personal interview, 26 October 2018.

47 Gabe, personal interview, 23 October 2018.

48 Elias Arens, personal interview, 24 October 2018.

49 Natali Seelig, personal interview, 24 October 2018.

50 Manuel Harder, personal interview, 27 October 2018.

51 Elias Arens, personal interview, 24 October 2018.

52 Manuel Harder, personal interview, 27 October 2018.

53 Gernot Böhme, "Atmosphere as Mindful Physical Presence in Space," *OASE* 91 (2013): 21–32.

54 Natali Seelig, personal interview, 24 October 2018.

55 Ibid.

56 Ibid.

57 Linda Pöppel, personal interview, 28 October 2018.

58 With the exception of two of the actors who at different times "play" the role of Peer Gynt and Peer Gynt's mother, although in a very abstract form.

59 Linda Pöppel, personal interview, 28 October 2018.

60 Marcel Kohler, personal interview, 26 October 2018.

61 This way of working is very similar to Impulse Training, a component of Physical Theatre.

62 Elias Arens, personal interview, 24 October 2018.

63 German theatre does not have previews, the *Premiere* is the first performance in front of an audience.

64 Linda Pöppel, personal interview, 28 October 2018.

65 Ibid.

66 As noted by *Premiere* audience members that were friends of Linda Pöppel. Linda Pöppel, personal interview, 28 October 2018.

67 "*Hunger. Peer Gynt* after Knut Hamsen/Henrik Ibsen," Media, www.deutschestheater. de/programm/a-z/hunger_peer/.

68 Bruno, personal interview, 26 October 2018.

69 Henrik, personal interview, 26 October 2018.

70 Bruno, personal interview, 26 October 2018.

71 Ibid.

72 Caroline Heim, *Audience as Performer: The Changing Role of Theatre Audiences in the Twenty-First Century* (London and New York: Routledge, 2016).

73 Henrik, personal interview, 26 October 2018.

74 Lisa, personal interview, 23 October 2018.

75 Bruno, personal interview, 26 October 2018.

76 Felix, personal interview, 23 October 2018.

77 Claudia, personal interview, 26 October 2018.

78 Fabian, personal interview, 23 October 2018.

79 Gabe, personal interview, 23 October 2018.

80 Bruno, personal interview, 26 October 2018.

81 Serena, personal interview, 26 October 2018.

82 Ibid.

83 Chekhov, *To the Actor*, 62.

84 Heim, *Audience as Performer*.

85 Linda Pöppel, personal interview, 28 October 2018.

86 Elias Arens, personal interview, 24 October 2018.

87 Ibid.

88 Marcel Kohler, personal interview, 26 October 2018.

89 Elias Arens, personal interview, 24 October 2018.

90 Natali Seelig, personal interview, 24 October 2018.

91 Linda Pöppel, personal interview, 28 October 2018.

92 Gareth White, *Audience Participation in the Theatre: Aesthetics of the Invitation* (New York: Palgrave Macmillan, 2013).

93 Natali Seelig, personal interview, 24 October 2018.

94 "Hot in the brain" is another way of saying "always thinking." I have let Manuel's own translation stand as it seems fitting for this "hazardous" production.

95 Manuel Harder, personal interview, 27 October 2018.

96 Elias Arens, personal interview, 24 October 2018.

97 Ibid.

98 Manuel Harder, personal interview, 27 October 2018.

99 These comments are not dissimilar to Keith Randolph Smith's comments in Chapter 2 when he relayed a dialogue he has with audiences when the play is abstract and difficult to understand. He too implores actors to "work with him."

100 When it comes to mainstream, commercial theatre, there does seem to be a divide in this perspective.

101 Heim, *Audience as Performer*.

102 Caroline Heim, "'Argue with Us!': Audience Co-creation through Post-Performance Discussions," *New Theatre Quarterly* 28, no. 2 (2012): 189–197.

103 In all, 106 interviews with audience members were undertaken for *Audience as Performer* in these cities.

104 Paul, personal interview, 23 October 2018.

105 Frank Castorf, Artistic Director at the Volkbühne 1992–2015.

106 Richard, personal interview, 23 October 2018.

107 Manuela, personal interview, 26 October 2018.

108 Fabian, personal interview, 23 October 2018.

109 I did not break their reverie to get their names.

110 Böhme, *Aesthetics of Atmospheres*, 31.

111 Natali Seelig, personal interview, 24 October 2018.

112 Linda performs in a lot of post-dramatic theatre productions.

113 Linda Pöppel, personal interview, 28 October 2018.

114 Marcel Kohler, personal interview, 26 October 2018.

115 Linda Pöppel, personal interview, 28 October 2018.

116 I did not witness this incident as I was interviewing audience members. Bruno, who I interviewed at the end of the production, relayed the quote and described what happened.

117 Marcel Kohler, personal interview, 26 October 2018.

118 Some plays have performances once or twice a week, or even once fortnight.

119 Claus Caesar, personal interview, 26 October 2018.

120 Manuel Harder, personal interview, 27 October 2018.

121 Böhme, *Aesthetics of Atmospheres*, 32.

122 Linda Pöppel, personal interview, 28 October 2018.

123 Gabe, personal interview, 23 October 2018.

124 Manuel Harder, personal interview, 27 October 2018.

125 Ibid.

126 Manuel Harder, email correspondence, 30 October 2018.

127 Marcel Kohler, personal interview, 26 October 2018.

128 Linda Pöppel, personal interview, 28 October 2018.

129 Jacques Rancière, *The Emancipated Spectator*, trans. Gregory Elliott (London and New York: Verso, 2009), 19.

130 Ibid., 22.

131 Natali Seelig, personal interview, 24 October 2018.

132 Because of the heavy fog during this particular scene I could not ascertain which actors they were.

CONCLUSION

In this twenty-first century we live in a world dominated by two-dimensional screens. Screens that scream for attention, that give pleasurable but temporary dopamine hits, that make us bend our necks, lower our gaze and shut out the people in the flesh around us to immerse ourselves in an individual experience, a virtual reality. We connect online, rather than meet in person. We may have a sense of comfort in our own individual screen world, but do we experience the deep comfort of being at home? There is a certain deadness in this virtual world. Have we gone so far in individualism that we have forgotten how important we are to each other? Conversely, in the theatre we raise our necks and direct our gaze at actors in the flesh. We share an experience with others and join in the collective effervescence of laughter or applause. We are part of a real-time conversation. We can feel it in the air. There is something about the theatrical experience that reaches beyond the experience of, for example, viewing a movie, that is – as described by audience members and actors in this book – "alive not dead," "more real than in real life" and "home." This feeling of liveness, of reality and of home is found in the space co-created in the actor–audience conversations across the footlights. It is, at its core, relational.

This interconnectedness of actors onstage conversing with audience members in the auditorium is, for those interviewed in this book, a solace from the unconsummated and hollow world of a flat screen. Actor Lynn Cohen went so far as to argue that the relationship across the footlights "is a marriage between you and the audience."[1] Further, as this book has argued, the psychological and emotion thought conversations that take place between the performers onstage and in the audience can work to create almost a crackle in the air that is electric.

What was found in the rich descriptions provided by actors and audience members was multi-layered and, at times, revelatory. The actors and audience discourse went beyond descriptions of the play to touch on core aspects of the theatrical experience. Theatre emerged as a safe environment for many actors and audience members to express emotions that they could not in real life. The theatre told stories that enabled actors and audience members alike to not only learn about and perform human frailty, triumph and despair, but also revealed ways to help them become better human beings. In this the theatre can become more real than the experience of life itself. As actor Keith Randolph Smith explained, "You get one life to live. But by being an actor in theatre you get to experience all these other lives which teaches you how to use your one life to live better."[2] From the other side of the footlights, Rachel Strauber had a similar response: "I really challenge who I am when I go to the theatre."[3] The experience of theatre – its stories, characters, relationships – has the potential to challenge the central values of actors and audience members as they both invest in co-creation of the artwork through filling in the gaps of the narrative with myriad projections, emotions, transferences and stories of their own. These fill the air with an emotional radiance of undercurrents that tune the actors and audience members with each other creating, at times, an electric air experience.

The electric air

This book set out to describe the importance of theatre's electric air. It is a nascent step in describing a poorly understood phenomenon experienced by actors and audience members. The book did not set out to prove a scientific theory of the electric air. How do you capture the wind? As actor Marcel Kohler describes,

> When I close the door to the outside world, there is always a kind of wind between the real world and the theatre. That wind lets the real life into the theatre. I think it is the actors that walk into the theatre that make the theatre what it is. Without the actors it isn't a theatre, it's only a house or something like that. So the actors change the space into something which it was not beforehand. And on the other hand we have audience members and you have a kind of responsibility to them. So we create our own world with the audience because we are there in that shared space.[4]

In this description Marcel points to the two live troupes of performers in the theatre: actors and audience members. In the way that Marcel has spoken of the wind, I have spoken of an electric air. The electric air described in this book is psychologically real, emotionally real, and it is felt. As it is felt, it has physical manifestations just like the emotions of love, anger, fear and joy. The interviewed actors and audience members also readily described their experience of the physical atmosphere of the theatre and sometimes depicted it in terms of electricity. The purpose of this book has been to document some of the conversations that occur between actors and audience members in the co-created space of a theatre and to describe not only the nature of the conversations but also the experience of the atmosphere that is co-created during those conversations in that shared space.

In describing the electric air, I was expecting to discover a phenomenon that was ephemeral and vague. I was surprised to find that not only were the actors and audience members describing something that was very real to them, but they also found it so magnetic that it either attracted or repelled them. It was physical for some, psychological for others and both for the majority. Many audience members wanted to sit as close as they could to the front to "feel it"[5] more and experience "the liveness"[6] of it. If they sat in the back of the auditorium they could no longer "feel it." In their psychical distance, transference experiences so powerfully repelled some audience members that they "shut out the world, or maybe wanted to run away from the world."[7]

Similarly, actors were attracted and repelled. They described the physical atmosphere of the electric air as "charged,"[8] "exhilarating,"[9] and "magic."[10] For actors, the electric air of the theatre can be so seductive and all-consuming that distance from it is sometimes sought. As Michael Chekhov argues,

> [For some actors] the small space of the stage is an entire world permeated with an atmosphere so strong, so magnetic that they can hardly bear to part with it after the performance is over.[11]

This is certainly true for Natali Seelig who finds it difficult to make a clear break from the theatrical world:

> [I need to] get a distance from [the production] when I leave it, because I have real troubles with this and it's bugging me. I have been working in the Deutsches Theater for nine years. One part of it is like coming home every day. But sometimes it differs a lot from the world I am coming from because all of it is in here in my head, so its fluid. The boundaries are fluid sometimes. It's more like a constant state of mind. So that is the challenge for me, to get out of it. Otherwise it's not that healthy. At least in the long run.[12]

The electric air of the theatrical experience onstage can become so powerful for actors that they need to distance themselves from it lest they lose themselves in it. In Natali's comments, the idea of "where is home" can be seen to add to the actor's insecurity and sometime sense of displacement. Theatres around the world emerge as diasporic spaces. The realm the actors inhabit and its attending atmosphere is addictive, perhaps, because it is for them more real than the real world.

Certain descriptors and undercurrents of the electric air were hypothesised and predetermined at the commencement of this book and were, during the interviews and case studies, confirmed, refined or recontextualised. Atmosphere, liveness and electricity were discussed in all the interviews. Of the 11 undercurrents – suspension of disbelief, the encounter, ephemerality, narrative, transference, projection, identification, empathy, presence, celebrity magnetism and community – some emerged as vital undercurrents of the theatrical experience in all interviews and others were rarely mentioned.

The encounter – its nature, the anxiety it caused, its absence – was of paramount importance in all the case studies. In *Heisenberg*, narrative was interwoven with the audience's psychological conversations. Interestingly, narrative emerged as the point of encounter in *The Encounter*. The lack of narrative in *Hunger. Peer Gynt* created an electric air experience of its own detailed below. Presence as a space-filling phenomenon was discussed in all the interviews as an important factor in creating the electric air experience. The ekstases radiating from the actors and sometimes from the audience created a thrill in the air. The concept of presence of "being in the moment" added to the liveness of the event. Yet one of the most important findings was that actor presence was predominantly described by the actors and audience members alike as comfort and authenticity rather than charisma or drawing power. Transference, projection, identification and empathy were referred to in all the interviews. Due to the relational nature and intimacy of the staging of *Heisenberg*, these psychological undercurrents surfaced as the focus of the encounter in the case study. They were noticeably absent in *Hunger. Peer Gynt* as the actor–audience relationship was occluded. Suspension of disbelief emerged as a vital part of the theatrical experience for actors and audience members, though only in the productions that included a narrative. Interestingly, community became more crucial in the absence of a narrative, yet not communitas. In *Hunger. Peer Gynt*, community among the actors and among the audience members was concretised in onstage and offstage collective effervescence. Although in *The Encounter* Simon McBurney could feel some of a collective resonance from the audience as a whole, the technology nullified any sense of community among the audience. The unique presence of celebrity onstage clearly changed the energy in the house for some audience members in *Heisenberg*: attracting some and repelling others. Ephemerality was the least discussed undercurrent in the interviews, although some audience members described the tension that uncertainty and liveness created. As Peter York stated, "there is the fact that there's no certainty of what will happen because every audience is different as well as every performance being different."[13] Actors also emphasised how the different presence of audiences co-created different performance outcomes. *Hunger. Peer Gynt* was the most spontaneous of all the productions. Not only were the emotional beats different each night, no two lighting states, music excerpts, dialogues or attenuating combinations were ever the same performance to performance.

Another theatrical concept emerged during the interviews that could be seen as, perhaps, an additional undercurrent: double consciousness and the stage fright it engenders. The general question "who do you see on the stage/in the auditorium" in the first iteration of interviews naturally generated discussions regarding actor, character and casting the audience. The double consciousness of the actors and the audience added layers to the experience of the live thrill in the atmosphere as the audience alternated between seeing the actor or the character or blended the two. The fear of being judged as actor rather than character manifested in stage fright for many of the interviewed actors. The uncertainty and thrill of whether the audience member was seeing character, actor or both, and the uncertainty, insecurity and risk-taking of the actor attempting to live in the blend, adds to the electricity in the air. As further study is undertaken of the electric air experience, other undercurrents may emerge or converge. The electric air of the theatre materialised as Gernot Böhme's space-filling phenomena with various undercurrents adding to the liveness and electricity of the experience for actors and audience members. The electric air filled the atmosphere with a felt emotional radiance which was heightened by the various psychological and emotion conversations across the footlights.

The conversations

The psychological and emotional thought conversations between actors and audience members in the theatre create a fertile environment for actor–audience co-creation. No actor or audience member interviewed for this book expressed any difficulty in describing their phenomenological experience of the nature of the conversations and their relationships across the footlights between actor and audience member and/or character and audience member, or the "cast" audience. As actor Wolfgang Michalek described,

> Tonight we are talking about life and death: you make a connection with the audience. You speak to them like other people who have to go through these things with you. You get to a place where together, you are celebrating what the author's put together.[14]

A connection and celebration it is indeed. A connection that audience member Rita Haynes describes as "intimate: they are talking to you personally. It's a personal experience. It's a personal thing between who's on the stage and who is in the audience."[15]

Each of the productions in this book contained certain actor–audience conversations that dominated the relationships between stage and auditorium. Each production invoked a different atmosphere. *Heisenberg* created more of an emotional atmosphere. *The Encounter* created more of a virtual atmosphere. In *Hunger. Peer Gynt* there was more of a spatial atmosphere or *Stimmung*. Consequently, there were psychological conversations in *Heisenberg* and virtual conversations in *The Encounter*. In *Hunger. Peer Gynt* there were scant actor–audience thought conversations. It was the absence of conversations that led to the walkouts. There were, however, aesthetic conversations, actor–actor conversations and audience conversations.

Heisenberg was the most traditional of the productions. Psychological conversations pervaded the atmosphere and, for some audience members, continued well after their viewing of the performance. *The Encounter* and *Hunger. Peer Gynt* both attempted to subvert and re-articulate traditional theatre conventions and conversations. The conversations in *The Encounter* were, in many ways, more intimate than traditional theatrical actor–audience discourses. The relationship between char/actor and audience was, accordingly, intensely personal. The audience and the actor rode the wave of the narrative together which rhythmically ebbed and flowed building a highly charged experience in the virtual world. That it was a *theatrical* experience for the audience is questionable. I would argue that the absence of opportunity for audience community compromised this. It certainly was a theatrical experience and conversation for the actor Simon McBurney. The strong narrative was the thread that concretised the actor–audience bond.

In *Hunger. Peer Gynt* we are left with the question raised by one of the audience members: Does a play without a narrative "suck you out"[16] and why? To approach this contentious question, we need to return to atmosphere. In *Hunger. Peer Gynt* the air was pulsating with tension onstage among the actors. In the auditorium, gradually growing to a climax at interval, the atmosphere was electric. The anarchy, the confusion and the walkout contributed to this. The physical, spatial atmosphere radiating from the stage also contributed to the sense of liveness in the auditorium atmosphere. Audience and actors alike delighted in this spatial atmosphere. Yet one-third of the audience left. There was no narrative or characters to identify with, project onto, empathise with. There was no leap of faith needed to suspend disbelief and get caught up in the fictitious world. There was no opportunity for co-creation. In *Hunger. Peer Gynt*, Böhme's spatial and emotional atmospheres did not conflate. This production was a cogent illustration of how a physical atmosphere can be entirely separate to an emotional atmosphere.

As the audience members noted in the interviews, if you remove the narrative, you forfeit many actor–audience conversations and, consequently, much of the actor–audience relationship. As was seen in the previous chapter, some audience members laboured very hard to create their own narratives,[17] but it was only those who surrendered to the flow of the experience, rather than search for a narrative, that enjoyed the production. For these few, the production became a remarkable, aesthetic experience. On stage, the actors highly desired the audience to find a way in. They were, however, so identified with their industry onstage and the onstage atmosphere that they felt "you lose your connection with the audience a bit. It is quite difficult to find out what the energy is in the audience."[18] The actors did not have many opportunities to invite the audience in. I have said elsewhere[19] that the invitation to co-create has to come from the stage: Does this production illustrate that it also has to come from the narrative itself? As Patrice Pavis argues, "The theatrical relationship, a metaphor for the encounter between actor and spectator, and considered to be the essence of theatre according to Grotowski and Brook, does not really apply to the postdramatic."[20] Yet, in this piece, which was post-dramatic, both actors and audiences still craved for and sought this relationship. They sought an emotional and psychological encounter. Narrative and actor–audience relationship in the theatre are interrelated.

Conversations are reciprocal. This reciprocity was present in *Heisenberg*, less so in *The Encounter* and painfully absent in *Hunger. Peer Gynt*. Actors and audience members desire conversation. Conversations create something magical because they are live. In *Heisenberg* the audience felt almost onstage with the actors. There were myriad conversations. In the theatre of the mind of *The Encounter* the conversations with the char/actor were intimate and were for some too close. Yet there was a noted distance between the audience members. The audience could, perhaps, have experienced the performance from their homes rather than in a theatre.[21] In *Hunger. Peer Gynt* the audience did not like being cut off from the stage or "left out"[22] of the conversation. Many were trying to have conversations that were not possible. So they left. There is much gained in post-dramatic theatre: refined aesthetic experience, the opportunity to focus on issues rather than characters and, for the actors, a mode of self-expression. Yet, as discussed, there is much that is relinquished. Particularly the feeling of including someone in a conversation. Conversations are created through two troupes of performers in relationship across the footlights.

The conversations that begin at one theatrical event often affect future conversations. Regular theatregoers and veteran actors such as those interviewed in this book are part of an ongoing journey where *Heisenberg*, *The Encounter* and *Hunger. Peer Gynt* are just a few of the conversations that work to create the actors' theatrical *oeuvre* or are added to the audience's performance text library. Meaning-making will become the transference of the next production the actors and audience members perform in or see. The character the actor plays in one performance will inform the character played in the next performance. The actor watched in one performance will lay down a history for future performances as the audience member enthuses, "I saw her in […]." The conversations will continue across performances primarily because they are created by an interconnectedness that is felt in the air across the footlights: relationship.

Relationship

As we focus more on faceless-time or virtual faces on screens, relational engagement with embodied conversations is diminishing. Real-time experiences are becoming a precious commodity. Yet we humans are social creatures. We thrive on relationships. In our relationships, however, there is always the risk that something will go wrong, but always the hope that it will go right. As seen in this book, the theatrical relationships across the footlights contain these properties. Something can go wrong: as an audience member you can feel left out of the conversation or you may be confronted with your nemesis on stage in a character. As an actor, the audience can judge you, you may be out of tune or you may experience debilitating paralysis. There remains the hope, however, that it will go right: that both actor and audience member will have an electric air experience.

Theatre not only replicates life in telling life's stories, it also replicates life as an arena of relationship. Theatre stages relationships and generates conversations across the footlights inviting audience relationship with the char/actors: to feel, live, project, transfer, identify and radiate. Like any relationship, it is a risky venture, especially for actors. Like any relationship, it can be exhilarating, and it takes, and gives, energy. Every audience member I interviewed was willing to suspend disbelief to give their full attention and energy to the actors onstage and join in the collective effervescent laughter with fellow audience members. Every actor I interviewed was willing to give their full selves to their audience night after night and join in a collective effervescent performance with fellow actors.

Relationships in life, like in the theatre, only reach electric air experiences when both parties are in tune with each other, and each side is open to the extraordinary possibilities that can transpire in a magnetic attraction. As the interviewed actors who have to work on character relationships[23] onstage confirmed, relationships take work, they take time. Audience member Frank Lachmann described the relational of theatre succinctly:

> This is a moment with the actors and me that can never be repeated, can never be the same. In that sense it is precious. In the cinema that doesn't happen. That's a special feeling. You are sharing a moment in time with someone.[24]

A face-to-face relationship in life and in the theatre, as actor Abigail McKern emphasised, makes you feel "very, very alive."[25] It is a felt, dynamic experience. It is precious. Actors and audience members interviewed in this book attest to this.

In my theatre journey, I have had the opportunity to have a view from the stage of the conversations that create relationship in the theatre, and a view from the audience. As an actor, I had felt in relationship with the audience, but could not describe it. I delighted in suspending my own disbelief to share a narrative with an audience and yet was insecure about audience acceptance in the encounter, harbouring a deep fear of being judged which sometimes sabotaged my relationship with an audience. As an audience member, I continue to have psychological conversations that draw me into close relationship with the char/actors through transference, projection, identification and empathy.

Now, in writing this book and as a researcher, I have gained a view from the side to observe both stage and audience. It is only from this side view of the stage and the audience, looking across the *Grenzland* at that in-between space, that I have been able to fully appreciate how relational theatre is. It is not something you can measure in terms of box-office earnings, critical reviews, flashy marketing or the number of performances of canonical plays. As Jerzy Growtowski articulated, "theatre cannot exist without the actor-spectator relationship of perceptual, direct, 'live' communion."[26] You have to be there. You have to be present, on either side of the footlights, to feel it in the air.

Relational audience research

To discover this relational core of theatre, it is imperative to explore theatre from the inside perspective rather than the outside. It is a challenge for actor or audience studies to explore the relational, yet it is highly rewarding. This book has undertaken some steps towards a methodology of what I posit to be relational audience research.[27] Future relational research can be undertaken in some of the most exciting new frontiers of theatre such as immersive theatre, site-specific theatre and transcultural theatre. All of the undercurrents as well as double consciousness and psychical distance would be fascinating to explore in these spaces. A study of atmosphere as an emotional radiance in space has been one of the focuses of this book, and it also deserves much more attention, especially in the integration of scenography studies and audience research. There are limitations to relational audience research and there are vast arenas that have not been considered in this book due to scope. Age, gender, culture, race and myriad other aspects yet to be explored in research like this naturally affect the conversations and the relationships across the footlights.

I also hope to have highlighted the importance of actor research. Despite the numerous books on actor training and acting styles, not only has the actors' perspectives of audiences received insufficient attention, their insights into theatre's creation and its transformative competencies are often overlooked. As many of the intuitive comments in this book testify, actors live in the blend, not only of the char/actor, but the actor/audience blend and the real/theatrical world blend. They live in the *Grenzland* between truth and appearance, hope and fear, light and darkness, life and death. They are not only the tellers of stories, they also embody stories. As such they have profound insights to share and, as we have seen, many are not only artists but philosophers. Actors reach across the border to thicken, reify and tune their relationship with audiences. They know that audiences are co-creators and that, as Konstantin Stanislavski argued, "thin air" is not what creates a robust actor–audience relationship,[28] electric air is.

What has emerged from this study of the conversations between actors and audiences is that the electric air, at its heart, is relational. In a "precarious" world where, as Nicolas Bourriaud asserts, "transience, speed and fragility reign,"[29] theatre can do much to help us maintain our relational humanity. Actors tacitly understand that ekstatic realms of human experience can happen in relationship with an audience. As actor Chuck Cooper posits, "when we are being watched by an audience something, some alchemy exists, that propels the piece of theatre into a new realm."[30] For audience members, such as Rachel Strauber, the reason one goes to the theatre is for those electric air events: "you go to the theatre for the night when you are going to be blown away because that *does* happen. And when that happens, you remember it for the rest of your life."[31]

Notes

1 Lynn Cohen, personal interview, 9 November 2018.
2 Keith Randolph Smith, personal interview, 2018.
3 Rachel Strauber, personal interview, 27 October 2016.
4 Marcel Kohler, personal interview, 26 October 2018.
5 Michael Reichgott, personal interview, 31 October 2016.
6 Carol York, personal interview, 27 July 2017.
7 Leslie Tucker, personal interview, 1 November 2016.
8 Anita Gillette, personal interview, 21 September 2016.
9 Catherine Brunell, personal interview, 1 November 2016.

10 Chuck Cooper, personal interview, 29 October 2016; and Jay O. Sanders, personal interview, 5 November 2018.

11 Michael Chekhov, *To the Actor: On the Technique of Acting* (New York: Harper and Row, 1953), 47.

12 Natali Seelig, personal interview, 24 October 2018.

13 Peter York, personal interview, 27 July 2017.

14 Wolfgang Michalek, personal interview, 11 October 2016.

15 Rita Haynes, personal interview, 27 July 2017.

16 This audience member quoted in the previous chapter walked out because there was no narrative.

17 This was, perhaps, because it was on a mainstream stage with an audience accustomed to a narrative.

18 Linda Pöppel, personal interview, 28 October 2018.

19 Caroline Heim, *Audience as Performer: The Changing Role of Theatre Audiences in the Twenty-First Century* (London: Routledge, 2016).

20 Patrice Pavis, *The Routledge Dictionary of Performance and Contemporary Theatre* (New York and London: Routledge, 2016), 307.

21 This did indeed happen in one performance that was live-streamed.

22 Bruno, personal interview, 26 October 2018.

23 And often actor relationships backstage.

24 Frank Lachmann, personal interview, 3 November 2016.

25 Abigail McKern, personal interview, 6 July 2017.

26 Jerzy Grotowski and Eugenio Barba, *Towards a Poor Theatre* (New York: Routledge, 2002), 19.

27 Which could equally be called relational actor research or relational actor–audience research. I use "relational audience research" as audiences are my primary area of research. Further, there has been an explosion of audience research since Susan Bennett's seminal book *Theatre Audiences* in 1997.

28 Konstantin Stanislavski, *An Actor Prepares*, trans. Elizabeth Reynolds Hapgood (London: Bloomsbury, 2013), 178.

29 Nicolas Bourriaud, *The Radicant* (New York: Lukas and Sternberg, 2009), 85.

30 Chuck Cooper, personal interview, 29 October 2016; and Jay O. Sanders, personal interview, 5 November 2018.

31 Rachel Strauber, personal interview, 27 October 2016.

APPENDIX

Actor biographies

Elias Arens

American born Elias Arens is a theatre and film actor. He has been a member of the Deutsches Theater ensemble since 2009. He completed his acting training in the Department of Performing Arts and Film at Zurich University of the Arts, where he earned his Bachelor's degree in 2008. Elias was awarded the Studienpreis Schauspiel by Migros-Kulturprozent, a scholarship from the Friedl Wald Stiftung, a solo prize at the meeting of German-language drama schools in Rostock in 2008, and the Armin Ziegler Prize in 2011. At the Deutsches Theater he has worked with Lilja Rupprecht, Andreas Kriegenburg, Sebastian Hartmann, András Dömötör, Tom Kühnel and Anne Lenk. Elias's film credits include *November*, *The Divine Order* and *My Sisters*.

Denis Arndt

Denis Arndt is an American theatre, television and film actor. He served in the Vietnam War as a helicopter pilot and studied at the University of Washington. *Heisenberg* was Denis's Broadway debut. In 2017 Denis received a Tony nomination for Best Lead Actor in Play for his portrayal of Alex Priest in *Heisenberg*. He has performed in numerous other regional and off-Broadway productions including *The Ballad of Soapy Smith* and *Richard II* at the Public Theatre. Denis has appeared in over 30 television shows including *LA Law*, *How to Get Away with Murder*, *The Good Fight*, *Grey's Anatomy*, *Past Life*, *Boston Legal* and *Touched by an Angel*. He was a regular on *The Practice*, *Providence*, *Time of Your Life* and *Picket Fences*. His films include *Basic Instinct*, *S.W.A.T.* and *Bandidas*.

Ian Bartholomew

British actor Ian Bartholomew is a theatre, television and film actor. He spent three years at the National Theatre working in various productions such as *Pravda* with Anthony Hopkins, *The Government Inspector* and *Guys and Dolls*. Ian worked for the Royal Shakespeare Company playing Shylock in their international tour of *The Merchant of Venice* and performed in *The Front Page* directed by Sam Mendes at the Donmar Warehouse. West End credits include *The Iceman Cometh* alongside Kevin Spacey, *Dead Funny*, *Tommy* and *Shakespeare in Love*. He was nominated for four Olivier Awards for other West End productions: *Into the Woods*, *Radio Times*, *Half a Sixpence* and *Mrs Henderson Presents*. His television credits are numerous and include *Spooks*, *Florence Nightingale*, *Thieves Like Us*, *New Tricks*, *Minder*, *Bergerac*, *The Professionals*, *The Accused* and many more. On film he has appeared in *Shiner*, *Breakout*, *Max and Helen*, *Eisenstein* and *A Prayer for the Dying*.

Catherine Brunell

Catherine Brunell is an American theatre, musical theatre and television actor. During her studies at Northwestern University, she was asked to understudy Éponine and Cosette in the national tour of *Les Misérables* and then went on to play Éponine on Broadway. Other Broadway credits include Portia in *Something Rotten*, Mary Poppins in *Mary Poppins* and Millie in *Thoroughly Modern Millie*. Other Broadway credits include *Big River*, *A Tale of Two Cities* and *ELF*. Catherine has performed in multiple national tours and regional productions. She has performed in the Broadway concert series as a soloist in concert halls and theatre nationwide and is a frequent guest soloist for the Carolina Philharmonic. Catherine was nominated twice for the Kevin Kline Award for Best Actress for her portrayals of Laurey in *Oklahoma* and Eliza in *My Fair Lady* at the St Louis MUNY. Her television credits include *The Unbreakable Kimmy Schmidt* and *The Sound of Music LIVE!* with Carrie Underwood.

Lynn Cohen

Lynn Cohen is an American theatre, television and film actor. She made her acting debut at the Actors Theatre of Louisville in *Getting Out*. On Broadway she has appeared in *Orpheus Descending* and *Ivanov*. Lynn has worked extensively in theatre in New York, particularly with companies such as Circle Repertory Theatre, Primary Stages, Manhattan Theatre Club and New York Theatre Workshop, among others. She has been nominated for Drama League and Lucille Lortel Awards, and she won the 2009 Richard Seff Award for her performance in *Chasing Manet*. Lynn is best known for her recurring role as Magda on the television series *Sex and the City*, as well as in the films in that franchise. Other film credits include *Vanya on 42nd Street*, *Munich*, *Across the Universe*, *Eagle Eye* and *The Hunger Games: Catching*

Fire. She has also played Judge Elizabeth Mizener several times on *Law & Order.* Lynn has numerous other film and television credits.

Chuck Cooper

Chuck Cooper is an American theatre, television and film actor. He made his Broadway debut in *Amen Corner* and since then has appeared in multiple Broadway productions such as *Chicago, Passion, Someone to Watch Over Me, Rumors, Amen Corner, Getting Away with Murder, Badfoot in St. Louis Woman* and *The Cherry Orchard.* He won a Tony Award for Best Featured Actor for his portrayal of Memphis in the Broadway show *The Life.* His other awards include the Lucille Lortel Award for *The Piano Lesson,* the San Diego Critics' Circle Award for *Two Trains Running,* the Audelco Award for *Caroline or Change* and two Drama Desk Nominations for *Choir Boy* and *The Life.* He has appeared in multiple off-Broadway productions. Movie credits include *Our Song, Gloria, The Peacemaker* and *The Juror.* Chuck's most recent television credits include *The Good Wife, House of Cards, Madam Secretary, Gossip Girl* and *Law & Order.*

Stéphane Dauch

Stéphane Dauch is a French theatre, television and film actor. He studied at the University of Nice and then acting at the École Régionale d'Acteurs de Cannes. Stéphane has appeared in numerous plays in the classical repertoire including *Les Fourberies de Scapin, Le Bourgeois Gentleman, Le Médecin malgré lui* and *L'Avare* by Molière; *Horace* and *Le Cid* by Corneille; *Alexandre le Grande* by Racine and *Cyrano de Bergerac* by Rostand. His musical talents have also taken him into the world of opera and he has played Papagueno in *The Magic Flute* at the Variety Theatre. In film he has appeared in *Every Night.* In television he has had recurring roles in *Under the Sun* and *The Story of Saturday.*

Janet Fullerlove

Janet Fullerlove is a British theatre, film and television actor. She studied acting at Mountview Academy of Theatre Arts. Janet has appeared in multiple stage productions in the United Kingdom, including on the West End. Among other productions, her theatre credits include *Unexpected Joy* at the Southwark Playhouse, *Oxy and the Morons* at the New Wolsey, *Fiddler on the Roof* at the Royal Albert Hall (BBC Proms), *Shakespeare in Love* on the West End, *Fortune's Fool* at the Old Vic, *The Taming of the Shrew* with the Royal Shakespeare Company, *The Beggar's Opera* at the Regent's Park Open Air Theatre, *Fabrication* at the Print Room, *Macbeth* at Shakespeare's Globe and *Cheryomushki* at the Lyric Hammersmith. Janet has also worked as a facilitator in Forum Theatre for many years. Her television and film credits include *The Last Days of Lucille Ball, Holby City, Longford, Tipping the Velvet, The Jack the Ripper Diaries* and *Tomorrow La Scala!*

Anita Gillette

Anita Gillette is an American theatre, film and television actor with numerous Broadway credits. Anita studied performance at the Peabody Conservatory. She began her career with *Gypsy* on Broadway and performed on Broadway in productions such as *Cabaret, Carnival, Guys and Dolls, They're Playing Our Song, Brighton Beach Memoirs, Showboat* and *Chapter Two* for which she received a Tony nomination and an LA Drama Critics Circle award. She has multiple off-Broadway credits. Anita is best known for her role as Mona in the Film *Moonstruck*, and she has played major roles in films such as *The Fitzgerald Family Christmas, Shall We Dance, She's the One, Larger Than Life, The Guru* and *Bob Roberts*. She has had recurring roles in various television shows such as *CSI, Law & Order* and was a series regular on *Quincy, The Baxters* and *The War at Home*, among many others. Anita was also a regular foil for Johnny Carson on at least 50 Tonight Shows.

Manuel Harder

Chilean born Manuel Harder is a theatre, film and television actor who has been an ensemble member of the Deutsches Theater since 2017. Following his degree in theatre studies, contemporary German literature and actor training, he worked as an ensemble member at various theatres: Salzburger Landestheater, Schauspiel Dortmund, Centraltheater Leipzig, Schauspiel Frankfurt and Schauspiel Stuttgart. Manuel has had guest engagements at the Schaubühne Berlin and has worked with Sebastian Hartmann, Jürgen Kruse, René Pollesch, Robert Borgmann, Martin Laberenz, Karin Henkel, Armin Petras, Luk Perceval, Sascha Hawemann, SIGNA, Michael Gruner, Hermann Schmidt-Rahmer and others. Manuel has premiered plays by Rimbaud, Lasker-Schüler, Brandau, Paoli, Bonaventura and participated in international exchange projects. He has taught drama at the University of Music and Theatre "Felix Mendelssohn Bartholdy" in Leipzig, the HMDK State University of Music, Performing Arts Stuttgart and the Athanor Akademie. Film and television credits include *Brut, Lux: Warrior of Light, Tatort, Wilsberg, Gender Crisis* and *Sløborn*.

Edward Hibbert

Edward Hibbert is a theatre, television and film actor. He studied acting at the Royal Academy of Dramatic Art. Having worked in both the United Kingdom and the United States, Edward performed in the National Theatre production of *Noises Off* and has had major roles on Broadway in *The Drowsy Chaperone, Curtains, Mrs Warren's Profession* and *It Shoulda Been You*. In 1993 he won an Obie Award for his off-Broadway performance in *Jeffrey*. He is best known for his recurring role as the delightful Gil Chesterton in *Frasier* and for his portrayal of Faulconbridge in the BBC series *The Life and Death of King John*. His film credits include *The Prestige, Taking Woodstock* and *The First Wives Club*. He has guest-starred in numerous television shows, and as a voice-over artist was the voice of Zazu in *The Lion King II* and *The Lion King 1½*. Edward is also a literary agent.

Simon McBurney

Simon McBurney is a British theatre, film and television actor, and a writer and director. He studied English literature at Peterhouse Cambridge and theatre at the Jacques Lecoq Institute in Paris. He is the co-founder and artistic director of the UK-based theatre company, Complicité, where he has devised, directed, acted in and produced multiple theatre productions that have toured worldwide. These include productions such as *The Master and Margarita*, *The Magic Flute*, *A Dog's Heart*, *Shun-kin*, *A Disappearing Number*, *A Minute Too Late* and *Measure for Measure*. Complicité has won over 50 awards. Simon has worked extensively in film and his credits include *The Manchurian Candidate*, *Friends with Money*, *The Golden Compass*, *The Duchess*, *Robin Hood*, *Harry Potter and the Deathly Hallows: Part 1*, *Tinker Tailor Soldier Spy*, *Magic in the Moonlight*, *The Theory of Everything* and *Mission: Impossible – Rogue Nation*. He has also appeared in multiple television productions. In 2015 Simon was awarded an OBE (Officer of the Order of the British Empire) "for services to Drama."

Abigail McKern

Abigail McKern is a British theatre and television actor. Her first professional job was working with Alan Ayckbourn at his Stephen Joseph theatre in Scarborough. Her West End credits include *Shakespeare in Love*, *La Cage Aux Folles*, *Nicholas Nickleby*, *Death of a Salesman*, *The Merchant of Venice*, *Suddenly Last Summer*, *The Magistrate*, *The Cherry Orchard*, *Cat on a Hot Tin Roof* and *North by Northwest*. She has played leading roles at the Royal Shakespeare Company and also worked at the National Theatre, the Royal Court Theatre, the Almeida Theatre, the Young Vic and Sydney Theatre Company. She won an Olivier Award for Best Supporting Actress in *As You Like It* and won the London Theatre Critics Award for Best Newcomer. Her television credits include, among many others, *Midsomer Murders*, *The Night Manager*, *Doctors*, *Holby City*, *Psychos*, *Nicholas Nickleby* and two series of *Rumpole of the Bailey* with her father. Abigail has worked with many iconic actors and directors including Judi Dench, Dustin Hoffman, Ian McKellen, Sam Mendes, Faye Dunnaway, Peter Hall, Max Stafford Clark, Kenneth Branagh, Diana Rigg, and her father, Leo McKern.

Wolfgang Michalek

Wolfgang Michalek is a German theatre actor and director. He studied acting at the Vienna Conservatory. He has been an ensemble member at the Schauspielhaus Wien, the Theater in der Josefstadt in Vienna, the Stadttheater Klagenfurt and the Schauspiel Hannover. In 2009 he joined the ensemble of the Staatsschauspiel Dresden, until he moved to Schauspiel Stuttgart in 2013. He worked with numerous directors, including Frank Castorf, Nicolas Stemann, Lars-Ole Walburg, Sebastian Baumgarten, Matthias Hartmann, Stefan Bachmann, Sebastian Nübling and Armin

Petras. In 2016 he made his directorial debut at the Schauspiel Stuttgart, where he staged several plays including *Miss Else, Cabal and Love, The Misanthrope* and the family production *The Wizard of Oz.* Wolfgang has been part of the Düsseldorfer Schauspielhaus ensemble since 2018, where he is currently starring in *1984, A Look from the Bridge, Don Carlos* and *Fight Club.* His film and television credits include *Tatort, Lifeline* and *Inspector Rex.*

Jeremy Mockridge

Jeremy Mockridge is a German film, television and theatre actor. He joined the Deutsches Theater ensemble in 2017. Jeremy studied acting at the Academy of Dramatic Arts "Ernst Busch." Before joining the Deutsches Theater, he appeared in many television series including *Stolberg, Hotel 13 SOKO Wismar, Rosamunde Pilcher, Chaos-Queens, Crossing Lines, Cologne P. D.* and a recurring role in *Lindenstraße.* In film, Jeremy's name grew into prominence through his performances in the children's films *The Wild Chickens* and their sequels, directed by Vivian Naefe. He has most recently starred in Erik Schmitt's *Cleo: If I Could Turn Back Time.*

Maryann Plunkett

Maryann Plunkett is an American theatre, film and television actor. She graduated from the University of New Hampshire and was a founding member of Portland Stage repertory company in Maine. Her Broadway credits include *Sunday in the Park with George* (replacing Bernadette Peters as Dot), *The Crucible* opposite Martin Sheen, *Saint Joan, A Little Hotel on the Side* and *The Seagull.* Maryann won a Tony Award for Best Leading Actress in a Musical for her portrayal of Sally Smith in the Broadway production of *Me and My Girl.* With her husband Jay O. Sanders, she has appeared in all of Richard Nelson's *Apple Family Plays* and *The Gabriels Election Play Trilogy* at the Public Theatre. She was nominated for a Drama Desk Award for her role as Barbara Apple. Her feature films include *Claire Dolan* and *The Company of Men.* On television she has appeared in *L.A. Law, Murder She Wrote, Miami Vice, Star Trek: The Next Generation* and *Law & Order.*

Linda Pöppel

Linda Pöppel is a Berlin theatre, film and television actor who has been a member of the ensemble at the Deutsches Theater since 2016. Before studying she was a member of the Volkbühne's youth theatre group P14 in Berlin. She studied acting at the Westfälische Schauspielschule Bochum. After studying, Linda joined the ensemble at the Centraltheater Leipzig working with, among others, Sebastian Hartmann, Sebastian Baumgarten, Robert Borgmann, Alexander Eisenach, Michael Schweighöfer and Martin Laberenz. In the 2013 to 2016 seasons, Linda was an ensemble member at Schauspiel Frankfurt where she continued her collaboration with Sebastian Hartmann and Alexander Eisenach. She also worked with René Pollesch, Ersan Mondtag and Jürgen Kruse as well as appearing in the dance-theatre production *Macbeth* with the choreographer

Dave St-Pierre. She continues to maintain a close working relationship with Jürgen Kruse and Sebastian Hartmann. Film and television credits include *Papa Gold*, *Tornado* and *Tatort*.

Edouard Rouland

Edouard Rouland is a French theatre and film actor. In Paris he has performed in many plays in the classical repertoire including *Les Femmes cevantes*, *La Comtesse d'Escarbagnas et Les Précieuses Ridicules*, *Dom Juan* and *Le bourgeois Gentilhomme* by Molière; *Antigone* and *Thomas More* by Anouilh; *La seconde surprise de l'amour* and *Le prince travesti* by Marivaux; *Le barbier de Séville* by Beaumarchais; *Le Cid* by Corneille; *Cyrano de Bergerac* by Rostand and *Le Père Humilié* by Claudel. His film credits include *Born as Gods*, *Protection Line*, and *Indelible*. Edouard is regularly engaged in Language Replacement (dubbing) for many foreign films and television programmes.

Lea Ruckpaul

Lea Ruckpaul is a German theatre, television and film actor. She completed her acting studies at the College of Music and Theater "Felix Mendelssohn Bartholdy" in Leipzig. She belonged to the drama studio of the Staatsschauspiel Dresden before she moved to the local ensemble at the beginning of the 2013/14 season. She collaborated with directors such as Tilmann Köhler, Roger Vontobel, Jan Gehler, Simon Solberg, Volker Lösch and Sebastian Baumgarten. In 2016 she was engaged at the Schauspiel Stuttgart, where she played in productions by Armin Petras and Jan Bosse. She has appeared as Cordelia and as a fool in Shakespeare's *King Lear* directed by Claus Peymann and as Gretchen in Goethe's *Faust* directed by Stephan Kimmig. Lea has been an ensemble member at the Düsseldorfer Schauspielhaus since 2018. Her film and television credits include *Dina Foxx: Deadly Contact*, *Tatort*, *All in Friendship*, *The Criminalist*, *SOKO Leipzig*, *The Wedding Planners*, *A Break*, *Emergency Call Port* and *Police Call 110*.

Jay O. Sanders

Jay O. Sanders is an American theatre, film and television actor. After graduating with the first theatre class of the State University of New York, he began his career at New York's Shakespeare in the Park in *Henry V*. He has appeared on Broadway in *Loose Ends*, *The Caine Mutiny Court-Martial, Saint Joan* and *Pygmalion*. He won a Drama Desk Award for Actor in a Play for *Uncle Vanya*. With his wife, Maryann Plunkett, he has appeared in all of Richard Nelson's *Apple Family Plays* and *The Gabriels Election Play Trilogy* at the Public Theatre. Jay has appeared in more plays at Shakespeare in the Park than any other actor to date. His feature films include *The Day after Tomorrow, Half Nelson, JFK, Edge of Darkness, Tumbleweeds, Green Lantern, Revolutionary Road* and *Glory and Angels in the Outfield*. On television, he has been in *True Detective, Roseanne, Crime Story* and had recurring roles on *Person of Interest*,

American Odyssey and *Blind Spot*. Jay's voice can be heard narrating a long list of documentaries for PBS and National Geographic.

Natali Seelig

Natali Seelig is a German theatre, film and television actor and joined the Deutsches Theater ensemble in 2009. She studied acting at the Otto Falckenberg School in Munich, and her first positions were at the Staatstheater Hannover and the Bavarian State Theater. In Munich she began working with Andreas Kriegenburg. In 1998 she was voted actress of the year. This was followed by an appointment at the Vienna Burgtheater. From 2002 to 2009 Natali was a member of the ensemble at the Thalia Theater Hamburg. She continued her work with Andreas Kriegenburg in numerous productions. Natali also worked with directors Armin Petras, Jorinde Dröse and Alize Zandwijk. At the Deutsches Theater she has appeared in productions by Andreas Kriegenburg, Jette Steckel, Lilja Rupprecht, Philipp Arnold, Tom Kühnel and Jürgen Kuttner. Film and television credits include *After Five in the Jungle*, *Inspector Rex* and *Fragmente*.

Keith Randolph Smith

Keith Randolph Smith is an American theatre and film actor. He studied at the American Academy of Dramatic Art and has appeared on Broadway in *Jitney*, *American Psycho*, *Fences*, *Come Back Little Sheba*, *King Hedley II*, *Salome* and *Piano Lesson*. Keith starred in the international tour of *Jitney*, which opened at the National Theatre in London. He has multiple off-Broadway credits. His film credits include *Malcolm X* and *Girl Six* directed by Spike Lee, *Path to Paradise*, *Fallout*, *The Warrior Class*, *Backstreet Justice*, *Anesthesia* and *Dead Dogs Lie*. Keith is a company member of Quick Silver Theater Company and The Actors Center. He is also the recipient of acting fellowships from TCG/Fox Foundation and the Lunt-Fontanne Foundation. His television credits include *The Good Fight*, *Law & Order*, *Law & Order – Criminal Intent*, *Law & Order SVU*, *NY Undercover*, *I'll Fly Away*, *The Cosby Show*, *Onion Sports Desk*, *One Life to Live*, *All My Children* and *Another World*.

INDEX